# Desperados
# &
# Cow-Punchers

# Desperados & Cow-Punchers

The Making of the Western Frontier

ILLUSTRATED

The Story of the Outlaw

and

The Passing of the Frontier

Emerson Hough

LEONAUR

*Desperados*
&
*Cow-Punchers*
The Making of the Western Frontier
*The Story of the Outlaw*
and
*The Passing of the Frontier*
by Emerson Hough

ILLUSTRATED

FIRST EDITION

First published under the titles
*The Story of the Outlaw*
and
*The Passing of the Frontier*

Leonaur is an imprint of Oakpast Ltd

Copyright in this form © 2018 Oakpast Ltd

ISBN: 978-1-78282-728-3 (hardcover)
ISBN: 978-1-78282-729-0 (softcover)

http://www.leonaur.com

Publisher's Notes
The views expressed in this book are not necessarily those of the publisher.

# Contents

The Story of the Outlaw                          7

The Passing of the Frontier                    231

# The Story of the Outlaw

# Contents

| | |
|---|---|
| Preface | 11 |
| The Desperado | 15 |
| The Imitation Desperado | 23 |
| The Land of the Desperado | 27 |
| The Early Outlaw | 33 |
| The Vigilantes of California | 54 |
| The Outlaw of the Mountains | 66 |
| Henry Plummer | 70 |
| Boone Helm | 82 |
| Death Scenes of Desperadoes | 87 |
| Joseph A. Slade | 92 |
| The Desperado of the Plains | 96 |
| Wild Bill Hickok | 103 |
| Frontier Wars | 114 |
| The Lincoln County War | 119 |
| The Stevens County War | 138 |
| Biographies of Bad Men | 153 |
| The Fight of Buckshot Roberts | 168 |

| | |
|---|---:|
| The Man Hunt | 172 |
| Bad Men of Texas | 184 |
| Modern Bad Men | 198 |
| Bad Men of the Indian Nations | 214 |
| Desperadoes of the Cities | 225 |

# Preface

In offering this study of the American desperado, the author constitutes himself no apologist for the acts of any desperado; yet neither does he feel that apology is needed for the theme itself. The outlaw, the desperado—that somewhat distinct and easily recognisable figure generally known in the West as the "bad man"—is a character unique in our national history, and one whose like scarcely has been produced in any land other than this. It is not necessary to promote absurd and melodramatic impressions regarding a type properly to be called historic, and properly to be handled as such. The truth itself is thrilling enough, and difficult as that frequently has been of discovery, it is the truth which has been sought herein.

A thesis on the text of disregard for law might well be put to better use than to serve merely as exciting reading, fit to pass away an idle hour. It might, and indeed it may—if the reader so shall choose—offer a foundation for wider arguments than those suggested in these pages, which deal rather with premises than conclusions. The lesson of our dealings with our bad men of the past can teach us, if we like, the best method of dealing with our bad men today.

There are other lessons which we might take from an acquaintance with frontier methods of enforcing respect for the law; and the first of these is a practical method of handling criminals in the initial executive acts of the law. Never were American laws so strong as today, and never were our executive officers so weak. Our cities frequently are ridden with criminals or rioters. We set hundreds of policemen to restore order, but order is not restored. What is the average policeman as a criminal-taker? Cloddy and coarse of fibre, rarely with personal heredity of mental or bodily vigour, with no training at arms, with no sharp, incisive quality of nerve action, fat, unwieldy, unable to run a hundred yards and keep his breath, not skilled enough to kill his man even when he has him cornered, he is the archetype of all unseemliness as the agent of a law which today, (1905), needs a sterner unholding than ever was the case in all our national life. We use this sort of tools in handling criminals, when each of us knows, or ought to know, that the city which would select twenty Western peace officers of the old type and set them to work without restrictions as to the size of their imminent graveyards, would free itself of criminals in three months' time, and would remain free so long as its methods remained in force.

As for the subject-matter of the following work, it may be stated that, while attention has been paid to the great and well-known instances and epochs of outlawry, many of the facts given have not previously found their way into print. The story of the Lincoln County War of the Southwest is given truthfully for the first time, and after full acquaintance with sources of information now inaccessible or passing away. The Stevens County War of Kansas, which took place, as it were, but yesterday and directly at our doors, has had no history but a garbled one; and as much might be said of many border encounters whose chief use heretofore has been to curdle the blood in pennydreadfuls. Accuracy has been sought among the confusing statements purporting to constitute the record in such historic movements as those of the "vigilantes" of California and Montana mining days, and of the later cattle days when "wars" were common between thieves and outlaws, and the representatives of law and order,—themselves not always duly authenticated officers of the law.

No one man can have lived through the entire time of the American frontier; and any work of this kind must be in part a matter of compilation in so far as it refers to matters of the past. In all cases where practicable, however, the author has made up the records from stories of actual participants, survivors and eyewitnesses; and he is able in some measure to write of things and men personally known during twenty-five years of Western life. Captain Patrick F. Garrett, of New Mexico, central figure of the border fighting in that district in the early railroad days, has been of much service in extending the author's information on that region and time. Mr. Herbert M. Tonney, now, (1905), of Illinois, tells his own story as a survivor of the typical county-seat war of Kansas, in which he was shot and left for dead. Many other men have offered valuable narratives.

In dealing with any subject of early American history, there is no authority more incontestable than Mr. Alexander Hynds, of Dandridge, Tennessee, whose acquaintance with singular and forgotten bits of early frontier history borders upon the unique in its way. Neither does better authority exist than Hon. N. P. Langford, of Minnesota, upon all matters having to do with life in the Rocky Mountain region in the decade of 1860-1870. He was an Argonaut of the Rockies and a citizen of Montana and of other Western territories before the coming of the days of law. Free quotations are made from his graphic work, *Vigilante Days and Ways*, which is both interesting of itself and valuable as a historical record.

The stories of modern train-robbing bandits and outlaw gangs are taken partly from personal narratives, partly from judicial records, and partly from works frequently more sensational than accurate, and requiring much sifting and verifying in detail. Naturally, very many volumes of Western history and adventure have been consulted. Much of this labour has been one of love for the days and places concerned, which exist no longer as they once did. The total result, it is hoped, will aid in telling at least a portion of the story of the vivid and significant life of the West, and of that frontier whose van, if ever marked by human lawlessness, has, none the less, ever been led by the banner of human liberty. May that banner still wave today, and though blood be again the price, may it never permanently be replaced by that of license and injustice in our America.

Chapter 1

# The Desperado

Energy and action may be of two sorts, good or bad; this being as well as we can phrase it in human affairs. The live wires that net our streets are more dangerous than all the bad men the country ever knew, but we call electricity on the whole good in its action. We lay it under law, but sometimes it breaks out and has its own way. These outbreaks will occur until the end of time, in live wires and vital men. Each land in the world produces its own men Individually bad—and, in time, other bad men who kill them for the general good.

There are bad Chinamen, bad Filipinos, bad Mexicans, and Indians, and negroes, and bad white men. The white bad man is the worst bad man of the world, and the prize-taking bad man of the lot is the Western white bad man. Turn the white man loose in a land free of restraint—such as was always that Golden Fleece land, vague, shifting and transitory, known as the American West—and he simply reverts to the ways of Teutonic and Gothic forests. The civilized empire of the West has grown in spite of this, because of that other strange germ, the love of law, anciently implanted in the soul of the Anglo-Saxon. That there was little difference between the bad man and the good man who went out after him was frequently demonstrated in the early roaring days of the West. The religion of progress and civilization meant very little to the Western town marshal, who sometimes, or often, was a peace officer chiefly because he was a good fighting man.

We band together and "elect" political representatives who do not represent us at all. We "elect" executive officers who execute nothing but their own wishes. We pay innumerable policemen to take from our shoulders the burden of self-protection; and the policemen do not do this thing. Back of all the law is the undelegated personal right, that vague thing which, none the less, is recognised in all the laws and charters of the world; as England and France of old, and Russia today, (1905), may show. This undelegated personal right is in each of us, or ought to be. If there is in you no hot blood to break into flame and set you arbiter for yourself in some sharp, crucial moment, then God pity you, for no woman ever loved you if she could find anything else to love, and you are fit neither as man nor citizen.

As the individual retains an undelegated right, so does the body social. We employ politicians, but at heart most of us despise politicians and love fighting men. Society and law are not absolutely wise nor absolutely right, but only as a compromise relatively wise and right. The bad man, so called, may have been in large part relatively bad. This much we may say scientifically, and without the slightest cheapness. It does not mean that we shall waste any maudlin sentiment over a desperado; and certainly, it does not mean that we shall have anything but contempt for the pretender at desperadoism.

Who and what was the bad man? Scientifically and historically he was even as you and I. Whence did he come? From any and all places. What did he look like? He came in all sorts and shapes, all colours and sizes—just as cowards do. As to knowing him, the only way was by trying him. His reputation, true or false, just or unjust, became, of course, the herald of the bad man in due time. The "killer" of a Western town might be known throughout the state or in several states. His reputation might long outlast that of able statesmen and public benefactors.

What distinguished the bad man in peculiarity from his fellow-man? Why was he better with weapons? What is courage, in the last analysis? We ought to be able to answer these questions in a purely scientific way. We have machines for photographing relative quickness of thought and muscular action. We are able to record the varying speeds of Impulse transmission in the nerves of different individuals. If you were picking out a bad man, would you select one who, on the machine, showed a dilatory nerve response? Hardly. The relative fitness for a man to be "bad," to become extraordinarily quick and skilful with weapons, could, without doubt, be predetermined largely by these scientific measurements. Of course, having no thought-machines in the early West, they got at the matter by experimenting, and so, very often, by a graveyard route. You could not always stop to feel the pulse of a suspected killer.

The use of firearms with swiftness and accuracy was necessary in the calling of the desperado, after fate had marked him and set him apart for the inevitable, though possibly long-deferred, end. This skill with weapons was a natural gift in the case of nearly every man who attained great reputation whether as killer of victims or as killer of killers. Practice assisted in proficiency, but a Wild Bill or a Slade or a Billy the Kid was born and not made.

Quickness in nerve action is usually backed with good digestion, and hard life in the open is good medicine for the latter. This, however, does not wholly cover the case. A slow man also might be a brave man. Sooner or later. If he went into the desperado business on either side of the game, he would fall before the man who was brave as himself and a fraction faster with the gun.

There were unknown numbers of potential bad men who died mute and Inglorious after a life spent at a desk or a plough. They might have been bad If matters had shaped right for that. Each war brings out its own heroes from unsuspected places; each sudden emergency summons its own fit man. Say that a man took to the use of weapons, and found himself arbiter of life and death with lesser animals, and able to grant them either at a distance. He went on, pleased with his growing skill with firearms. He discovered that as the sword had in one age of the world lengthened the human arm, so did the six-shooter—that epochal instrument, invented at precisely that time of the American life when the human arm needed lengthening—extend and strengthen his arm, and make him and all men equal. The user of weapons felt his powers increased.

So now, in time, there came to him a moment of danger. There was his enemy. There was the affront, the challenge. Perhaps it was male against male, a matter of sex, prolific always in bloodshed. It might be a matter of property, or perhaps it was some taunt as to his own personal courage. Perhaps alcohol came into the question, as was often the case. For one reason or the other, it came to the ordeal of combat. It was the undelegated right of one individual against that of another. The law was not invoked—the law would not serve. Even as the quicker set of nerves flashed into action, the arm shot forward, and there smote the point of flame as did once the point of steel. The victim fell, his own weapon clutched in his hand, a fraction too late. The law cleared the killer. It was "self-defence." "It was an even break," his fellowmen said; although thereafter they were more reticent with him and sought him out less frequently.

"It was an even break," said the killer to himself—"an even break, him or me." But, perhaps, the repetition of this did not serve to blot out a certain mental picture. I have had a bad man tell me that he killed his second man to get rid of the mental image of his first victim.

But this exigency might arise again; indeed, most frequently did arise. Again, the embryo bad man was the quicker. His self-approbation now, perhaps, began to grow. This was the crucial time of his life. He might go on now and become a bad man, or he might cheapen and become an imitation desperado. In either event, his third man left him still more confident. His courage and his skill in weapons gave him assuredness and ease at the time of an encounter. He was now becoming a specialist. Time did the rest, until at length they buried him.

The bad man of genuine sort rarely looked the part assigned to him in the popular imagination. The long-haired blusterer, adorned with a dialect that never was spoken, serves very well in fiction about the West, but that is not the real thing. The most dangerous man was apt to be quiet and smooth-spoken. When an antagonist blustered and threatened, the most dangerous man only felt rising in his own soul, keen and stern, that strange exultation which often comes with combat for the man naturally brave. A Western officer of established reputation once said to me, while speaking of a recent personal difficulty into which he had been forced:

> I hadn't been in anything of that sort for years, and I wished I was out of it. Then I said to myself, 'Is it true that you are getting old—'have you lost your nerve?' Then all at once the old feeling came over me, and I was just like I used to be. I felt calm and happy, and I laughed after that. I jerked my gun and shoved it into his stomach. He put up his hands and apologised. 'I will give you a hundred dollars now,' he said, 'If you will tell me where you got that gun.' I suppose I was a trifle quick for him.

The virtue of the "drop" was eminently respected among bad men. Sometimes, however, men were killed in the last desperate conviction that no man on earth was as quick as they. What came near being an incident of that kind was related by a noted Western sheriff.

> Down on the edge of the Pecos valley, a dozen miles below old Fort Sumner, there used to be a little saloon, and I once captured a man there. He came in from somewhere east of our territory, and was wanted for murder. The reward offered for him was twelve hundred dollars. Since he was a stranger, none of us knew him, but the sheriff's descriptions sent in said he had a freckled face, small hands, and a red spot in one eye. I heard

that there was a new saloon-keeper in there, and thought he might be the man, so I took a deputy and went down one day to see about it.

I told my deputy not to shoot until he saw me go after my gun. I didn't want to hold the man up unless he was the right one, and I wanted to be sure about that identification mark in the eye. Now, when a bartender is waiting on you, he will never look you in the face until just as you raise your glass to drink. I told my deputy that we would order a couple of drinks, and so get a chance to look this fellow in the eye. When he looked up, I did look him in the eye, and there was the red spot!

I dropped my glass and jerked my gun and covered him, but he just wouldn't put up his hands for a while. I didn't want to kill him, but I thought I surely would have to. He kept both of his hands resting on the bar, and I knew he had a gun within three feet of him somewhere. At last slowly he gave in. I treated him well, as I always did a prisoner, told him we would square it if we had made any mistake. We put irons on him and started for Las Vegas with him in a wagon. The next morning, out on the trail, he confessed everything to me. We turned him over, and later he was tried and hung. I always considered him to be a pretty bad man. So far as the result was concerned, he might about as well have gone after his gun. I certainly thought that was what he was going to do. He had sand. I could just see him stand there and balance the chances in his mind.

The same officer went on, reflectively:

Another of the nerviest men I ever ran up against, I met when I was sheriff of Doña Aña County. New Mexico. I was in Las Cruces, when there came in a sheriff from over in the Indian Nations looking for a fugitive who had broken out of a penitentiary after killing a guard and another man or so. This sheriff told me that the criminal in question was the most desperate man he had ever known, and that no matter how we came on him, he would put up a fight and we would have to kill him before we could take him. We located our man, who was cooking on a ranch six or eight miles out of town. I told the sheriff to stay in town, because the man would know him and would not know us. I had a Mexican deputy along with me.

I put out my deputy on one side of the house and went in. I

found my man just wiping his hands on a towel after washing his dishes. I threw down on him, and he answered by smashing me in the face, and then jumping through the window like a squirrel. I caught at him and tore the shirt off his back, but I didn't stop him. Then I ran out of the door and caught him on the porch. I did not want to kill him, so I struck him over the head with the handcuffs I had ready for him. He dropped, but came up like a flash, and struck me so hard with his fist that I was badly jarred. We fought hammer and tongs for a while, but at length he broke away, sprang through the door, and ran down the hall. He was going to his room after his gun.

At that moment my Mexican came in, and having no sentiment about it, just whaled away and shot him in the back, killing him on the spot. The doctors when they examined this man's body that he as the most perfect physical specimen they had ever seen. I can testify that he was a fighter. The sheriff offered me the reward, but I wouldn't take any of it. I told him that I would be over in his country some time, and that I was sure he would do as much for me if I needed his help. I hope that if I do have to go after his particular sort of bad people, I'll be lucky in getting the first start on my man. That man was as desperate a fighter as I ever saw or expect to see. Give a man of that stripe any kind of a show and he's going to kill you, that's all. He knows that he has no chance under the law.

Sometimes they got away with desperate chances, too, as many a peace officer has learned to his cost. The only way to go after such a man is to go prepared, and then to give him no earthly show to get the best of you. I don't mean that an officer ought to shoot down a man if he has a show to take his prisoner alive; but I do mean that he ought to remember that he may be pitted against a man who is just as brave as he is, and just as good with a gun, and who is fighting for his life.

Of course, such a man as this, whether confronted by an officer of the law or by another man against whom he has a personal grudge, or who has in any way challenged him to the ordeal of weapons, was steadfast in his own belief that he was as brave as any, and as quick with weapons. Thus, until at length he met his master in the law of human progress and civilization, he simply added to his own list of victims, or was added to the list of another of his own sort. For a very long

THE SCENE OF MANY LITTLE WARS

More men have been killed in this street than in any other in America time, moreover, there existed a great region on the frontier where the law could not protect. There was good reason, therefore, for a man's learning to depend upon his own courage and strength and skill. He had nothing else to protect him, whether he was good or bad. In the typical days of the Western bad man, life was the property of the Individual, and not of society, and one man placed his life against another's as the only way of solving hard personal problems. Those days and those conditions brought out some of the boldest and most reckless men the earth ever saw. Before we freely criticize them, we ought fully to understand them.

Chapter 2

# The Imitation Desperado

The counterfeit bad man, in so far as he has a place in literature, was largely produced by Western consumptives for Eastern consumption. Sometimes he was in person manufactured in the East and sent West. It is easy to see the philosophical difference between the actual bad man of the West and the Imitation article. The bad man was an evolution; the Imitation bad man was an Instantaneous creation, a supply arising full panoplied to fill a popular demand. Silently there arose, partly in the West and partly in the East, men who gravely and calmly proceeded to look the part. After looking the part for a time, to their own satisfaction at least, and after taking themselves seriously as befitted the situation, they, in very many instances, faded away and disappeared in that Nowhere whence they came. Some of them took themselves too seriously for their own good. Of course, there existed for some years certain possibilities that any one of these bad men might run against the real thing.

There always existed in the real, sober, level-headed West a contempt for the West-struck man who was not really bad, but who wanted to seem "bad." Singularly enough, men of this type were not so frequently local products as immigrants. The "bootblack bad man" was a character recognised on the frontier—the city tough gone West with ambitions to achieve a bad eminence. Some of these men were partially bad for a while. Some of them, no doubt, even left behind them, after their sudden funerals, the impression that they had been wholly bad. You cannot detect all the counterfeit currency in the world, severe as the test for counterfeits was in the old West. There is, of course, no great amount of difference between the West and the East. All America, as well as the West, demanded of its citizens nothing so much as genuineness.

Yet the Western phrase, to "stand the acid," was not surpassed in graphic descriptiveness. When an imitation bad man came into a town of the old frontier, he had to "stand the acid" or get out. His hand would be called by someone. "My friend," said old Bob Bobo, the famous Mississippi bear hunter, to a man who was doing some pretty loud talking, "I have always noticed that when a man goes out hunting for trouble in these bottoms, he almost always finds it." Two weeks later, this same loud talker threatened a calm man in simple jeans pants, who took a shotgun and slew him impulsively. Now, the West got its hot blood largely from the South, and the dogma of the Southern town was the same in the Western mining town or cow camp—the bad man or the would-be bad man had to declare himself before long, and the acid bottle was always close at hand.

That there were grades in counterfeit bad men was accepted as a truth on the frontier. A man might be known as dangerous, as a murderer at heart, and yet be despised. The imitation bad man discovered that it is comparatively easy to terrify a good part of the population of a community. Sometimes a base imitation of a desperado is exalted in the public eye as the real article. A few years ago, (at 1905), four misled hoodlums of Chicago held up a street-car barn, killed two men, stole a sum of money, killed a policeman and another man, and took refuge in a dugout in the sand hills below the city, comporting themselves according to the most accepted dime-novel standards. Clumsily arrested by one hundred men or so, instead of being tidily killed by three or four, as would have been the case on the frontier, they were put in jail, given columns of newspaper notice, and worshiped by large crowds of maudlin individuals. These men probably died in the belief that they were "bad." They were not bad men, but Imitations, counterfeit, and, indeed, nothing more than cheap and dirty little murderers.

Of course, we all feel able to detect the mere notoriety hunter, who poses about in cheap pretentiousness; but now and then in the West there turned up something more difficult to understand. Perhaps the most typical case of imitation bad man ever known, at least in the Southwest, was Bob Ollinger, who was killed by Billy the Kid in 1881, when the latter escaped from jail at Lincoln, New Mexico. That Ollinger was a killer had been proved beyond the possibility of a doubt. He had no respect for human life, and those who knew him best knew that he was a murderer at heart. His reputation was gained otherwise than through the severe test of an "even break." Some say that he killed Chavez, a Mexican, as he offered his own hand in greeting. He killed another man. Hill, in a similarly treacherous way. Later, when, as a peace officer, he was with a deputy, Pierce, serving a warrant on one Jones, he pulled his gun and, without need or provocation, shot Jones through. The same bullet, passing through Jones's body, struck Pierce in the leg and left him a cripple for life.

Again, Ollinger was out as a deputy with a noted sheriff in pursuit of a Mexican criminal, who had taken refuge in a ditch. Ollinger wanted only to get into a position where he could shoot the man, but his superior officer crawled alone up the ditch, and, rising suddenly, covered his man and ordered him to surrender. The Mexican threw down his gun and said that he would surrender to the sheriff, but that he was sure Ollinger would kill him. This fear was justified. The sheriff said:

> When I brought out the man, Ollinger came up on the run, with his cocked six-shooter in his hand. His long hair was flying behind him as he ran, and I never in my life saw so devilish a look on any human being's face. He simply wanted to shoot that Mexican, and he chased him around me until I had to tell him I would kill him if he did not stop.

The sheriff added later:

> Ollinger was a born murderer at heart, I never slept out with him that I did not watch him. After I had more of a reputation, I think Ollinger would have been glad to kill me for the notoriety of it. I never gave him a chance to shoot me in the back or when I was asleep. Of course, you will understand that we had to use for deputies such material as we could get.

Ollinger was the sort of imitation desperado that looks the part. He wore his hair long and affected the ultra-Western dress, which today is despised in the West. He was one of the very few men at that time—twenty-five years ago—who carried a knife at his belt. When he was in such a town as Las Vegas or Sante Fé, he delighted to put on a buckskin shirt, spread his hair out on his shoulders, and to walk through the streets, picking his teeth with his knife, or once in a while throwing it in such a way that it would stick up in a tree or a board. He presented an eye-filling spectacle, and was indeed the ideal imitation bad man. This being the case, there may be interest in following out his life to its close, and in noting how the bearing of the bad man's title sometimes exacted a very high price of the claimant.

Ollinger, who had made many threats against Billy the Kid, was very cordially hated by the latter. Together with Deputy Bell, of White Oaks, Ollinger had been appointed to guard the Kid for two weeks previous to the execution of the death sentence which had been imposed upon the latter. The Kid did not want to harm Bell, but he dearly hated Ollinger, who never had lost an opportunity to taunt him. Watching his chance, the Kid at length killed both Bell and Ollinger, shooting the latter with Ollinger's own shotgun, with which Ollinger had often menaced his prisoner.

Other than these two men, the Kid and Ollinger, I know of no better types each of his own class. One was a genuine bad man, and the other was the genuine Imitation of a bad man. They were really as far apart as the poles, and they are so held in the tradition of that bloody country today, (at 1905). Throughout the West there are two sorts of wolves—the coyote and the grey wolf. Either will kill, and both are lovers of blood. One is yellow at heart, and the other is game all the way through. In outward appearance both are wolves, and in appearance they sometimes grade toward each other so closely that it is hard to determine the species. The grey wolf is a warrior and is respected. The coyote is a sneak and a murderer, and his name is a term of reproach throughout the West.

Chapter 3

# The Land of the Desperado

There was once a vast empire, almost unknown, west of the Missouri River. The white civilization of this continent was three hundred years in reaching it. We had won our independence and taken our place among the nations of the world before our hardiest men had learned anything whatever of this Western empire. We had bought this vast region and were paying for it before we knew what we had purchased. The wise men of the East, leading men in Congress, said that it would be criminal to add this territory to our already huge domain, because it could never be settled. It was not dreamed that civilization would ever really subdue it. Even much later, men as able as Daniel Webster deplored the attempt to extend our lines farther to the West, saying that these territories could not be States, that the East would suffer

If we widened our West, and that the latter could never be of value to the union! So far as this great West was concerned. It was spurned and held in contempt, and it had full right to take Itself as an outcast. Decreed to the wilderness forever, it could have been forgiven for running wild. Denominated as unfit for the occupation of the Eastern population, it might have been expected that it would gather to Itself a population all its own.

It did gather such a population, and in part that population was a lawless one. The frontier, clear across to the Pacific, has at one time or another been lawless; but this was not always the fault of the men who occupied the frontier. The latter swept Westward with such unexampled swiftness that the machinery of the law could not always keep up with them. Where there are no courts, where each man is judge and jury for himself, protecting himself and his property by his own arm alone, there always have gathered also the lawless, those who do not wish the day of law to come, men who want license and not liberty, who wish crime and not lawfulness, who want to take what is not theirs and to enforce their own will in their own fashion.

There are two states of society perhaps equally bad for the promotion of good morals and virtue—the densely populated city and the wilderness. In the former, a single individual loses his identity in the mass, and, being unnoticed, is without the view of the public, and can, to a certain extent, commit crimes with impunity. In the latter, the population is sparse and, the strong arm of the law not being extended, his crimes are in a measure unobserved, or, if so, frequently power is wanting to bring him to justice. Hence, both are the resort of desperadoes. In the early settlement of the West, the borders were Infested with desperadoes flying from justice, suspected or convicted felons escaped from the grasp of the law, who sought safety. The counterfeiter and the robber there found a secure retreat or a new theatre for crime.

The foregoing words were written in 1855 by a historian to whom the West of the trans-Missouri remained still a sealed book; but they cover very fitly the appeal of a wild and unknown land to a bold, a criminal, or an adventurous population. Of the trans-Missouri as we of today, (1905), think of it, no one can write more accurately and understandingly than Theodore Roosevelt, President of the United States, who thus describes the land he knew and loved.

Some distance beyond the Mississippi, stretching from Texas to North Dakota, and westward to the Rocky mountains, lies the plains country. This is a region of light rainfall, where the ground is clad with short grass, while Cottonwood trees fringe the courses of the winding plains streams; streams that are alternately turbid torrents and mere dwindling threads of water. The great stretches of natural pasture are broken by grey sage-brush plains, and tracts of strangely shaped and coloured Bad Lands; sun-scorched wastes in summer, and in winter arctic in their iron desolation. Beyond the plains rise the Rocky Mountains, their flanks covered with coniferous woods; but the trees are small, and do not ordinarily grow very close together.
Toward the north the forest becomes denser, and the peaks higher; and glaciers creep down toward the valleys from the fields of everlasting snow. The brooks are brawling, trout-filled

torrents; the swift rivers roam over rapid and cataract, on their way to one or other of the two great oceans.

Southwest of the Rockies evil and terrible deserts stretch for leagues and leagues, mere waterless wastes of sandy plain and barren mountain, broken here and there by narrow strips of fertile ground. Rain rarely falls, and there are no clouds to dim the brazen sun. The rivers run in deep canyons, or are swallowed by the burning sand; the smaller watercourses are dry throughout the greater part of the year.

Beyond this desert region rise the sunny Sierras of California, with their flower-clad slopes and groves of giant trees; and north of them, along the coast, the rain-shrouded mountain chains of Oregon and Washington, matted with the towering growth of the mighty evergreen forest. (*The Wilderness Hunters*.)

Such, then, was this Western land, so long the home of the outdweller who foreran civilization, and who sometimes took matters of the law into his own hands. For purposes of convenience, we may classify him as the bad man of the mountains and the bad man of the plains; because he was usually found in and around the crude localities where raw resources in property were being developed; and because, previous to the advent of agriculture, the two vast wilderness resources were minerals and cattle. The mines of California and the Rockies; the cattle of the great plains—write the story of these and you have much of the story of Western desperadoism. For, in spite of the fact that the ideal desperado was one who did not rob or kill for gain, the most usual form of early desperadoism had to do with attempts at unlawfully acquiring another man's property.

The discovery of gold in California caused a flood of bold men, good and bad, to pour into that remote region from all corners of the earth. Books could be written, and have been written, on the days of terror in California, when the Vigilantes took the law into their own hands. There came the time later when the rich placers of Montana and other territories were pouring out a stream of gold rivalling that of the days of '49; and when a tide of restless and reckless characters, resigning or escaping from both armies in the Civil War, mingled with many others who heard also the imperious call of a land of gold, and rolled westward across the plains by every means of conveyance or locomotion then possible to man.

The next great days of the wild West were the cattle days, which also reached their height soon after the end of the great war, when the North was seeking new lands for its young men, and the Southwest was hunting an outlet for the cattle herds, which had enormously multiplied while their owners were off at the wars. The cattle country had been passed over unnoticed by the mining men for many years, and dismissed as the Great American Desert, as it had been named by the first explorers, who were almost as ignorant about the West as Daniel Webster himself. Into this once barren land, a vast region unsettled and without law, there now came pouring up the great herds of cattle from the South, in charge of men wild as the horned kine they drove. Here was another great wild land that drew, as a magnet, wild men from all parts of the country.

This last home of the bad man, the old cattle range, is covered by a passage from *The Story of the Cowboy*:

> The braiding of a hundred minor pathways, the Long Trail lay like a vast rope connecting the cattle country of the South with that of the North. Lying loose or coiling, it ran for more than two thousand miles along the eastern ridge of the Rocky Mountains, sometimes close in at their feet, again hundreds of miles away across the hard table-lands or the well-flowered prairies. It traversed in a fair line the vast land of Texas, curled over the Indian Nations, over Kansas, Colorado, Nebraska, Wyoming and Montana, and bent in wide overlapping circles as far west as Utah and Nevada; as far east as Missouri, Iowa, Illinois; and as far north as the British possessions.
>
> Even today you may trace plainly its former course, from its faint beginnings in the lazy land of Mexico, the Ararat of the cattle range. It is distinct across Texas, and multifold still in the Indian lands. Its many intermingling paths still scar the iron surface of the Neutral Strip, and the ploughs have not buried all the old furrows in the plains of Kansas. Parts of the path still remain visible in the mountain lands of the far North. You may see the ribbons banding the hillsides today along the valley of the Stillwater, and along the Yellowstone and toward the source of the Missouri. The hoof marks are beyond the Musselshell, over the Bad Lands and the coulees and the flat prairies; and far up into the land of the long cold you may see, even today if you like, the shadow of that unparalleled pathway, the Long Trail of the cattle range. History has no other like it.

This was really the dawning of the American cattle industry. The Long Trail now received a gradual but unmistakable extension, always to the north, and along the line of the intermingling of the products of the Spanish and the Anglo-Saxon civilizations. The thrust was always to the north. Chips and flakes of the great Southwestern herd began to be seen in the northern states. Meantime the AngloSaxon civilization was rolling swiftly toward the upper West. The Indians were being driven from the plains. A solid army was pressing behind the vanguard of soldier, scout and plainsman. The railroads were pushing out into a new and untracked empire. In 1871 over six hundred thousand cattle crossed the Red River for the Northern markets. Abilene, Newton, Wichita, Ellsworth, Great Bend, "Dodge," flared out into a swift and sometime evil blossoming.

The Long Trail, which long ago had found the black corn lands of Illinois and Missouri, now crowded to the West, until it had reached Utah and Nevada, and penetrated every open park and mesa and valley of Colorado, and found all the high plains of Wyoming. Cheyenne and Laramie became common words now, and drovers spoke wisely of the dangers of the Platte as a year before they had mentioned those of the Red River or the Arkansas. Nor did the Trail pause in its irresistible push to the north until it had found the last of the five great trans-continental lines, far in the British provinces. The Long Trail of the cattle range was done. By magic the cattle industry had spread over the entire West.

By magic, also, the cattle industry called to itself a population unique and peculiar. Here were great values to be handled and guarded. The cowboy appeared, summoned out of the shadows by the demand of evolution. With him appeared also the cattle thief, making his living on free beef, as he had once on the free buffalo of the plains. The immense domain of the West was filled with property held under no better or more obvious mark than the imprint of a hot iron on the hide. There were no fences. The owner might be a thousand miles away.

The temptation to theft was continual and urgent. It seemed easy and natural to take a living from these great herds which no one seemed to own or to care for. The "rustler" of the range made his appearance, bold, hardy, unprincipled; and the story of his undoing by the law is precisely that of the finish of the robbers of the mines by the Vigilantes.

Now, too, came the days of transition, which have utterly changed all the West. The railroad sprang across this great middle country of the plains. The intent was to connect the two sides of this continent; but, incidentally, and more swiftly than was planned, there was built a great midway empire on the plains, now one of the grandest portions of America.

This building of the trans-continental lines was a rude and dangerous work. It took out into the West mobs of hard characters, not afraid of hard work and hard living. These men would have a certain amount of money as wages, and would assuredly spend these wages as they made them; hence, the gambler followed the rough settlements at the "head of the rails." The murderer, the thief, the prostitute, the social outcast and the fleeing criminal went with the gamblers and the toughs. Those were the days when it was not polite to ask a man what his name had been back in the States.

A very large percentage of this population was wild and lawless, and it impressed those who joined it instead of being altered and improved by them. There were no wilder days in the West than those of the early railroad building. Such towns as Newton, Kansas, where eleven men were killed in one night; Fort Dodge, where armed encounters among cowboys and gamblers, deputies and desperadoes, were too frequent to attract attention; Caldwell, on the Indian border; Hays City, Abilene, Ellsworth—any of a dozen cow camps, where the head of the rails caught the great northern cattle drives, furnished chapters lurid enough to take volumes in telling—Indeed, perhaps, gave that stamp to the West which has been apparently so ineradicable.

These were flourishing times for the Western desperado, and he became famous, and, as it were, typical, at about this era. Perhaps this was due in part to the fact that the railroads carried with them the telegraph and the newspaper, so that records and reports were made of what had for many years gone unreported. Now, too, began the influx of transients, who saw the wild West hurriedly and wrote of it as a strange and dangerous country. The wild citizens of California and Montana in mining days passed almost unnoticed except in fiction. The wild men of the middle plains now began to have a record in facts, or partial facts, as brought to the notice of the reading public which was seeking news of the new lands. A strange and turbulent day now drew swiftly on.

## Chapter 4

# The Early Outlaw

Before passing to the review of the more modern days of wild life on the Western frontier, we shall find it interesting to note a period less known, but quite as wild and desperate as any of later times. Indeed, we might also say that our own desperadoes could take lessons from their ancestors of the past generation who lived in the forests of the Mississippi valley.

Those were the days when the South was breaking over the Appalachians and exploring the middle and lower West. Adventurers were dropping down the old river roads and "traces" across Kentucky, Tennessee, and Mississippi, into Louisiana and Texas. The flatboat and keel-boat days of the great rivers were at their height, and the population was in large part transient, migratory, and bold; perhaps holding a larger *per cent*, of criminals than any Western population since could claim. There were no organised systems of common carriers, no accepted roads and highways.

The great National Road, from Wheeling west across Ohio, paused midway of Indiana. Stretching for hundreds of miles in each direction was the wilderness, wherein man had always been obliged to fend for himself. And, as ever, the wilderness had its own wild deeds. Flatboats were halted and robbed; caravans of travellers were attacked; lonely wayfarers plodding on horseback were waylaid and murdered. In short, the story of that early day shows our first frontiersman no novice in crime.

About twenty miles below the mouth of the Wabash river, there was a resort of robbers such as might belong to the most lurid dime-novel list—the famous Cave-in-the-Rock, in the bank of the Ohio river. This cavern was about twenty-five feet in height at its visible opening, and it ran back into the bluff two hundred feet, with a width

TYPES OF BORDER BARRICADES

of eighty feet. The floor of this natural cavern was fairly flat, so that it could be used as a habitation. From this lower cave a sort of aperture led up to a second one, immediately above it in the bluff wall, and these two natural retreats of wild animals offered attractions to wild men which were not unaccepted. It was here that there dwelt for some time the famous robber Meason, or Mason, who terrorised the flatboat trade of the Ohio at about 1800.

Meason was a robber king, a giant in stature, and a man of no ordinary brains. He had associated with him his two sons and a few other hard characters, who together made a band sufficiently strong to attack any party of the size usually making up the boat companies of that time, or the average family traveling, mounted or on foot, through the forest-covered country of the Ohio valley. Meason killed and pillaged pretty much as he liked for a term of years, but as travel became too general along the Ohio, he removed to the wilder country south of that stream, and began to operate on the old "Natchez and Nashville Trace," one of the roadways of the South at that time, when the Indian lands were just opening to the early settlers.

Lower Tennessee and pretty much all of Mississippi made his stamping-grounds, and his name became a terror there, as it had been along the Ohio. The governor of the State of Mississippi offered a reward for his capture, dead or alive; but for a long time, he escaped all efforts at apprehension. Treachery did the work, as it has usually in bringing such bold and dangerous men to book. Two members of his gang proved traitors to their chief. Seizing an opportunity, they crept behind him and drove a tomahawk into his brain. They cut off the head and took it along as proof; but as they were displaying this at the seat of government, the town of Washington, they themselves were recognised and arrested, and were later tried and executed; which ended the Meason gang, one of the early and once famous desperado bands.

From the earliest days there have been border counterfeiters of coin. One of the first and most remarkable was the noted Sturdevant, who lived in lower Illinois, near the Ohio River, in the first quarter of the last century. Sturdevant was also something of a robber king, for he could at any time wind his horn and summon to his side a hundred armed men. He was ostensibly a steady farmer, and lived comfortably, with a good corps of servants and tenants about him; but his ablest assistants did not dwell so close to him. He had an army of confederates all over the middle West and South, and issued more counterfeit money than any man before, and probably than any man since. He always exacted a regular price for his money—sixteen dollars for a hundred in counterfeit—and such was the looseness of currency matters at that time that he found many willing to take a chance in his trade.

He never allowed any confederate to pass a counterfeit bill in his own state, or in any other way to bring himself under the surveillance of local law; and they were all obliged to be especially circumspect in the county where they lived. He was a very smug sort of villain, in the trade strictly for revenue, and he was so careful that he was never caught by the law, in spite of the fact that it was known that his farm was the source of a flood of spurious money. He was finally "regulated" by the citizens, who arose and made him leave the country. This was one of the early applications of lynch law in the West. Its results were, as usual, salutary. There was no more counterfeiting in that region. A very noted desperado of these early days was Harpe, or Big Harpe, as he was called, to distinguish him from his brother and associate, Little Harpe. Big Harpe made a wide region of the Ohio valley dangerous to travellers. The events connected with his vicious life are thus given by that always interesting old-time chronicler, Henry Howe:

> In the fall of the year 1801 or 1802, a company consisting of two men and three women arrived in Lincoln county, Ky., and encamped about a mile from the present town of Stanford. The appearance of the individuals composing this party was wild and rude in the extreme. The one who seemed to be the leader of the band was above the ordinary stature of men. His frame was bony and muscular, his breast broad, his limbs gigantic. His clothing was uncouth and shabby, his exterior weather-beaten and dirty, indicating continual exposure to the elements, and designating him as one who dwelt far from the habitations of men, and mingled not in the courtesies of civilized life.
> 
> His countenance was bold and ferocious, and exceedingly repulsive, from its strongly marked expression of villainy. His face, which was larger than ordinary, exhibited the lines of ungovernable passion, and the complexion announced that the ordinary feelings of the human breast were in him extinguished. Instead of the healthy hue which indicates the social emotions, there was a livid, unnatural redness, resembling that of a dried and lifeless skin. His eye was fearless and steady, but it was also artful and audacious, glaring upon the beholder with an un-

pleasant fixedness and brilliancy, like that of a ravenous animal gloating on its prey. He wore no covering on his head, and the natural protection of thick, coarse hair, of a fiery redness, uncombed and matted, gave evidence of long exposure to the rudest visitations of the sunbeam and the tempest.

He was armed with a rifle, and a broad leathern belt, drawn closely around his waist, supported a knife and a tomahawk. He seemed, in short, an outlaw, destitute of all the nobler sympathies of human nature, and prepared at all points of assault or defence. The other man was smaller in size than him who lead the party, but similarly armed, having the same suspicious exterior, and a countenance equally fierce and sinister. The females were coarse and wretchedly attired.

These men stated in answer to the inquiry of the inhabitants, that their name was Harpe, and that they were emigrants from North Carolina. They remained at their encampment the greater part of two days and a night, spending the time in rioting, drunkenness and debauchery. When they left, they took the road leading to Green River.

The day succeeding their departure, a report reached the neighbourhood that a young gentleman of wealth from Virginia, named Lankford, had been robbed and murdered on what was then called and is still known as the "Wilderness Road," (1905), which runs through the Rock-castle hills. Suspicion Immediately fixed upon the Harpes as the perpetrators, and Captain Ballenger at the head of a few bold and resolute men, started in pursuit. They experienced great difficulty in following their trail, owing to a heavy fall of snow, which obliterated most of their tracks, but finally came upon them while encamped in a bottom on Green River, near the spot where the town of Liberty now stands.

At first, they made a show of resistance, but upon being informed that if they did not immediately surrender, they would be shot down, they yielded themselves prisoners. They were brought back to Stanford, and there examined. Among their effects were found some fine linen shirts, marked with the initials of Lankford. One had been pierced by a bullet and was stained with blood. They had also a considerable sum of money in gold. It was afterward ascertained that this was the kind of money Lankford had with him. The evidence against them being thus conclusive, they were confined in the Stanford jail, but were afterward sent for trial to Danville, where the district court was in session. Here they broke jail, and succeeded in making their escape.

They were next heard of in Adair County, near Columbia. In passing through the country, they met a small boy, the son of Colonel Trabue, with a pillow-case of meal or flour, an article they probably needed. This boy. It is supposed they robbed and then murdered, as he was never afterward heard of. Many years afterward human bones answering the size of Colonel Trabue's son at the time of his disappearance, were found in a sink hole near the place where he was said to have been murdered.

The Harpes still shaped their course toward the mouth of Green River, marking their path by murders and robberies of the most horrible and brutal character. The district of country through which they passed was at that time very thinly settled, and from this reason, their outrages went unpunished. They seemed inspired with the deadliest hatred against the whole human race, and such was their implacable misanthropy, that they were known to kill where there was no temptation to rob. One of their victims was a little girl, found at some distance from her home, whose tender age and helplessness would have been protection against any but incarnate fiends. The last dreadful act of barbarity, which led to their punishment and expulsion from the country, exceeded in atrocity all the others.

Assuming the guise of Methodist preachers, they obtained lodgings one night at a solitary house on the road. Mr. Stagall, the master of the house, was absent, but they found his wife and children, and a stranger, who, like themselves, had stopped for the night. Here they conversed and made inquiries about the two noted Harpes who were represented as prowling about the country. When they retired to rest, they contrived to secure an axe, which they carried with them into their chamber. In the dead of night, they crept softly downstairs, and assassinated the whole family, together with the stranger, in their sleep, and then setting fire to the house, made their escape.

When Stagall returned, he found no wife to welcome him; no home to receive him. Distracted with grief and rage, he turned his horse's head from the smouldering ruins, and repaired to the house of Captain John Leeper. Leeper was one of the most powerful men in his day, and fearless as powerful. Collecting four or five men well-armed, they mounted and started in pursuit of vengeance. It was agreed that Leeper should attack 'Big Harpe,' leaving 'Little Harpe' to be disposed of by Stagall. The others were to hold themselves in readiness to assist Leeper and Stagall, as circumstances might require.

This party found the women belonging to the Harpes, attending to their little camp by the roadside; the men having gone aside into the woods to shoot an unfortunate traveller, of the name of Smith, who had fallen into their hands, and whom the women had begged might not be dispatched before their eyes. It was this halt that enabled the pursuers to overtake them. The women immediately gave the alarm, and the miscreants mounting their horses, which were large, fleet and powerful, fled in separate directions. Leeper singled out the 'Big Harpe,' and being better mounted than his companions, soon left them far behind. 'Little Harpe' succeeded in escaping from Stagall, and he, with the rest of his companions, turned and followed on the track of Leeper and the 'Big Harpe.'

After a chase of about nine miles, Leeper came within gunshot of the latter and fired. The ball entering his thigh, passed through it and penetrated his horse and both fell. Harpe's gun escaped from his hand and rolled some eight or ten feet down the bank. Reloading his rifle, Leeper ran to where the wounded outlaw lay weltering in his blood, and found him with one thigh broken, and the other crushed beneath his horse. Leeper rolled the horse away, and set Harpe in an easier position. The robber begged that he might not be killed. Leeper told him that he had nothing to fear from him, but that Stagall was coming up, and could not probably be restrained.

Harpe appeared very much frightened at hearing this, and implored Leeper to protect him. In a few moments, Stagall appeared, and without uttering a word, raised his rifle and shot Harpe through the head. They then severed the head from the body, and stuck it upon a pole where the road crosses the creek, from which the place was then named and is yet called Harpe's Head. Thus, perished one of the boldest and most noted freebooters that has ever appeared in America. Save courage, he was without one redeeming quality, and his death freed the country from a terror which had long paralyzed its boldest spirits.

The 'Little Harpe' afterward joined the band of Meason, and became one of his most valuable assistants in the dreadful trade of robbery and murder. He was one of the two bandits that, tempted by the reward for their leader's head, murdered him, and eventually themselves suffered the penalty of the law as previously related.

Thus, it would seem that the first quarter of the last century on the frontier was not without its own interest. The next decade, or that ending about 1840, however, offered a still greater instance of outlawry, one of the most famous ones indeed of American history, although little known today, (1905). This had to do with that genius in crime, John A. Murrell, long known as the great Western land-pirate; and surely no pirate of the seas was ever more enterprising or more dangerous.

Murrell was another man who, in a decent walk of life, would have been called great. He had more than ordinary energy and intellect. He was not a mere brute, but a shrewd, cunning, scheming man, hesitating at no crime on earth, yet animated by a mind so bold that mere personal crime was not enough for him. When it is added that he had a gang of robbers and murderers associated with him who were said to number nearly two thousand men, and who were scattered over the entire South below the Ohio River, it may be seen how bold were his plans; and his ability may further be shown in the fact that for years these men lived among and mingled with their fellows in civil life, unknown and unsuspected. Some of them were said to have been of the best families of the land; and even yet there come to light strange and romantic tales, perhaps not wholly true, of death-bed confessions of men prominent in the South who admitted that once they belonged to Murrell's gang, but had later repented and reformed.

A prominent Kentucky lawyer was one of these. Murrell and his confederates would steal horses and mules, or at least the common class, or division, known as the "strikers," would do so, although the members of the Grand Council would hardly stoop to so petty a crime. For them was reserved the murdering of travellers or settlers who were supposed to have money, and the larger operations of negro stealing.

The theft of slaves, the claiming of the runaway rewards, the later re-stealing and re-selling and final killing of the negro in order to destroy the evidence, are matters which Murrell reduced to a system that has no parallel in the criminal records of the country. But not even here did this daring outlaw pause. It was not enough to steal a negro here and there, and to make a few thousand dollars out of each negro so handled. The whole state of organised society was to be overthrown by means of this same black population. So at least goes one story of his life. We know of several so-called black insurrections that were planned at one time or another in the South—as, for instance, the Turner insurrection in Virginia; but this Murrell enterprise was the biggest of them all.

The plan was to have the uprising occur all over the South on the same day, Christmas of 1835. The blacks were to band together and march on the settlements, after killing all the whites on the farms where they worked. There they were to fall under the leadership of Murrell's lieutenants, who were to show them how to sack the stores, to kill the white merchants, and take the white women. The banks of all the Southern towns were to become the property of Murrell and his associates. In short, at one stroke, the entire system of government, which had been established after such hard effort in that fierce wilderness along the old Southern "traces," was to be wiped out absolutely. The land was indeed to be left without law. The entire fruits of organised society were to belong to a band of outlaws. This was probably the best and boldest Instance ever seen of the narrowness of the line dividing society and savagery.

Murrell was finally brought to book by his supposed confederate, Virgil A. Stewart, the spy, who went under the name of Hues, whose evidence, after many difficulties, no doubt resulted in the breaking up of this, the largest and most dangerous band of outlaws this country ever saw; although Stewart himself was a vain and ambitious notoriety seeker. Supposing himself safe, Murrell gave Stewart a detailed story of his life. This was later used in evidence against him; and although Stewart's account needs qualification, it is the best and fullest record obtainable today. (*Life and Adventures of Virgil A. Stewart.*)

Murrell personally stated:

> I was born in Middle Tennessee. My parents had not much property, but they were intelligent people; and my father was an honest man I expect, and tried to raise me honest, but I think none the better of him for that. My mother was of the pure grit; she learned me and all her children to steal as soon as we could walk and would hide for us whenever she could. At ten

years old I was not a bad hand. The first good haul I made was from a pedler who lodged at my father's house one night.

I began to look after larger spoils and ran several fine horses. By the time I was twenty I began to acquire considerable character, and concluded to go off and do my speculation where I was not known, and go on a larger scale; so, I began to see the value of having friends in this business. I made several associates; I had been acquainted with some old hands for a long time, who had given me the names of some royal fellows between Nashville and Tuscaloosa, and between Nashville and Savannah in the state of Georgia and many other places.

Myself and a fellow by the name of Crenshaw gathered four good horses and started for Georgia. We got in company with a young South Carolinian just before we reached Cumberland Mountain, and Crenshaw soon knew all about his business. He had been to Tennessee to buy a drove of hogs, but when he got there pork was dearer than he calculated, and he declined purchasing. We concluded he was a prize. Crenshaw winked at me; I understood his idea. Crenshaw had travelled the road before, but I never had; we had travelled several miles on the mountain, when we passed near a great precipice; just before we passed it, Crenshaw asked me for my whip, which had a pound of lead in the butt; I handed it to him, and he rode up by the side of the South Carolinian, and gave him a blow on the side of the head, and tumbled him from his horse; we lit from our horses and fingered his pockets; we got twelve hundred and sixty-two dollars.

Crenshaw said he knew of a place to hide him, and gathered him under the arms, and I by his feet, and conveyed him to a deep crevice in the brow of the precipice, and tumbled him into it; he went out of sight. We then tumbled in his saddle, and took his horse with us, which was worth two hundred dollars. We turned our course for South Alabama, and sold our horse for a good price. We frolicked for a week or more and were the highest larks you ever saw. We commenced sporting and gambling, and lost every cent of our money.

We were forced to resort to our profession for a second raise. We stole a negro man, and pushed for Mississippi. We had promised him that we would conduct him to a free state if he would let us sell him once as we went on our way; we also agreed to give him part of the money. We sold him for six hundred dollars; but, when we went to start, the negro seemed to be very uneasy, and appeared to doubt our coming back for him as we had promised. We lay in a creek bottom, not far from the place where we had sold the negro, all the next day, and after dark we went to the china-tree in the lane where we were to meet Tom; he had been waiting for some time. He mounted his horse, and we pushed with him a second time. We rode twenty miles that night to the house of a friendly speculator.

I had seen him in Tennessee, and had given him several lifts. He gave me his place of residence, that I might find him when I was passing. He is quite rich, and one of the best kind of fellows. Our horses were fed as much as they would eat, and two of them were foundered the next morning. We were detained a few days, and during that time our friend went to a little village in the neighbourhood, and saw the negro advertised, with a description of the two men of whom he had been purchased, and with mention of them as suspicious personages. It was rather squally times, but any port in a storm; we took the negro that night to the bank of a creek which runs by the farm of our friend, and Crenshaw shot him through the head. We took out his entrails and sunk him in the creek; our friend furnished us with one fine horse, and we left him our foundered horses. We made our way through the Choctaw and Chickasaw Nations, and then to Williamson County, in this state. We should have made a fine trip if we had taken care of all we got.

I had become a considerable libertine, and when I returned home I spent a few months rioting in all the luxuries of forbidden pleasures with the girls of my acquaintance. My stock of cash was soon gone, and I put to my shift for more. I commenced with horses, and fan several from the adjoining counties. I had got associated with a young man who had professed to be a preacher among the Methodists, and a sharper he was; he was as slick on the tongue as goose-grease. I took my first lessons in divinity from this young preacher. He was highly respected by all who knew him, and well calculated to please; he first put me in the notion of preaching, to aid me in my speculations.

I got into difficulty about a mare that I had taken, and was Imprisoned for near three years. I shifted it from court to court, but was at last found guilty, and whipped. During my confinement I read the scriptures, and became a good judge of theology. I had not neglected the criminal laws for many years before that time. When they turned me loose I was prepared for anything; I wanted to kill all but those of my own grit; and I will die by the side of one of them before I will desert.

My next speculation was in the Choctaw region; myself and brother stole two fine horses, and made our way into this country. We got in with an old negro man and his wife, and three sons, to go off with us to Texas, and promised them that, if they would work for us one year after we got there, we would let them go free, and told them many fine stories. The old negro became suspicious that we were going to sell him, and grew quite contrary; so, we landed one day by the side of an island, and I requested him to go with me round the point of the island to hunt a good place to catch some fish.

After we were hidden from our company I shot him through the head, and then ripped open his belly and tumbled him into the river. I returned to my company, and told them that the negro had fallen into the river, and that he never came up after he went under. We landed fifty miles above New Orleans, and went into the country and sold our negroes to a Frenchman for nineteen hundred dollars.

We went from where we sold the negroes to New Orleans, and dressed ourselves like young lords. I mixed with the loose characters at the *swamp* every night. One night, as I was returning to the tavern where I boarded, I was stopped by two armed men, who demanded my money. I handed them my pocketbook, and observed that I was very happy to meet with them, as we were all of the same profession.

One of them observed, 'D——d if I ever rob a brother chip. We have had our eyes on you and the man that has generally come with you for several nights; we saw so much rigging and glittering jewellery, that we concluded you must be some wealthy dandy, with a surplus of cash; and had determined to rid you of the trouble of some of it; but, if you are a robber, here is your pocketbook, and you must go with us tonight, and we will give you an introduction to several fine fellows of the block; but stop, do you understand this motion?' I answered it, and thanked them for their kindness, and turned with them. We went to old Mother Surgick's, and had a real frolic with her girls. That night was the commencement of my greatness in what the world calls villainy. The two fellows who robbed me were named Haines and Phelps; they made me known to all the speculators that visited New Orleans, and gave me the name of every fellow who would speculate that lived on the Mississippi River, and many of its tributary streams, from New Orleans up to all the large Western cities.

I had become acquainted with a Kentuckian, who boarded at the same tavern I did, and I suspected he had a large sum of money; I felt an inclination to count it for him before I left the city; so, I made my notions known to Phelps and my other new comrades, and concerted our plan. I was to get him off to the swamp with me on a spree, and when we were returning to our lodgings, my friends were to meet us and rob us both. I had got very intimate with the Kentuckian, and he thought me one of the best fellows in the world. He was very fond of wine; and I had him well fumed with good wine before I made the proposition for a frolic.

When I invited him to walk with me he readily accepted the invitation. We cut a few shines with the girls, and started to the tavern. We were met by a band of robbers, and robbed of all our money. The Kentuckian was so mad that he cursed the whole city, and wished that it would all be deluged in a flood of water so soon as he left the place. I went to my friends the next morning, and got my share of the spoil money, and my pocketbook that I had been robbed of. We got seven hundred and fifty dollars of the bold Kentuckian, which was divided among thirteen of us.

I commenced traveling and making all the acquaintances among the speculators that I could. I went from New Orleans to Cincinnati, and from there I visited Lexington, in Kentucky. I found a speculator about four miles from Newport, who furnished me with a fine horse the second night after I arrived at his house. I went from Lexington to Richmond, in Virginia, and from there I visited Charleston, in the State of South Carolina; and from thence to Milledgeville, by the way of Savannah and Augusta, in the State of Georgia. I made my way from Milledgeville to Williamson county, the old stamping-ground. In all the route I only robbed eleven men but I preached some fine sermons, and scattered some counterfeit United States paper among my brethren.

After I returned home from the first grand circuit I made among my speculators, I remained there but a short time, as I could not rest when my mind was not actively engaged in some speculation. I commenced the foundation of this mystic clan on that tour, and suggested the plan of exciting a rebellion among the negroes, as the sure road to an inexhaustible fortune to all who would engage in the expedition. The first mystic sign which is used by this clan was in use among robbers before I was born; and the second had its origin from myself, Phelps, Haines, Cooper, Doris, Bolton, Harris, Doddridge, Celly, Morris, Walton, Depont, and one of my brothers, on the second night after my acquaintance with them in New Orleans.

We needed a higher order to carry on our designs, and we adopted our sign, and called it the sign of the Grand Council of the Mystic Clan; and practised ourselves to give and receive the new sign to a fraction before we parted; and, in addition to this improvement, we invented and formed a mode of corresponding, by means of ten characters, mixed with other matter, which has been very convenient on many occasions, and especially when any of us get into difficulties. I was encouraged in my new undertaking, and my heart began to beat high with the hope of being able one day to visit the pomp of the Southern and Western people in my vengeance; and of seeing their cities and towns one common scene of devastation, smoked walls and fragments.

I decoyed a negro man from his master in Middle Tennessee, and sent him to Mill's Point by a young man, and I waited to see the movements of the owner. He thought his negro had run off. So, I started to take possession of my prize. I got another friend at Mill's Point to take my negro in a skiff, and convey him to the mouth of Red River, while I took passage on a steamboat. I then went through the country by land, and sold my negro for nine hundred dollars, and the second night after I sold him I stole him again, and my friend ran him to the Irish bayou in Texas; I followed on after him, and sold my negro in Texas for five hundred dollars. I then resolved to visit South America, and see if there was an opening in that country for a speculation; I had also concluded that I could get some strong friends in that quarter to aid me in my designs relative to a negro rebellion; but of all people in the world, the Spaniards are the most treacherous and cowardly; I never want them concerned in any matter with me; I had rather take the negroes in this country to fight than a Spaniard.

I stopped in a village, and passed as a doctor, and commenced practising medicine. I could ape the doctor first-rate, having read Ewel, and several other works on primitive medicine. I became a great favourite of an old Catholic; he adopted me as his son in the faith, and introduced me to all the best families as a young doctor from North America. I had been with the old Catholic but a very short time before I was a great Roman Catholic, and bowed to the cross, and attended regularly to all the ceremonies of that persuasion; and, to tell you the fact, Hues, all the Catholic religion needs to be universally received, is to be correctly represented; but you know I care nothing for religion.

I had been with the old Catholic about three months, and was getting a heavy practice, when an opportunity offered for me to rob the good man's secretary of nine hundred and sixty dollars in gold, and I could have got as much more in silver if I could have carried it. I was soon on the road for home again; I stopped three weeks in New Orleans as I came home, and had some high fun with old Mother Surgick's girls.

I collected all my associates in New Orleans at one of my friend's houses in that place, and we sat in council three days before we got all our plans to our notion; we then determined to undertake the rebellion at every hazard, and make as many friends as we could for that purpose. Every man's business being assigned him, I started for Natchez on foot. Having sold my horse in New Orleans with the intention of stealing another after I started, I walked four days, and no opportunity offered for me to get a horse. The fifth day, about twelve o'clock, I had become very tired, and stopped at a creek to get some water and rest a little.

While I was sitting on a log, looking down the road I had come, a man came in sight riding a good-looking horse. The very moment I saw him I determined to have his horse if he was in the garb of a traveller. He rode up, and I saw from his equipage that he was a traveller. I arose from my seat and drew an elegant rifle pistol on him, and ordered him to dismount. He did so, and I took his horse by the bridle, and pointed down the creek, and ordered him to walk before me. We went a few hundred yards and stopped. I hitched his horse, then made him undress himself, all to his shirt and drawers, and ordered him to turn his back to me. He asked me if I was going to shoot him. I ordered him the second time to turn his back to me.

He said, 'If you are determined to kill me, let me have time to pray before I die.' I told him I had no time to hear him pray. He turned round and dropped on his knees, and I shot him through the back of the head. I ripped open his belly, and took out his entrails, and sunk him in the creek. I then searched his pockets, and found four hundred and one dollars and thirty-seven cents, and a number of papers that I did not take time to examine. I sunk the pocketbook and papers and his hat in the creek. His boots were brand new, and fitted me very genteelly, and I put them on, and sunk my old shoes in the creek to atone for them. I rolled up his clothes and put them into his portmanteau, as they were quite new cloth of the best quality. I mounted as fine a horse as ever I straddled, and directed my course to Natchez in much better style than I had been for the last five days.

I reached Natchez, and spent two days with my friends at that place and the girls under the Hill together. I then left Natchez for the Choctaw nation, with the Intention of giving some of them a chance for their property. As I was riding along between Benton and Rankin, planning for my designs, I was overtaken by a tall and good-looking young man, riding an elegant horse, which was splendidly rigged off; and the young gentleman's apparel was of the gayest that could be had, and his watchchain and other jewellery were of the richest and best. I was anxious to know If he intended to travel through the Choctaw nation, and soon managed to learn. He said he had been to the lower country with a drove of negroes, and was returning home to Kentucky.

We rode on, and soon got very intimate for strangers, and agreed to be company through the Indian nation. We were two fine-looking men, and, to hear us talk, we were very rich. I felt him on the subject of speculation, but he cursed the speculators, and said he was in a bad condition to fall into the hands of such villains, as he had the cash with him that twenty negroes had sold for; and that he was very happy that he happened to get in company with me through the nation.

I concluded he was a noble prize, and longed to be counting his cash. At length we came into one of those long stretches in the Nation, where there was no house for twenty miles, on the third day after we had been in company with each other. The country was high, hilly, and broken, and no water; just about the time I reached the place where I intended to count my companion's cash, I became very thirsty, and insisted on turning down a deep hollow, or dale, that headed near the road, to hunt some water.

We had followed down the dale for near four hundred yards, when I drew my pistol and shot him through. He fell dead; I commenced hunting for his cash, and opened his large pocketbook, which was stuffed very full; and when I began to open it I thought it was a treasure indeed; but oh! the contents of that book! it was richly filled with the copies of love-songs, the forms of love-letters, and some of his own composition,—but no cash. I began to cut off his clothes with my knife, and examine them for his money. I found four dollars and a half in change in his pockets, and no more. And is this the amount for which twenty negroes sold? thought I.

I recollected his watch and jewellery, and I gathered them in; his chain was rich and good, but it was swung to an old brass watch. He was a puff for true, and I thought all such fools ought to die as soon as possible. I took his horse, and swapped him to an Indian native for four ponies, and sold them on the way home. I reached home, and spent a few weeks among the girls of my acquaintance, in all the enjoyments that money could afford.

My next trip was through Georgia, South Carolina, North Carolina, Virginia, and Maryland, and then back to South Carolina, and from there round by Florida and Alabama. I began to conduct the progress of my operations, and establish my emissaries over the country in every direction.

I have been going ever since from one place to another, directing and managing; but I have others now as good as myself to manage. This fellow, Phelps, that I was telling you of before, he is a noble chap among the negroes, and he wants them all free; he knows how to excite them as well as any person; but he will not do for a robber, as he cannot kill a man unless he has received an injury from him first. He is now in jail at Vicksburg, and I fear will hang. I went to see him not long since, but he is so strictly watched that nothing can be done. He has been in the habit of stopping men on the highway, and robbing them, and letting them go on; but that will never do for a robber; after I rob a man he will never give evidence against me, and there is but one safe plan in the business, and that is to kill—if I could not afford to kill a man, I would not rob.

The great object that we have in contemplation is to excite a rebellion among the negroes throughout the slave-holding states. Our plan is to manage so as to have it commence everywhere at the same hour. We have set on the 25th of December, 1835, for the time to commence our operations. We design having our companies so stationed over the country, in the vicinity of the banks and large cities, that when the negroes commence their carnage and slaughter, we will have detachments to fire the towns and rob the banks while all is confusion and dismay. The rebellion taking place everywhere at the same time, every part of the country will be engaged in its own defence; and one part of the country can afford no relief to another, until many places will be entirely overrun by the negroes, and our pockets replenished from the banks and the desks of rich merchants' houses. It is true that in many places in the slave states the negro population is not strong, and would be easily overpowered; but, back them with a few resolute leaders from our clan, they will murder thousands, and huddle the remainder into large bodies of stationary defence for their own preservation; and then, in many other places, the black population is much the strongest, and under a leader would overrun the country before any steps could be taken to suppress them.

We do not go to every negro we see and tell him that the negroes Intend to rebel on the night of the 25th of December, 1835. We find the most vicious and wickedly disposed on large farms, and poison their minds by telling them how they are mistreated. When we are convinced that we have found a bloodthirsty devil, we swear him to secrecy and disclose to him the secret, and convince him that every other state and section of country where there are any negroes intend to rebel and slay all the whites they can on the night of the 25th of December,

1835, and assure him that there are thousands of white men engaged in trying to free them, who will die by their sides in battle. We have a long ceremony for the oath, which is administered in the presence of a terrific picture painted for that purpose, representing the monster who is to deal with him should he prove unfaithful in the engagements he has entered Into. This picture is highly calculated to make a negro true to his trust, for he is disposed to be superstitious at best.

Our black emissaries have the promise of a share in the spoils we may gain, and we promise to conduct them to Texas should we be defeated, where they will be free; but we never talk of being defeated. We always talk of victory and wealth to them. There is no danger in any man. If you can ever get him once Implicated or engaged in a matter. That is the way we employ our strikers in all things; we have them Implicated before we trust them from our sight.

This may seem too bold, but that is what I glory in. All the crimes I have ever committed have been of the most daring; and I have been successful in all my attempts as yet; and I am confident that I will be victorious in this matter, as in the robberies which I have in contemplation; and I will have the pleasure and honour of seeing and knowing that by my management I have glutted the earth with more human gore, and destroyed more property, than any other robber who has ever lived in America, or the known world. I look on the American people as my common enemy.

My clan is strong, brave, and experienced, and rapidly increasing in strength every day. I should not be surprised if we were to be two thousand strong by the 25th of December, 1835; and, in addition to this, I have the advantage of any other leader of banditti that has ever preceded me, for at least one-half of my Grand Council are men of high standing, and many of them in honourable and lucrative offices.

The number of men, more or less prominent, in the different states included: sixty-one from Tennessee, forty-seven from Mississippi, forty-six from Arkansas, twenty-five from Kentucky, twenty-seven from Missouri, twenty-eight from Alabama, thirty-three from Georgia, thirty-five from South Carolina, thirty-two from North Carolina, twenty-one from Virginia, twenty-seven from Maryland, sixteen from

Florida, thirty-two from Louisiana. The transient members who made a habit of travelling from place to place numbered twenty-two; Murrell said that there was a total list of two thousand men in his band, including all classes.

To the foregoing sketch of Murrell's life Mr. Alexander Hynds, historian of Tennessee, adds some facts and comments which will enable the reader more fully to make his own estimate as to this singular man:

> The central meeting place of Murrell's band was near an enormous cottonwood tree in Mississippi County, Arkansas. It was standing in 1890, and is perhaps still standing in the wilderness shortly above Memphis. His widely scattered bands had a system of signs and passwords. Murrell himself was married to the sister of one of his gang. He bought a good farm near Denmark, Madison county, Tennessee, where he lived as a plain farmer, while he conducted the most fearful schemes of rapine and murder from New Orleans up to Memphis, St. Louis and Cincinnati.
>
> Nature had done much for Murrell. He had a quick mind, a fine natural address and great adaptability; and he was as much at ease among the refined and cultured as with his own gang. He made a special study of criminal law, and knew something of medicine. He often palmed himself off as a preacher, and preached in large camp-meetings—and some were converted under his ministry! He often used his clerical garb in passing counterfeit money. With a clear head, cool, fine judgment, and a nature utterly without fear, moral or physical, his power over his men never waned. To them he was just, fair and amiable. He was a kind husband and brother, and a faithful friend. He took great pride in his position and in the operations of his gang. This conceit was the only weak spot in his nature, and led to his downfall.
>
> "Stewart, who purports to be Murrell's biographer, made Murrell's acquaintance, pretended to join his gang, and playing on his vanity, attended a meeting of the gang at the rendezvous at the Big Cottonwood, and saw the meeting of the Grand Council. He had Murrell arrested, and he was tried, convicted and sent to the Tennessee penitentiary in 1834 for ten years. There he worked in the blacksmith shops, but by the time he got out, was broken down in mind and body, emerging an imbecile and

an invalid, to live less than a year.

Stewart's account holds Inconsistencies and Inaccuracies, such as that many men high in social and official life belonged to Murrell's gang, which his published lists do not show. He had perhaps 440 to 450 men, scattered from New Orleans to Cincinnati, but his downfall spread fear and distrust among them.

At Vicksburg, on July 4, 1835, a drunken member of the gang threatened to attack the authorities, and was tarred and feathered. Others of the gang, or at least several well-known gamblers, collected and defied the citizens, and killed the good and brave Dr. Bodley. Five men were hung, Hullams, Dutch Bill, North, Smith and McCall. The news swept like wildfire through the Mississippi Valley and gave heart to the lovers of law and order. At one or two other places some were shot, some were hanged, and now and then one or two were sent to prison, and thus an end was put to organised crime in the Southwest forever; and this closed out the reign of the river cutthroats, pirates and gamblers as well.

Thus, as in the case of Sturdevant, lynch law put an effectual end to outlawry that the law itself could not control.

CHAPTER 5

# The Vigilantes of California

The world will never see another California. Great gold stampedes there may be, but under conditions far different from those of 1849. Transportation has been so developed, travel has become so swift and easy, that no section can now long remain segregated from the rest of the world. There is no corner of the earth which may not now be reached with a celerity impossible in the days of the great rush to the Pacific Coast. The whole structure of civilization, itself based upon transportation, goes swiftly forward with that transportation, and the tent of the miner or adventurer finds immediately erected by its side the temple of the law.

It was not thus in those early days of our Western history. The law was left far behind by reason of the exigencies of geography and of wilderness travel. Thousands of honest men pressed on across the plains and mountains inflamed, it is true, by the madness of the lust for gold, but carrying at the outset no wish to escape from the watch-care of the law. With them went equal numbers of those eager to escape all restraints of society and law, men intending never to aid in the up-rearing of the social system in new wild lands. Both these elements, the law-loving and the law-hating, as they advanced *pari-passu* farther and farther from the staid world which they had known, noticed the development of a strange phenomenon: that law, which they had left behind them, waned in importance with each passing day. The standards of the old home changed, even as customs changed.

A week's journey from the settlements showed the Argonaut a new world. A month hedged it about to itself, alone, apart, with ideas and values of its own and independent of all others. A year sufficed to leave that world as distinct as though it occupied a planet all its own. For that world the divine fire of the law must be rediscovered, evolved, nay, evoked fresh from chaos even as the savage calls forth fire from the dry and sapless twigs of the wilderness.

In the gold country all ideas and principles were based upon new conditions. Precedents did not exist. Man had gone savage again, and it was the beginning. Yet this savage, willing to live as a savage in a land which was one vast encampment, was the Anglo-Saxon savage, and therefore carried with him that chief trait of the American character, the principle that what a man earns—not what he steals, but what he earns—is his and his alone. This principle sowed in ground forbidding and unpromising was the seed of the law out of which has sprung the growth of a mighty civilization fit to be called an empire of its own. The growth and development of law under such conditions offered phenomena not recorded in the history of any other land or time.

In the first place, and even while in transit, men organised for the purpose of self-protection, and in this necessary act, law-abiding and criminal elements united. After arriving at the scenes of the gold fields, such organisation was forgotten; even the parties that had banded together in the Eastern states as partners rarely kept together for a month after reaching the region where luck, hazard and opportunity, inextricably blended, appealed to each man to act for himself and with small reference to others. The first organisations of the mining camps were those of the criminal element. They were presently met by the organisation of the law and order men.

Hard upon the miners' law came the regularly organised legal machinery of the older states, modified by local conditions, and irretrievably blended with a politics more corrupt than any known before or since. Men were busy in picking up raw gold from the earth, and they paid small attention to courts and government. The law became an unbridled instrument of evil. Judges of the courts openly confiscated the property of their enemies, or sentenced them with no reference to the principles of justice, with as great disregard for life and liberty as was ever known in the Revolutionary days of France. Against this manner of government presently arose the organisations of the law-abiding, the justice-loving, and these took the law into their own stern hands. The executive officers of the law, the sheriffs and constables, were in league to kill and confiscate; and against these the new agency of the actual law made war, constituting themselves into an arm of essential government, and openly called themselves Vigilantes.

In turn criminals used the cloak of the Vigilantes to cover their own deeds of lawlessness and violence. The Vigilantes purged themselves of the false members, and carried their own title of opprobrium, the "stranglers," with unconcern or pride. They grew in numbers, the love of justice their lodestone, until at one time they numbered more than five thousand in the city of San Francisco alone, and held that community in a grip of lawlessness, or law, as you shall choose to term it. They set at defiance the chief executive of the state, erected an armed castle of their own, seized upon the arms of the militia, defied the government of the United States and even the United States Army! They were, as you shall choose to call them, criminals, or great and noble men. Seek as you may today, (1905), you will never know the full roster of their names, although they made no concealment of their identity; and no one, to this day, has ever been able to determine who took the first step in their organisation. They began their labours in California at a time when there had been more than two thousand murders—five hundred in one year—and not five legal executions.

Their task included the erection of a fit structure of the law, and, Incidentally, the destruction of a corrupt and unworthy structure claiming the title of the law. In this strange, swift panorama there is all the story of the social system, all the picture of the building of that temple of the law which, as Americans, we now revere, or, at times, still despise and desecrate. At first the average gold seeker concerned himself little with law, because he intended to make his fortune quickly and then hasten back East to his former home; yet, as early as the winter of 1849, there was elected a legislature which met at San Jose, a Senate of sixteen members and an Assembly of thirty-six. In this election the new American vote was in evidence. The miners had already tired of the semi-military phase of their government, and had met and adopted a state constitution. The legislature enacted one hundred and forty new laws in two months, and abolished all former laws; and then, satisfied with its labours, it left the enforcement of the laws, in the good old American fashion, to whomsoever might take an interest in the matter. (Tuthill: *History of California*). This is our custom even today, (1905). Our great cities of the East are practically all governed, so far as they are governed at all, by civic leagues, civic federations, citizens' leagues, business men's associations—all protests at non-enforcement of the law. This protest in '49 and on the Pacific coast took a sterner form.

At one time the city of San Francisco had three separate and distinct city councils, each claiming to be the only legal one. In spite of the new state organisation, the law was much a matter of go as you please. Under such conditions it was no wonder that outlawry began to show its head in bold and well-organised forms. A party of ruffians, who called themselves the "Hounds," banded together to run all foreigners out of the rich camps, and to take their diggings over for themselves. A number of Chileans were beaten or shot, and their property was confiscated or destroyed. This was not in accordance with the saving grace of American justice, which devoted to a man that which he had earned.

A counter organisation was promptly formed, and the "Hounds" found themselves confronted with two hundred "special constables," each with a good rifle. A mass meeting sat as a court, and twenty of the "Hounds" were tried, ten of them receiving sentences that never were enforced, but which had the desired effect. So now, while far to the eastward the Congress was hotly arguing the question of the admission of California as a state, she was beginning to show an interest in law and justice when aroused thereto.

It was difficult material out of which to build a civilized community. The hardest population of the entire world was there; men savage or civilized by tradition, heathen or Christian once at least, but now all Californian. Wealth was the one common thing. The average daily return in the work of mining ranged from twenty to thirty dollars, and no man might tell when his fortune might be made by a blow of a pick. Some nuggets of gold weighing twenty-five pounds were discovered. In certain diggings men picked pure gold from the rock crevices with a spoon or a knife point. As to values, they were guessed at, the only currency being gold dust or nuggets. Prodigality was universal.

All the gamblers of the world met in vulture concourse. There was little in the way of home; of women almost none. Life was as cheap as gold dust. Let those who liked bother about statehood and government and politics; the average man was too busy digging and spending gold to trouble over such matters. The most shameless men were those found in public office. Wealth and commerce waxed great, but law and civilization languished. The times were ripening for the growth of some system of law which would offer proper protection to life and property. The measure of this need may be seen from the figures of the production of gold. From 1848 to 1856 California produced between five hundred and six hundred million dollars in virgin gold. What wonder the courts were weak; and what wonder the Vigilantes became strong!

There were in California three distinct Vigilante movements, those of 1849, 1851 and 1856, the earliest applying rather to the outlying mining camps than to the city of San Francisco. In 1851, seeing that the courts made no attempt to punish criminals, a committee was formed which did much toward enforcing respect for the principles of justice. If not of law. On June 11 they hanged John Jenkins for robbing a store. A month later they hanged James Stuart for murdering a sheriff. In August of the same summer they took out of jail and hanged Whittaker and McKenzie, Australian ex-convicts, whom they had tried and sentenced, but who had been rescued by the officers of the law. Two weeks later this committee disbanded.

They paid no attention to the many killings that were going on over land titles and the like, but confined themselves to punishing men who had committed intolerable crimes. Theft was as serious as murder, perhaps more so, in the creed of the time and place. The list of murders reached appalling dimensions. The times were sadly out of joint. The legislature was corrupt, graft was rampant—though then unknown by that name—and the entire social body was restless, discontented, and uneasy. Politics had become a fine art. The judiciary, lazy and corrupt, was held in contempt. The dockets of the courts were full, and little was done to clear them effectively. Criminals did as they liked and went unwhipped of justice. It was truly a day of violence and license.

Once more the sober and law-loving men of California sent abroad word, and again the Vigilantes assembled. In 1853 they hanged two Mexicans for horse stealing, and also a bartender who had shot a citizen near Shasta. At Jackson they hanged another Mexican for horse stealing, and at Volcano, in 1854, they hanged a man named Macy for stabbing an old and helpless man. In this instance vengeance was very swift, for the murderer was executed within half an hour after his deed. The haste caused certain criticism when, in the same month one Johnson was hanged for stabbing a man named Montgomery, at Iowa Hill, who later recovered.

At Los Angeles three men were sentenced to death by the local court, but the Supreme Court issued a stay for two of them, Brown and Lee. The people asserted that all must die together, and the mayor of the city was of the same mind. The third man, Alvitre, was hanged legally on January 12, 1855. On that day the mayor resigned his office to join the Vigilantes. Brown was taken out of jail and hanged in spite of the decision of the Supreme Court. The people were out-running the law. That same month they hanged another murderer for killing the treasurer of Tuolumne county. In the following month they hanged three more cattle thieves in Contra Costa county, and followed this by hanging a horse thief in Oakland.

A larger affair threatened in the following summer, when thirty-six Mexicans were arrested for killing a party of Americans. For a time, it was proposed to hang all thirty-six, but sober counsel prevailed and only three were hanged; this after formal jury trial. Unknown bandits waylaid and killed Isaac B. Wall and T. S. Williamson of Monterey, and, that same month U. S. Marshal William H. Richardson was shot by Charles Cora in the streets of San Francisco. The people grumbled. There was no certainty that justice would ever reach these offenders. The reputation of the state was ruined, not by the acts of the Vigilantes, but by those of unscrupulous and unprincipled men in office and upon the bench. The government was run by gamblers, ruffians, and thugs. The good men of the state began to prepare for a general movement of purification and the installation of an actual law. The great Vigilante movement of 1856 was the result.

The immediate cause of this last organisation was the murder of James King, editor of the *Bulletin*, by James P. Casey. Casey, after shooting King, was hurried off to jail by his own friends, and there was protected by a display of military force. King lingered for six days after he was shot, and the state of public opinion was ominous. Cora, who had killed Marshal Richardson, had never been punished, and there seemed no likelihood that Casey would be. The local press was divided. The religious papers, the *Pacific* and the *Christian Advocate*, both openly declared that Casey ought to be hanged. The clergy took up the matter sternly, and one minister of the Gospel, Rev. J. A. Benton, of Sacramento, gave utterance to this remarkable but well-grounded statement:

> A people can be justified in recalling delegated power and resuming its exercise.

Before we hasten to criticize sweepingly under the term "mob law" such work as this of the Vigilantes, it will be well for us to weigh that utterance, and to apply it to conditions of our own times; today, (1905), is well-nigh as dangerous to American liberties as were the wilder days of California.

Now, summoned by some unknown command, armed men appeared in the streets of San Francisco, twenty-four companies in all, with perhaps fifty men in each company. The Vigilantes had organised again. They brought a cannon and placed it against the jail gate, and demanded that Casey be surrendered to them. There was no help for it, and Casey went away handcuffed, to face a court where political influence would mean nothing. An hour later the murderer Cora was taken from his cell, and was hastened away to join Casey in the headquarters building of the Vigilantes. A company of armed and silent men marched on each side of the carriage containing the prisoner. The two men were tried in formal session of the Committee, each having counsel, and all evidence being carefully weighed.

King died on May 20, 1856, and on May 22nd was buried with popular honours, a long procession of citizens following the body to the cemetery. A popular subscription was started, and in a brief time over thirty thousand dollars was raised for the benefit of his widow and children. When the long procession filed back into the city, it was to witness, swinging from a beam projecting from a window of Committee headquarters, the bodies of Casey and Cora.

The Committee now arrested two more men, not for a capital crime, but for one which lay back of a long series of capital crimes—the stuffing of ballot-boxes and other election frauds. These men were Billy Mulligan and the prize-fighter known as Yankee Sullivan. Although advised that he would have a fair trial and that the death penalty would not be passed upon him, Yankee Sullivan committed suicide in his cell. The entire party of lawyers and judges were arrayed against the Committee, naturally enough. Judge Terry, of the Supreme Court, issued a writ of *habeas corpus* for Mulligan.

The Committee ignored the sheriff who was sent to serve the writ. They cleared the streets in front of headquarters, established six. cannon in front of their rooms, put loaded swivels on top of the roof and mounted a guard of a hundred riflemen. They brought bedding and provisions to their quarters, mounted a huge triangle on the roof for a signal to their men all over the city, arranged the interior of their rooms in the form of a court and, in short, set themselves up as the law, openly defying their own Supreme Court of the state. So far from being afraid of the vengeance of the law, they arrested two more men for election frauds, Chas. P. Duane and "Woolly" Kearney. All their prisoners were guarded in cells within the headquarters building.

The opposition to the Committee now organised in turn under the name of the "Law and Order Men," and held a public meeting. This was numerously attended by members of the Vigilante Committee, whose books were now open for enrolment. Not even the criticism of their own friends stayed these men in their resolution. They went even further. Governor Johnson issued a proclamation to them to disband and disperse. They paid no more attention to this than they had to Judge Terry's writ of *habeas corpus*. The governor threatened them with the militia, but it was not enough to frighten them. General Sherman resigned his command in the state militia, and counselled moderation at so dangerous a time.

Many of the militia turned in their rifles to the Committee, which got other arms from vessels in the harbour, and from carelessly guarded armouries. Halting at no responsibility, a band of the Committee even boarded a schooner which was carrying down a cargo of rifles from the governor to General Howard at San Francisco, and seized the entire lot. Shortly after this they confiscated a second shipment which the governor was sending down from Sacramento in the same way; thus, seizing property of the federal government. If there was such a crime as high treason, they committed it, and did so openly and without hesitation.

Governor Johnson contented himself with drawing up a statement of the situation, which was sent down to President Pierce at Washington, with the request that he instruct naval officers on the Pacific station to supply arms to the State of California, which had been despoiled by certain of its citizens. President Pierce turned over the matter to his attorney-general, Caleb Cushing, who rendered an opinion saying that Governor Johnson had not yet exhausted the state remedies, and that the United States Government could not interfere.

Little remained for the Committee to do to show its resolution to act as the State *pro tempore*. That little it now proceeded to do by practically suspending the Supreme Court of California. In making an arrest of a witness wanted by the Committee, Sterling A. Hopkins, one of the policemen retained for work by the Committee, was stabbed in the throat by Judge Terry, of the Supreme Bench, who was very bitter against all members of the Committee. It was supposed that the wound would prove fatal, and at once the Committee sounded the call for general assembly. The city went into two hostile camps, Terry and his friend, Dr. Ashe, taking refuge in the armoury where the "Law and Order" faction kept their arms.

The members of the Vigilante Committee besieged this place, and presently took charge of Terry and Ashe, as prisoners. Then the scouts of the Committee went out after the arms of all the armouries belonging to the governor and the "Law and Order" men who supported him, the lawyers and politicians who felt that their functions were being usurped. Two thousand rifles were taken, and the opposing party was left without arms. The entire state, so to speak, was now in the hands of the "Committee of Vigilance," a body of men, quiet, law-loving, law-enforcing, but of course technically traitors and criminals. The parallel of this situation has never existed elsewhere in American history.

Had Hopkins died the probability is that Judge Terry would have been hanged by the Committee, but fortunately he did not die. Terry lay a prisoner in the cell assigned him at the Committee's rooms for seven weeks, by which time Hopkins had recovered from the wound given him by Terry. The case became one of national interest, and tirades against "the Stranglers" were not lacking; but the Committee went on enrolling men. And it did not open its doors for its prisoners, although appeal was made to Congress in Terry's behalf—an appeal which was referred to the Committee on Judiciary, and so buried.

Terry was finally released, much to the regret of many of the Committee, who thought he should have been punished. The executive committee called together the board of delegates, and issued a statement showing that death and banishment were the only penalties optional with them. Death they could not inflict, because Hopkins had recovered; and banishment they thought impractical at that time, as it might prolong discussion indefinitely, and enforce a longer term in service than the Committee cared for. It was the earnest wish of all to disband at the first moment that they considered their state and city fit to take care of themselves, and the sacredness of the ballot-box again insured. To assure this latter fact, they had arrayed themselves against the federal government, as certainly they had against the state government.

The Committee now hanged two more murderers—Hetherington and Brace—the former a gambler from St. Louis, the latter a youth of New York parentage, twenty-one years of age, but hardened enough to curse volubly upon the scaffold. By the middle of August, 1856, they had no more prisoners in charge, and were ready to turn the city over to its own system of government. Their report, published in the following fall, showed they had hanged four men and banished many others, besides frightening out of the country a large criminal population that did not tarry for arrest and trial.

If opinion was divided to some extent in San Francisco, where those stirring deeds occurred, the sentiment of the outlying communities of California was almost a unit in favour of the Vigilantes, and their action received the sincere flattery of Imitation, as half a score of criminals learned to their sorrow on Impromptu scaffolds. There was no large general organisation in any other community, however. After a time, some of the banished men came back, and many damage suits were argued later in the courts; but small satisfaction came to those claimants, and few men who knew of the deeds of the "Committee of Vigilance" ever cared to discuss them. Indeed, it was practically certain that any man who ever served on a Western vigilance committee finished his life with sealed lips. Had he ventured to talk of what he knew he would have met contempt or something harsher.

A political capital was made out of the situation in San Francisco. The "Committee of Vigilance" felt that it had now concluded its work and was ready to go back to civil life. On August 18, 1856, the Committee marched openly in review through the streets of the city, five thousand one hundred and thirty-seven men in line, with three companies of artillery, eighteen cannon, a company of dragoons, and a medical staff of forty odd physicians. There were in this body one hundred and fifty men who had served in the old Committee in 1851.

After the parade the men halted, the assemblage broke up into companies, the companies into groups; and thus, quietly, with no vaunting of themselves and no concealment of their acts, there passed away one of the most singular and significant organisations of American citizens ever known. They did this with the quiet assertion that if their services were again needed, they would again assemble; and they printed a statement covering their actions in detail, showing to any fair-minded man that what they had done was indeed for the good of the whole community, which had been wronged by those whom it had elected to power, those who had set themselves up as masters where they had been chosen as servants.

The "Committee of Vigilance" of San Francisco was made up of men from all walks of life and all political parties. It had any amount of money at its command that it required, for its members were of the best and most influential citizens. It maintained, during its existence, quarters unique in their way, serving as arms-room, trial court, fortress, and prison. It was not a mob, but a grave and orderly band of men, and its deliberations were formal and exact, its labours being divided among proper sub-committees and boards. The quarters were kept open day and night, always ready for swift action, if necessary.

It had an executive committee, which upon occasion conferred with a board of delegates composed of three men from each subdivision of the general body. The executive committee consisted of thirty-three members, and its decision was final; but it could not enforce a death penalty except on a two-thirds vote of those present. It had a prosecuting attorney, and it tried no prisoner without assigning to him competent counsel. It had also a police force, with a chief of police and a sheriff with several deputies. In short, it took over the government, and was indeed the government, municipal and state in one. Recent as was its life, its deeds today are well-nigh forgotten. Though opinion may be still divided in certain quarters, California need not be ashamed of this "Committee of Vigilance." She should be proud of it, for it was largely through its unthanked and dangerous safeguarding of the public interests that California gained her social system of today, (1905).

In all the history of American desperadoism and of the movements which have checked it, there is no page more worth study than this from the story of the great Golden State. The moral is a sane, clean, and strong one. The creed of the "Committee of Vigilance" is one which we might well learn today; and its practice would leave us with more dignity of character than we can claim, so long as we content ourselves merely with outcry and criticism, with sweeping accusation of our unfaithful public servants, and without seeing that they are punished. There is nothing but manhood and freedom and justice in the covenant of the Committee. That covenant all American citizens should be ready to sign and live up to:

> We do bind ourselves each unto the other by a solemn oath to do and perform every just and lawful act for the maintenance of law and order, *and to sustain the laws when faithfully and properly administered.* But we are determined that no thief, burglar, incendiary, assassin, *ballot-box stuffer or other disturber of the peace,* shall escape punishment, either by quibbles of the law, the carelessness of the police or a laxity of those who pretend to administer justice.

What a man earns, that is his—such was the lesson of California. Self-government is our right as a people—that is what the Vigilantes said. When the laws failed of execution, then it was the people's right to resume the power that they had delegated, or which had been usurped from them—that is their statement as quoted by one of the ablest of many historians of this movement. The people might withdraw authority when faithless servants used it to thwart justice—that was what the Vigilantes preached. It is good doctrine today, (1905).

CHAPTER 6

# The Outlaw of the Mountains

The greatest of American gold stampedes, and perhaps the greatest of the world, not even excepting that of Australia, was that following upon the discovery of gold in California. For twenty years all the West was mad for gold. No other way would serve but the digging of wealth directly from the soil. Agriculture was too slow, commerce too tame, to satisfy the bold population of the frontier. The history of the first struggle for mining claims in California—one stampede after another, as this, that and the other "strike" was reported in new localities—was repeated all over the vast region of the auriferous mountain lands lying between the plains and California, which were swiftly prospected by men who had now learned well the prospector's trade.

The gold-hunters lapped back on their own trails, and, no longer content with California, began to prospect lower Oregon, upper Idaho, and Western Montana. Walla Walla was a supply point for a time. Florence was a great mountain market, and Lewiston. One district after another sprang into prominence, to fade away after a year or two of feverish life. The placers near Bannack caught a wild set of men, who surged back from California. Oro Fino was a temporary capital; then the fabulously rich placer which made Alder Gulch one of the quickly perished but still unforgotten diggings.

The flat valley of this latter gulch housed several "towns," but was really for a dozen miles a continuous string of miners' cabins. The city of Helena is built on the tailings of these placer washings, and its streets are literally paved with gold even today, (1905). Here in 1863, while the great conflict between North and South was raging, a great community of wild men, not organised into anything fit to be called society, divided and fought bitterly for control of the apparently exhaustless wealth which came pouring from the virgin mines.

These clashing factions repeated, in Intensified form, the history of California. They were even more utterly cut off from all the world. Letters and papers from the states had to reach the mountains by way of California, *via* the Horn or the Isthmus. Touch with the older civilization was utterly lost; of law there was none.

Upon the social horizon now appeared the sinister figure of the trained desperado, the professional bad man. The business of outlawry was turned into a profession, one highly organised, relatively safe and extremely lucrative. There was wealth to be had for the asking or the taking. Each miner had his buckskin purse filled with native gold. This dust was like all other dust. It could not be traced nor identified; and the old saying, "*'Twas mine, 'tis his*," might here of all places in the world most easily become true. Cheques, drafts, currency as we know it now, all the means by which civilized men keep record of their property transactions, were unknown. The gold-scales established the only currency, and each man was his own banker, obliged to be his own peace officer, and the defender of his own property.

Now our desperado appeared, the man who had killed his man, or, more likely, several men, and who had not been held sternly to an accounting for his acts; the man with the six-shooter and the skill to use it more swiftly and accurately than the average man; the man with the mind which did not scruple at murder. He found much to encourage him, little to oppose him.

The crowd from both East and West had now arrived. The town was full of gold-hunters. Expectation lighted up the countenance of every newcomer. Few had yet realised the utter despair of failure in a mining camp. In the presence of vice in all its forms, men who were staid and exemplary at home laid aside their morality like a useless garment, and yielded to the seductive influences spread for their ruin. The gambling-shops and hurdy-gurdy saloons—beheld for the first time by many of these fortune-seekers—lured them on step by step, until many of them abandoned all thought of the object they had in pursuit for lives of shameful and criminal indulgence. The condition of society thus produced was fatal to all attempts at organisation, either for protection or good order.

Yet the same condition made opportunity for those who did not wish to see a society established. Wherever the law-abiding did not organise, the bandits did; and the strength of their party, the breadth and boldness of its operations, and the length of time it carried on its unmolested operations, form one of the most extraordinary Incidents in American history. They killed, robbed, and terrorised over hundreds of miles of mountain country, for years setting at defiance all attempts at their restraint. They recognised no command except that of their "chief," whose title was always open to contest, and who gained his own position only by being more skilful, more bloodthirsty, and more unscrupulous than his fellows.

Henry Plummer, the most important captain of these cut-throats of the mountains, had a hundred or more men in his widely scattered criminal confederacy. More than one hundred murders were committed by these *banditti* in the space of three years. Many others were, without doubt, committed and never traced. Dead bodies were common in those hills, and often were unidentified. The wanderer from the States usually kept his own counsel. None knew who his family might be; and that family, missing a member who disappeared into the maw of the great West of that day of danger, might never know the fate of the one mysteriously vanished.

These robbers had their confederates scattered in all ranks of life. Plummer himself was sheriff of his county, and had confederates in deputies or city marshals. This was a strange feature of this old desperadoism in the West—It paraded often in the guise of the law. We shall find further instances of this same; phenomenon. *Employés*, friends, officials—there was none that one might trust. The organisation of the robbers even extended to the stage lines, and a regular system of communication existed by which the allies advised each other when and where such and such a passenger was going, with such and such an amount of gold upon him.

The holding up of the stage was something regularly expected, and the traveller who had any money or valuables drew a long breath when he reached a region where there was really a protecting law. Men were shot down in the streets on little or no provocation, and the murderer boasted of his crime and defied punishment. The dance-halls were run day and night. The drinking of whiskey, and, moreover, bad whiskey, was a thing universal. Vice was everywhere and virtue was not. Those few who had an aim and an ambition in life were long in the minority and, in the welter of a general license, they might not recognise each other and join hands. Murder and pillage ruled, until at length the spirit of law and order, born anew of necessity, grew and gained power as it did in most early communities of the West. How these things in time took place may best be seen by reference to the bloody biographies of some of the most reckless desperadoes ever seen in any land.

CHAPTER 7

# Henry Plummer

Henry Plummer was for several years in the early '60's the "chief" of the widely extended band of robbers and murderers who kept the placer-mining fields of Montana and Idaho in a state of terror. Posing part of the time as an officer of the law, he was all the time the leader in the reign of lawlessness. He was always ready for combat, and he so relied upon his own skill that he would even give his antagonist the advantage—or just enough advantage to leave himself sure to kill him. His victims in duels of this sort were many, and, as to his victims in cold-blooded robbery, in which death wiped out the record, no one will ever know the list.

Plummer was born in Connecticut in 1837, and, until his departure as a young man for the West, he was all that might be expected of one brought up under the chastening influences of a New England home. He received a good education, and became a polished, affable, and gentlemanly appearing man. He was about five feet ten, possibly five feet eleven inches in height, and weighed about one hundred and sixty pounds, being rather slender in appearance. His face was handsome and his demeanour always frank and open, although he was quiet and did not often talk unless accosted. His voice was low and pleasant, and he had no bravado or swagger about him. His eye was light in colour and singularly devoid of expression.

Two features gave him a sinister look—his forehead, which was low and brutish, and his eye, which was cold and fish-like. His was a strong, well-keyed nervous organisation. He was quick as a cat when in action, though apparently suave and easy in disposition. He was a good pistol shot, perhaps the best of all the desperadoes who infested Idaho and Montana at that time. Not even in his cups did he lose control of voice and eye and weapon. He was always ready—a cool, quiet, self-possessed, well-regulated killing machine.

At the date of Plummer's arrival in the mining country, the town of Lewiston, Idaho, was the emporium of a wide region then embraced under the name of Idaho Territory; the latter also including Montana at that time. Where his life had been spent previous to that is not known, but it is thought that he came over from California. Plummer set up as a gambler, and this gave him the key to the brotherhood of the bad. Gamblers usually stick together pretty closely, and institute a sort of free-masonry of their own; so that Plummer was not long in finding, among men of his own profession and their associates, a number of others whom he considered safe to take into his confidence. Every man accepted by Plummer was a murderer. He would have no weaklings.

No one can tell how many victims his associates had had before they went into his alliance; but it is sure that novices in man-killing were not desired, nor any who had not been proved of nerve. Plummer soon had so many men that he set up a rendezvous at points on all the trails leading out from Lewiston to such mines as were producing any gold. One robbery followed another, until the band threw of all restraint and ran the towns as they liked, paying for what they took when they felt like it, and laughing at the protests of the minority of the population, which was placed in the hard strait of being in that country and unable to get out without being robbed. It was the intention to seize the property of every man who was there and who was not accepted as a member of the gang.

One killing after another occurred on the trails, and man after man was lost and never traced. Assaults were made upon many men who escaped, but no criminal could be located, and. Indeed, there was no law by which any of them could be brought to book. The express riders were fired upon and robbed and the pack trains looted. No man expected to cross the mountain trails without meeting some of the robbers, and, when he did meet them, he expected to be killed if he made resistance, for they outnumbered the parties they attacked in nearly all Instances. The outlaws were now indeed about three times as numerous as those not in sympathy with them.

Rendered desperate by this state of affairs, a few resolute citizens who wanted law and order found each other out at last and organised into a vigilance committee, remembering the success of the Vigilantes of California, whose work was still recent history. Plummer himself was among the first to join this embryonic vigilante movement, as was the case in so many other similar movements in other parts of the West, where the criminal joined the law-loving in order to find out what the latter intended to do. His address was such as to disarm completely all suspicion, and he had full knowledge of facts which enabled him to murder for vengeance as well as for gain.

After Oro Fino was worked out as a placer field, the prospectors located other grounds east of the Salmon River range, at Elk City and Florence, and soon Lewiston was forsaken, all the population trooping off over the mountains to the new fields. This broke up the vigilante movement in its infancy, and gave Plummer a longer lease of life for his plans. All those who had joined the vigilante movement were marked men. One after another they were murdered, none knew by whom, or why. Masked robbers were seen every day along the trails leading between one remote mining camp and another, but no one suspected Henry Plummer, who was serving well in his double role.

Meantime, additional placer grounds had been discovered a hundred and fifty miles south of Florence, on the Boise River, and some valuable strikes were also made far to the north, at the upper waters of the Beaverhead. All the towns to the westward were now abandoned, and the miners left Florence as madly as they had rushed to it from Oro Fino and Elk City. West Bannack and East Bannack were now all the cry. To these new points, as may be supposed, the organised band of robbers fled with the others. Plummer, who had tried Elk City, Deer Lodge, and other points, now appeared at Bannack.

One after another reports continued to come of placers discovered here and there in the upper Rockies. Among all these, the strikes on Gold Creek proved to be the most extensive and valuable. A few Eastern men, almost by accident, had found fair "pay" there, and returned to that locality when they found themselves unable to get across the snow-covered mountains to Florence. These few men at the Gold Creek diggings got large additions from expeditions made up in Denver and bound for Florence, who also were unable to get across the Salmon River mountains. Yet others came out in the summer of 1862, by way of the upper plains and the Missouri River, so that the accident of the season, so to speak, turned aside the traffic intended to reach Florence into quite another region. This fact, as events proved, had much to do with the later fate of Henry Plummer and his associates.

These Eastern men were different from those who had been schooled in the mines of the Pacific Slope. They still clung to law and order; and they did not propose to be robbed. The first news of the strikes brought over the advance guard of the roughs who had been running the other camps; and, as soon as these were unmasked by acts of their own, the little advance guard of civilization shot one of them, Arnett, and hung two others, Jernigan and Spillman. This was the real beginning of a permanent vigilante force in Montana. It afforded perhaps the only known instance of a man being buried with a six-shooter in one hand and a hand of cards in the other. Arnett was killed in a game of cards, and died with his death grip thus fixed.

The new diggings did not at first prove themselves, and the camp at Bannack, on Grasshopper Creek, was more prosperous. Henry Plummer, therefore, elected Bannack as his headquarters. Others of the loosely connected *banditti* began to drop into Bannack from other districts, and Plummer was soon surrounded by his clan and kin in crime. George Ives, Bill Mitchell, Charlie Reeves, Cy Skinner, and others began operations on the same lines which had so distinguished them at the earlier diggings, west of the range. In a few weeks Bannack was as bad as Lewiston or Florence had ever been. In fact, it became so bad that the Vigilantes began to show their teeth, although they confined their sentences to banishment. The black sheep and the white began now to be segregated.

Plummer, shrewd to see the drift of opinion, saw that he must now play his hand out to the finish, that he could not now reform. He accordingly laid his plans to kill Jack Crawford, who was chosen as miners' sheriff. Plummer undertook one expedient after another to draw Crawford into a quarrel, in which he knew he could kill him; for Plummer's speed with the pistol had been proved when he killed Jack Cleveland, one of his own best gun-fighters. Rumour ran that he was the best pistol shot in the Rockies and as bad a man as the worst.

Plummer thought that Crawford suspected him of belonging to the bandits, and so doomed him. Crawford was wary, and defeated three separate attempts to waylay and kill him, besides avoiding several quarrels that were thrust upon him by Plummer or his men. Dick Phleger, a friend of Crawford, was also marked by Plummer, who challenged him to fight with pistols, as he frequently had challenged Crawford. Phleger was a braver man than Crawford, but he declined the duel. Plummer would have killed them both. He only wanted the appearance of an "even break," with the later plea of "self-defence," which has shielded so many bad men from punishment for murder.

Plummer now tried treachery, and told Crawford they would be friends. All the time he was hunting a chance to kill him. At length he held Crawford up in a restaurant, and stood waiting for him with a rifle. A friend handed Crawford a rifle, and the latter slipped up and took a shot from the corner of the house at Plummer, who was across the street. The ball struck Plummer's right arm and tore it to pieces. Crawford missed him with a second shot, and Plummer walked back to his own cabin. Here he had a long siege with his wound, refusing to allow his arm to be amputated, since he knew he might as well be dead as so crippled.

He finally recovered, although the ball was never removed and the bone never knit. The ball lodged in his wrist and was found there after his death, worn smooth as silver by the action of the bones. Crawford escaped down the Missouri River, to which he fled at Fort Benton. He never came back to the country. Plummer went on practising with the six-shooter with his left hand, and became a very good left-hand shot. He knew that his only safety lay in his skill with weapons.

Plummer's physician was Dr. Glick, who operated under cover of a shotgun, and with the cheerful assurance that if he killed Plummer by accident, he himself would be killed. After that Glick dressed the wounds of more than one outlaw, but dared not tell of it. Plummer admitted to him at last that these were his men and told Glick he would kill him if he ever breathed a word of this confidence. So, the knowledge of the existence of the *banditti* was known to one man for a long time.

As to Bannack, it was one of the wildest camps ever known in any land. Pistol fire was heard incessantly, and one victim after another was added to the list. George Ives, Johnny Cooper, George Carrhart, Hayes Lyons, Cy Skinner, and others of the toughs were now open associates of the leading spirit, Plummer. The condition of lawlessness and terror was such that all the decent men would have gone back to the States, but the same difficulties that had kept them from getting across to Florence now kept them from getting back East. The winter held them prisoners.

Henry Plummer was now elected sheriff for the Bannack mining district, to succeed Crawford, whom he had run out of the country. It seems very difficult to understand how this could have occurred; but it will serve to show the numerical strength of Plummer's party. The latter, now married, professed to have reformed. In reality, he was deeper in deviltry than ever in his life.

The diggings at Gold Creek and Bannack were now eclipsed by

the sensational discoveries on the famous Alder Gulch, one of the phenomenal placers of the world, and the most productive ever known in America. The stampede was fast and furious to these new diggings. In ten days the gulch was staked out for twelve miles, and the cabins of the miners were occupied for all of that distance, and scattered over a long, low flat, whose vegetation was quickly swept away. The new camp that sprung up on one end of this bar was called Virginia City. It need not be said that among the first settlers there were the outlaws earlier mentioned, with several others: Jack Gallagher, Buck Stinson, Ned Ray, and others, these three named being "deputies" of "Sheriff" Plummer. A sort of court was formed for trying disputed mining claims.

Charley Forbes was clerk of this court, and incidentally one of Plummer's band! This clerk and these deputies killed one Dillingham, whom they suspected of informing a friend of a robbery planned to make away with him on the trail from Bannack to Virginia City. They were "tried" by the court and freed. Hayes Lyons admitted privately that Plummer had told him to kill the Informer Dillingham. The invariable plan of this bloodthirsty man was to destroy unfavourable testimony by means of death. The unceasing flood of gold from the seemingly exhaustless gulch caused three or four more little camps or towns to spring up; but Virginia City now took the palm for frontier reputation in hardness. Ten millions in "dust" was washed out in one year. Everyone had gold, sacks and cans of it.

The wild license of the place was unspeakably vitiating. Fights with weapons were incessant. Rude dance-halls and saloons were crowded with truculent, armed men in search of trouble. Churches and schools were unknown. Tents, log cabins, and brush shanties made the residences.

> Hacks rattled to and fro between the several towns, freighted with drunken and rowdy humanity of both sexes. Citizens of acknowledged respectability often walked, more often perhaps rode side by side on horseback, with noted courtesans, in open day, through the crowded streets, and seemingly suffered no harm in reputation. Pistols flashed, bowie-knives flourished, oaths filled the air. This was indeed the reign of unbridled license, and men who at first regarded it with disgust and terror, by constant exposure soon learned to become part of it, and to forget that they had ever been aught else. Judges, lawyers, doc-

tors, even clergymen, could not claim exemption.

This was in 1863. At that time, the nearest capitals were Olympia, on Puget Sound; Yankton, two thousand miles away; and Lewiston, seven hundred miles away. What machinery of the law was there to hinder Plummer and his men? What better field than this one, literally overflowing with gold, could they have asked for their operations? And what better chief than Plummer?

His next effort was to be appointed deputy United States marshal, and he received the indorsement of the leading men of Bannack. Plummer afterward tried several times to kill Nathaniel P. Langford, who caused his defeat, but was unsuccessful in getting the opportunity he sought.

From Bannack to Salt Lake City was about five hundred miles. Mails by this time came in from Salt Lake City, which was the supply point. If a man wanted to send out gold to his people in the States, it had to go over this long trail across the wild regions. There was no mail service, and no express office nearer than Salt Lake. Merchants sent out their funds by private messenger. Every such journey was a risk of death. Plummer had clerks in every institution that was making money, and these kept him posted as to the times when shipments of dust were about to be made; they also told him when any well-staked miner was going out to the States. Plummer's men were posted all along these mountain trails. No one will ever know how many men were killed in all on the Salt Lake trail.

There was a stage also between Bannack and Virginia City, and this was regarded as a legitimate and regular booty producer by the gang. Whenever a rich passenger took stage, a confederate at the place put a mark on the vehicle so that it could be read at the next stop. At this point there was sure to be others of the gang, who attended to further details. Sometimes two or three thousand dollars would be taken from a single passenger. A stage often carried fifteen or twenty thousand dollars in dust. Plummer knew when and where and how each stage was robbed, but in his capacity as sheriff covered up the traces of all his associates.

The robbers who did the work were usually masked, and although suspicions were rife and mutterings began to grow louder, there was no actual evidence against Plummer until one day he held up a young man by name of Tilden, who voiced his belief that he knew the man who had held him up. Further evidence was soon to follow. A pack-

PLUMMER'S MEN HOLDING UP THE BANNACK STAGE

to meet retribution. The others then in custody were allowed to go under milder sentences.

The Vigilantes now organised with vigour and determination. One bit of testimony was added to another, and one man now dared to voice his suspicions to another. Twenty-five determined men set out to secure others of the gang now known to have been united in this long brotherhood. Some of these men were now fleeing the country, warned by the fate of Ives; but the Vigilantes took Red Yager and Buck Stinson and Ned Ray, two of them Plummer's deputies, as well as another confederate named Brown. The party stopped at the Lorain Ranch, near a cottonwood grove, and tried their prisoners without going into town. Red Yager confessed in full before he was hung, and it was on his testimony that the whole secret league of robbers was exposed and eventually brought to justice. He gave the following list:

Henry Plummer was chief of the gang; Bill Bunton, stool-pigeon and second in command; George Brown, secretary; Sam Bunton, roadster; Cyrus Skinner, fence, spy and roadster; George Shears, horse thief and roadster; Frank Parish, horse thief and roadster; Bill Hunter, telegraph man and roadster; Ned Ray, council-room keeper at Bannack City; George Ives, Stephen Marshland, Dutch John (Wagner), Alex Carter, Whiskey Bill (Graves), Johnny Cooper, Buck Stinson, Mexican Frank, Bob Zachary, Boone Helm, Clubfoot George (Lane), Billy Terwilllger, Gad Moore, were roadsters.

The noose was now tightening around the neck of the outlaw, Henry Plummer, whose adroitness had so long stood him in good stead. The honest miners found that their sheriff was the leader of the outlaws! His doom was said then and there, with that of all these others.

A party of the Virginia City law and order men slipped over to Bannack, Henry Plummer's home. In a few hours the news had spread of what had happened at the other camps, and a branch organisation of the Vigilantes was formed for Bannack. Stinson and Ray were now arrested, and then Plummer himself, the chief, the brains of all this long-secret band of marauders. He was surprised with his coat and arms off, and taken prisoner. A few moments later, he was facing a scaffold, where, as sheriff, he had lately hung a man. The law had no delays. No court could quibble here. Not all Plummer's wealth could save him now, nor all his intellect and cool audacity.

An agony of remorse and fear now came upon the outlaw' chief. He fell upon his knees, called upon God to save him, begged, pleaded, train, bound for Salt Lake, had no less than eighty thousand dollars in dust in its charge, and Plummer had sent out Dutch John and Steve Marshland to hold up the train. The freighters were too plucky, and both the bandits were wounded, and so marked, although for the time they escaped. George Ives also was recognised by one or two victims and began to be watched on account of his numerous open murders.

At length, the dead body of a young man named Tiebalt was found in a thicket near Alder Gulch, under circumstances showing a revolting murder. At last the slumbering spirit of the Vigilantes began to awaken. Two dozen men of the camp went out and arrested Long John, George Ives, Alex Carter, Whiskey Bill, Bob Zachary, and Johnny Cooper. These men were surprised in their camp, and among their long list of weapons were some that had been taken from men who had been robbed or murdered. These weapons were identified by friends. Old Tex was another man taken in charge, and George Hilderman yet another. All these men wanted a "jury trial," and wanted it at Virginia City, where Plummer would have official influence enough to get his associates released! The captors, however, were men from Nevada, the other leading camp in Alder Gulch, and they took their prisoners there.

At once a Plummer man hastened out on horseback to get the chief on the ground, riding all night across the mountains to Bannack to carry the news that the citizens had at last rebelled against anarchy, robbery, and murder. On the following morning, two thousand men had gathered at Nevada City, and had resolved to try the outlaws. As there was rivalry between Virginia and Nevada camps, a jury was made up of twenty-four men, twelve from each camp. The miners' court, most dread of all tribunals, was in session.

Some forms of the law were observed. Long John was allowed to turn state's evidence. He swore that George Ives had killed Tiebalt, and declared that he shot him while Tiebalt was on his knees praying, after he had been told that he must die. Then a rope was put around his neck and he was dragged to a place of concealment in the thicket where the body was found. Tiebalt was not dead while so dragged, for his hands were found full of grass and twigs which he had clutched. Ives was condemned to death, and the law and order men were strong enough to suppress the armed disturbance at once started by his friends, none of whom could realise that the patient citizens were at last taking the law into their own hands. A scaffold was improvised and Ives was hung,—the first of the Plummer gang wept like a child, declared that he was too wicked to die thus soon and unprepared. It was useless. The full proof of all his many crimes was laid before him.

Ray, writhing and cursing, was the first to be hanged. He got his finger under the rope around his neck and died hard, but died. Stinson, also cursing, went next. It was then time for Plummer, and those who had this work in hand felt compunction at hanging a man so able, so urbane and so commanding. None the less, he was told to prepare. He asked for time to pray, and was told to pray from the crossbeam. He said goodbye to a friend or two, and asked his executioners to "give him a good drop." He seemed to fear suffering, he who had caused so much suffering. To oblige him, the men lifted his body high up and let it fall, and he died with little struggle.

To cut short a long story of bloody justice, it may be added that of the men named as guilty by Yager everyone was arrested, tried, and hung by the Vigilantes. Plummer for some time must have dreaded detection, for he tried to cover up his guilt by writing back home to the States that he was in danger of being hanged on account of his Union sympathies. His family would not believe his guilt, and looked on him as a martyr. They sent out a brother and sister to look into the matter, but these too found proof which left them no chance to doubt. The whole ghastly revelation of a misspent life lay before them. Even Plummer's wife, whom he loved very much and who was a good woman, was at last convinced of what at first, she could not believe. Plummer had been able to conceal from even his wife the least suspicion that was not an honourable man. His wife was east in the States at the time of his death.

Plummer went under his true name. George Ives was a Wisconsin boy from near Racine. Both he and Plummer were twenty-seven years of age when killed, but they had compressed much evil into so short a span. Plummer himself was a master of men, a brave and cool spirit, an expert with weapons, and in all not a bad specimen of the bad man at his worst. He was a murderer, but after all was not enough a murderer. No outlaw of later years so closely resembled the great outlaw, John A. Murrell, as did Henry Plummer, but the latter differed in one regard:—he spared victims, who later arose to accuse him.

The frontier has produced few bloodier records than Plummer's. He was principal or accessory, as has been stated, in more than one hundred murders, not to mention innumerable robberies and thefts. His life was lived out in scenes typical of the early Western frontier.

The madness of adventure in new wild fields, the lust of gold and its unparalleled abundance drove to crime men who might have been respected and of note in proper ranks of life and in other surroundings.

## Chapter 8

# Boone Helm

Henry Plummer was what might be called a good instance of the gentleman desperado, if such a thing be possible; a man of at least a certain amount of refinement, and certainly one who, under different surroundings, might have led a different life. For the sake of contrast. If for nothing else, we may take the case of Boone Helm, one of Plummer's gang, who was the opposite of Plummer in every way except the readiness to rob and kill. Boone Helm was bad, and nothing in the world could ever have made him anything but bad. He was, by birth and breeding, low, coarse, cruel, animal-like and utterly depraved, and for him no name but ruffian can fitly apply.

Helm was born in Kentucky, but his family moved to Missouri during his early youth, so that the boy was brought up on the borderland between civilization and the savage frontier; for this was about the time of the closing days of the old Santa Fé Trail, and the towns of Independence and Westport were still sending out their wagon trains to the far mountain regions. By the time Boone Helm was grown, and soon after his marriage, the great gold craze of California broke out, and he joined the rush westward. Already he was a murderer, and already he had a reputation as a quarrelsome and dangerous man. He was of powerful build and turbulent temper, delighting in nothing so much as feats of strength, skill, and hardihood. His community was glad to be rid of him, as was, indeed, any community in which he ever lived.

In the California diggings, Helm continued the line of life mapped out for him from birth. He met men of his own kidney there, and was ever ready for a duel with weapons. In this way he killed several men, no one knows how many; but this sort of thing was so common in the case of so many men in those days that little attention was paid to it. It must have been a very brutal murder which at length caused him to flee the Coast to escape the vengeance of the miners. He headed north and east, after a fashion of the times following the California boom, and was bound for the mountain placers in 1853, when he is recorded as appearing at the Dalles, Oregon. He and a half-dozen companions, whom he had picked up on the way, and most of whom were strangers to each other, now started out for Fort Hall, Idaho, intending to go from there to a point below Salt Lake City.

The beginning of the terrible mountain winter season caught these men somewhere west of the main range in eastern Oregon, in the depths of as rugged a mountain region as any of the West. They were on horseback, and so could carry small provisions; but in some way they pushed on deeper and deeper into the mountains, until they got to the Bannack River, where they were attacked by Indians and chased into a country none of them knew. At last they got over east as far as the Soda Springs on the Bear river, where they were on well-known ground. By this time, however, their horses had given out, and their food was exhausted. They killed their horses, made snowshoes with the hides, and sought to reach Fort Hall. The party was now reduced to one of those awful starving marches of the wilderness which are now and then chronicled in Western life. This meant that the weak must perish where they fell.

The strength of Helm and one of the others, Burton, enabled them to push on ahead, leaving their companions behind in the mountains. Almost within reach of Fort Hall, Burton gave out and was left behind in an abandoned cabin. Helm pushed on into the old stockade, but found it also abandoned for the winter season, and he could get no food there. He then went back to where he had left Burton, and, according to his own report, he was trying to get wood for a fire when he heard a pistol-shot and returned to find that Burton had killed himself. He stayed on at this spot, and, like a hyena, preyed upon the dead body of his companion. He ate one leg of the body, and then, wrapping up the other in a piece of old shirt, threw it across his shoulder and started on further east.

He had, before this on the march, declared to the party that he had practiced cannibalism at an earlier time, and proposed to do so again if it became necessary on this trip across the mountains. His calm threat was now verified. Helm was found at last at an Indian camp by John W. Powell, who learned that he was as hard a character as he had ever run across. None the less, he took care of Helm, gave him food and clothes, and took him to the settlements around Salt Lake. Powell found that Helm had a bag containing over fourteen hundred dollars in coin, which he had carried across the divide with him through all his hardships. He would take no pay from Helm, and the latter never even thanked him for his kindness, but left him as soon as he reached the Mormon settlements.

Here the abandoned ruffian boasted of what he had done, and settled down for a brief time to the customary enjoyments of the rough when in town. He spent his money, hired out as a Danite, killed a couple of men whom the Mormons wanted removed, and soon got so bad that he had to leave. Once more he headed west to California, and once more he started back north from San Francisco, for reasons satisfactory to himself. While in California, as was later learned, he undertook to rob and kill a man at an outlying ranch, who had taken him in and befriended him when he was in need and in flight from vengeance. He showed no understanding of the feeling of gratitude, no matter what was done for him or how great was his own extremity.

In Oregon Helm went back to robbery as his customary means of support, and he killed several men at this time of his life, how many will never be known. In 1862, as the mountain placers were now beginning to draw the crowds of mining men, it was natural that Boone Helm should show up at Florence. Here he killed a man in cold blood, in treachery, while his enemy was not armed, and after their quarrel had been compromised. This victim was Dutch Fred, a man of reputation as a fighter, but he had never offended Helm, who killed him at the instigation of an enemy of his victim, and possibly for hire. He shot Fred while the latter stood looking him in the face, unarmed, and, missing him with the first shot, took deliberate aim with the second and murdered his man in cold blood.

This was pretty bad even for Florence, and he had to leave. That fall he turned up far to the north, on the Fraser River, in British Columbia. Here he was once more reduced to danger on a starving foot march in the wilderness, and here, once more, he was guilty of eating the body of his companion, whom he is supposed to have slain. He was sent back by the British authorities, and for a time was held at Portland, Oregon, for safe keeping. Later he was tried at Florence for killing Dutch Fred, but the witnesses had disappeared, and people had long ago lost interest in the crime by reason of others more recent. Helm escaped justice and was supposed to have gone to Texas; but he soon appeared in the several settlements which have been mentioned in the foregoing pages, and moved from one to the other. He killed many more men, how many in all was never known.

The courage and hardihood of Boone Helm were in evidence to the close of his life. Three men of the Vigilantes did the dangerous work of arresting him, and took him by closing in on him as he stood in the street talking. "If I'd had a chance," said he, "or If I had guessed what you all were up to, you'd never have taken me." He claimed not to know what was wanted of him when brought before the judges of the Vigilante court, and solemnly declared that he had never killed a man in all his life! They made him kiss the Bible and swear to this over again just to see to what lengths his perjured and depraved soul would go. He swore on the Bible with perfect calmness!

His captors were not moved by this, and indeed Helm was little expectant that they would be. He called aside one of them whom he knew, declined a clergyman, and confessed to a murder or so in Missouri and in California, admitted that he had been imprisoned once or twice, but denied that he had been a road agent. He accused some of his warmest friends of the latter crime. Jack Gallegher, also under arrest, heard him thus incriminate himself and others of the gang and called him all the names in the calendar, telling him he ought to die.

"I have looked at death in all forms," said Helm, coolly, "and I am not afraid to die." He then asked for a glass of whiskey, as did a good many of these murderers when they were brought to the gallows. From that time on he was cool and unconcerned, and showed a finish worthy of one ambitious to be thought wholly bad.

There were six thousand men assembled in Virginia City to see the executions of these criminals, who were fast being rounded up and hung by the citizens. The place of execution was in a half-finished log building. The ropes were passed over the ridge-pole, and, as the front of the building was open, a full view was offered of the murderers as they stood on the boxes arranged for the drops. Boone Helm looked around at his friends placed for death, and told Jack Gallegher to "stop making such a fuss." "There's no use being afraid to die," said he; and indeed, there probably never lived a man more actually devoid of all sense of fear. He valued neither the life of others nor his own. He saw that the end had come, and was careless about the rest. He had a sore finger, which was tied up, and this seemed to trouble him more than anything else. There was some delay about the confessions and the last offices of those who prayed for the condemned, and this seemed to irritate Boone Helm.

"For God's sake," said he, "if you're going to hang me, I want you to do it and get through with it. If not, I want you to tie up my finger for me."

"Give me that overcoat of yours, Jack," he said to Gallegher, as the latter was stripped for the noose.

"You won't need it now," replied Gallegher, who was dying blasphemous. About then, George Lane, one of the line of men about to be hung, jumped off his box on his own account.

"There's one gone to hell," remarked Boone Helm, philosophically. Gallegher was hanged next, and as he struggled his former friend watched him calmly. "Kick away, old fellow," said Boone Helm. Then, as though suddenly resolved to end it, he commented, "My turn next. I'll be in hell with you in a minute!"

Boone Helm was a Confederate and a bitter one, and this seems to have remained with him to the last. "Every man for his principles!" he shouted. "Hurrah for Jeff Davis! Let her rip!" He sprang off the box; and so, he finished, utterly hard and reckless to the last.

CHAPTER 9

# Death Scenes of Desperadoes

There is always a grim sort of curiosity regarding the way in which notoriously desperate men meet their end; and perhaps this is as natural as is the curiosity regarding the manner in which they lived. "Did he die game?" is one of the questions asked by bad men among themselves. "Did he die with his boots on?" is another. The last was the test of actual or, as it were, of professional badness. One who admitted himself bad was willing to die with his boots on. Honest men were not, and more than one early Western man fatally shot had his friends take off his boots before he died, so that he might not go with the stain of desperadoism attached to his name.

Some bad men died unrepentant and defiant. Others broke down and wept and begged. A great oblivion enshrouds most of these utterances, for few Vigilante movements ever reached importance enough to permit those who participated to make publicly known their own participation in them. Indeed, no man ever concerned in a law and order execution ever liked to talk about it. Tradition, however, has preserved the exact utterances of many bad men. Report is preserved, in a general way, of many of the rustlers hung by the cattle men in the "regulator" movement in Montana, Wyoming, and Nebraska in the late '70's. "Give me a chew of tobacco, folks," said one. "Meet you in hell, fellows," remarked others of these rustlers when the last moment arrived. "So-long, boys," was a not infrequent remark as the noose tightened. Many of these men were brave, and some of them were hung for what they considered no crime.

Henry Plummer, whose fate has been described in a previous chapter, was one of those who died in a sense of guilt and terror. His was a nature of some sensitiveness, not callous like that of Boone Helm. Plummer begged for life on any terms, asked the Vigilantes to cut off his ears and hands and tongue, anything to mark him and leave him helpless, but to leave him alive. He protested that he was too wicked to die, fell on his knees, cried aloud, promised, besought. On the whole, his end hardly left him enshrouded with much glamor of courage; although the latter term is relative in the bad man, who might be brave at one time and cowardly at another, as was often proved.

Ned Ray and Buck Stinson died full of profanity and curses, heaping upon their executioners all manner of abuse. They seemed to be animated by no understanding of a life hereafter, and were concerned only in their animal Instinct to hold on to this one as long as they might. Yet Stinson, of a good Indiana family, was a bright and studious and well-read boy, of whom many good things had been predicted.

Dutch John, when faced with death, acted much as his chief, Henry Plummer, had done. He begged and pleaded, and asked for mutilation, disfigurement, anything, if only he might still live. But, like Plummer, at the very last moment he pulled together and died calmly. "How long will it take me to die?" he asked. "I have never seen anyone hanged." They told him it would be very short and that he would not suffer much, and this seemed to please him. Nearly all these desperadoes seemed to dread death by hanging. The Territory of Utah allowed a felon convicted under death penalty to choose the manner of his death, whether by hanging, beheading, or shooting; but no record remains of any prisoner who did not choose death by shooting. A curiosity as to the sensation of hanging was evinced in the words of several who were hung by Vigilantes.

In the largest hanging made in this Montana work, there were live men executed one after the other: Clubfoot George, Hayes Lyons, Jack Gallegher, Boone Helm, and Frank Parish, all known to be members of the Plummer gang. George and Parish at first declared that they were innocent—the first word of most of these men when they were apprehended. Parish died silent. George had spent some hours with a clergyman, and was apparently repentant. Just as he reached the box, he saw a friend peering through a crack in the wall. "Goodbye, old fellow," he called out, and sprang to his own death without waiting for the box to be pulled from under his feet.

Hayes Lyons asked to see his mistress to say goodbye to her before he died, but was refused. He kept on pleading for his life to the very last instant, after he had told the men to take his body to his mistress for burial. This woman was really the cause of Lyons' undoing. He had been warned, and would have left the country but for her. A woman

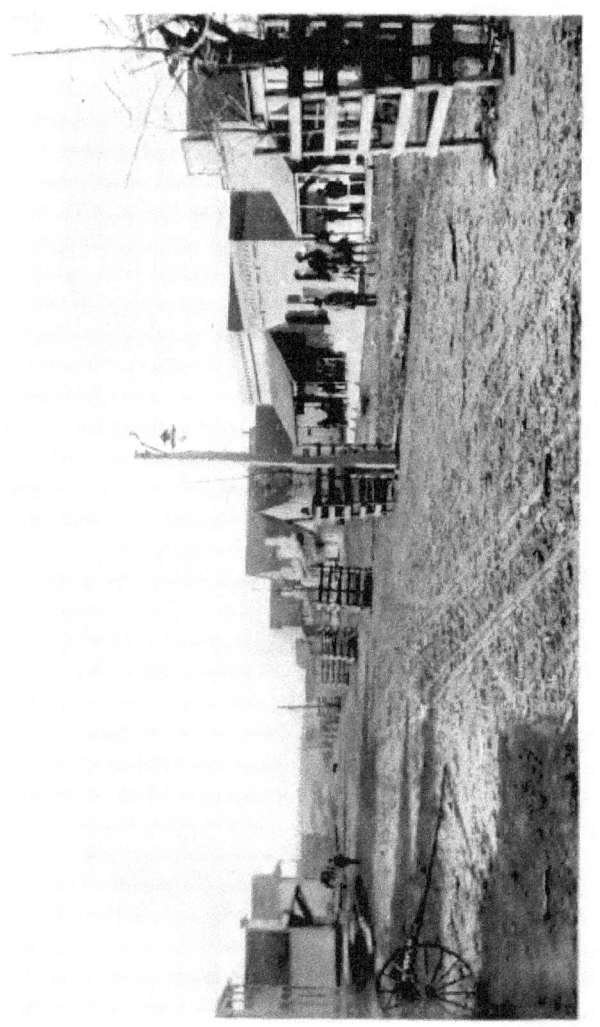
THE SCENE OF MANY HANGINGS

was very often the cause of a desperado's apprehension.

Jack Gallegher in his last moments was, if possible, more repulsive even than Boone Helm. The latter was brave, but Gallegher was a coward, and spent his time in cursing his captors and pitying himself. He tried to be merry. "How do I look with a halter around my neck?" he asked facetiously of a bystander. He asked often for whiskey and this was given him. A moment later he said, "I want one more drink of whiskey before I die." This was when the noose was tight around his neck, and the men were disgusted with him for the remark. One remarked, "Give him the whiskey"; so, the rope, which was passed over the beam above him and fastened to a side log of the building, was loosened to oblige him. "Slack off the rope, can't you," cried Gallegher, "and let a man have a parting drink." He bent his head down against the rope and drank a tumblerful of whiskey at a gulp. Then he called down curses on the men who were about him, and kept it up until they cut him short by jerking away the box from under his feet.

A peculiar instance of unconscious, but grim, humour was afforded at Gallegher's execution. Just as he was led to the box and ordered to climb up, he drew a pocketknife and declared he would kill himself and not be hanged in public. A Vigilante covered him with a six-shooter. "Drop that Jack," he exclaimed, "or I'll blow your head off." So Gallegher, having the choice of death between shooting, hanging or beheading, chose hanging after all! He was a coward.

Cy Skinner, when on the way to the scaffold, broke and ran, calling on his captors to shoot. They declined, and hanged him. Alex Carter, who was on the fatal line with Skinner in that lot, was disgusted with him for running. He asked for a smoke while the men were waiting, and died with a lie on his lips—"I am Innocent." That is not an infrequent declaration of criminals at the last. The lie is only a blind clinging to the last possible means of escape, and is the same as the instinct for self-preservation, a crime swallowed up in guilt.

Johnny Cooper wanted a "good smoke" before he died, and was given it. Bob Zachary died without fear, and praying forgiveness on his executioners. Steve Marshland asked to be pardoned because of his youth. "You should have thought of that before," was the grim reply. He was adjudged old enough to die, as he had been old enough to kill.

George Shears was one of the gamest of the lot. He seemed indifferent about it all after his capture, and, when he was told that he was to be hanged, he remarked that he ought to be glad it was no worse. He was executed in the barn at a ranch where he was caught, and, conveniences being few, a ladder was used instead of a box or other drop. He was told to ascend the latter, and did so without the least hesitation or evidence of concern. "Gentlemen," said he, "I am not used to this business, never having been hung before. Shall I jump off or slide off?" They told him to "jump, of course," and he took this advice. "All right. Goodbye!" he said, and sprang off with unconcern.

Whiskey Bill was not given much chance for last words. He was hung from horseback, the noose being dropped down from a tree to his neck as he sat on a horse behind one of the Vigilantes. "Goodbye, Bill," was the remark of the latter, as he spurred his horse and left Bill hanging.

One of the most singular phenomena of these executions was that of Bill Hunter, who, while hanging by the neck, went through all the motions of drawing and firing his six-shooter six times. Whether the action was conscious or unconscious it is impossible to tell.

Bill Bunton resisted arrest and was pugnacious, of course declaring his innocence. At the last he showed great gameness. He was particular about the manner in which the knot of the rope was adjusted to his neck, seeming, as did many of these men, to dread any suffering while hanging. He asked if he might jump off the platform himself, and was told he might if he liked. "I care no more for hanging," he explained, "than I do for taking a drink of water, but I'd like to have my neck broken. I'd like to have a mountain three hundred feet high to jump off from. Now, I'll give you the time: One—two—three. Here goes!"

CHAPTER 10

# Joseph A. Slade

One of the best-known desperadoes the West ever produced was Joseph A. Slade, agent of the Overland stage line on the central or mountain division, about 1860, and hence in charge of large responsibilities in a strip of country more than six hundred miles in extent, which possessed all the ingredients for trouble in plenty. Slade lived, in the heyday of his career, just about the time when men from the East were beginning to write about the newly discovered life of the West. Bret Harte had left his indelible stamp upon the literature of the land, and Mark Twain was soon to spread widely his impressions of life as seen in *Roughing It*; while countless newspaper men and book writers were edging out and getting hearsay stories of things known at first hand by a very few careful and conscientious writers.

The hearsay man engaged in discovering the West always clung to the regular lines of travel; and almost everyone who passed across the mountains on the Overland stage line would hear stories about the desperate character of Slade. These stories grew by newspaper multiplication, until at length the man was owner of the reputation of a fiend, a ghoul, and a murderer. There was a wide difference between this and the truth. As a matter of fact, there were many worse desperadoes on the border.

Slade was born at Carlisle, Illinois, and served in the Mexican War in 1848. He appears to have gone into the Overland service in 1859. At once he plunged into the business of the stage line, and soon became a terror to the thieves and outlaws, several of whom he was the means of having shot or hung, although he himself was nothing of a man-hunter at the time; and indeed, in all his life he killed but one man—a case of a reputation beyond desert, and an instance of a reputation fostered by admiring but ignorant writers.

Slade was reported to have tied one of his enemies, Jules Reni, more commonly called Jules, to the stake, and to have tortured him for a day, shooting him to pieces bit by bit, and cutting off his ears, one of which he always afterward wore in his pocket as a souvenir. There was little foundation for this reputation beyond the fact that he did kill Jules, and did it after Jules had been captured and disarmed by other men. But he had been threatened time and again by Jules, and was once shot and left for dead by the latter, who emptied a pistol and a shotgun at Slade, and left him lying with thirteen bullets and buckshot in his body. Jules thought he did not need to shoot Slade any more after that, and gave directions for his burial as soon as he should have died.

At that Slade rose on his elbow and promised Jules he would live and would wear one of his, Jules', ears on his watch chain; a threat which no doubt gave rise to a certain part of his ghastly reputation. Jules was hung for a while by the stage people, but was let down and released on promise of leaving the country never to return. He did not keep his promise, and it had been better for him If he had.

Jules Reni was a big Frenchman, one of that sort of early ranchers who were owners of small ranches and a limited number of cattle and horses—just enough to act as a shield for thefts of livestock, and to offer encouragement to such thefts. Before long Jules was back at his old stamping-grounds, where he was looked on as something of a bully; and at once he renewed his threats against Slade.

Slade went to the officers of the military post at Laramie, the only kind of authority then in the land, which had no sort of courts or officers, and asked them what he should do. They told him to have Jules captured and then to kill him, else Jules would do the same for him. Slade sent four men out to the ranch where Jules was stopping, about twelve miles from Laramie, while he followed in the stagecoach. These men captured Jules at a ranch a little farther down the line, and left him prisoner at the stage station. Here Slade found him in the corral, a prisoner, unarmed and at his mercy, and without hesitation he shot him, the ball striking him in the mouth.

His victim fell and feigned death, but Slade—who was always described as a good pistol shot—saw that he was not killed, and told him he should have time to make his will if he desired. There is colour in the charge of deliberate cruelty, but perhaps rude warrant for the cruelty, under the circumstances of treachery in which Jules had pursued Slade. At least, some time elapsed while a man was running back and forward from the house to the corral with pen and ink and paper. Jules never signed his will. When the last penful of ink came out to the corral, Jules was dead, shot through the head by Slade. This looks like cruelty of an unnecessary sort, and like taunting a helpless victim; but here the warrant for all the Slade sort of stories seems to end, and there is no evidence of his mutilating his victim, as was often described.

Slade went back to the officers of Fort Laramie, and they said he had done right and did not detain him. Nor did any of Jules' friends ever molest him. He returned to his work on the Overland. After this he grew more turbulent, and was guilty of high-handed outrages and of a general disposition to run things wherever he went. The officers at Fort Halleck arrested him and refused to turn him over to the stage line unless the latter agreed to discharge him. This was done, and now Slade, out of work, began to be bad at heart. He took to drink and drifting, and so at last turned up at the Beaverhead diggings in 1863, not much different from many others of the bad folk to be found there.

Quiet enough when sober, Slade was a maniac in drink, and this latter became his habitual condition. Now and again he sobered up, and he always was a business man and animated by an ambition to get on in the world. He worked here and there in different capacities, and at last settled on a ranch, a dozen miles or so from Virginia City, where he lived with his wife, a robust, fine-looking woman of great courage and very considerable beauty, of whom he was passionately fond; although she lived almost alone in the remote cabin in the mountains, while Slade pursued his avocations, such as they were, in the settlements along Alder Gulch.

Slade now began to grow ugly and hard, and to exult in terrorising the hard men of those hard towns. He would strike a man in the face while drinking with him, would rob his friends while playing cards, would ride into the saloons and break up the furniture, and destroy property with seeming exultation at his own maliciousness. He was often arrested, warned, and fined; and sometimes he defied such officers as went after him and refused to be arrested. His whole conduct made him a menace to the peace of this little community, which was now endeavouring to become more decent, and he fell under the fatal scrutiny of the Vigilantes, who concluded that the best thing to do was to hang Slade. He had never killed anyone as yet, although he had abused many; but it was sure that he would kill someone if allowed to run on; and, moreover, it was humiliating to have one man trying to run the town and doing as he pleased.

Slade was to learn what society means, and what the social compact means, as did many of these wild men who had been running as savages outside of and independent of the law. Slade got wind of the deliberations of the Committee, as well he might when six hundred men came down from Nevada Camp to Virginia City to help in the court of the miners, before which Slade was now to come. It was the Nevada Vigilantes who were most strongly of the belief that death and not banishment was the proper punishment for Slade. The leader of the marching men calmly told Slade that the Committee had decided to hang him; and, once the news was sure, Slade broke out into lamentations.

This was often the case with men who had been bullies and terrors. They weakened when in the hands of a stronger power. Slade crept about on his hands and knees, begging like a baby. "My God! My God!" he cried. "Must I die? Oh, my poor wife, my poor wife! My God, men, you can't mean that I'm to die!"

They did mean it, and neither his importunities nor those of his friends had avail. His life had been too rough and violent and was too full of menace to others. He had had his fair frontier chance and had misused it. Some wept at his prayers, but none relented. In broad daylight, the procession moved down the street, and soon Slade was swinging from the beam of a corral gate, one more example of the truth that when man belongs to society he owes duty to society and else must suffer at its hands. This was the law.

Slade's wife was sent for and reached town soon after Slade's body was cut down and laid out. She loaded the Vigilantes with imprecations, and showed the most heartbroken grief. The two had been very deeply attached. She was especially regretful that Slade had been hanged and not shot. He was worth a better death than that, she protested.

Slade's body was preserved in alcohol and kept out at the lone ranch cabin all that winter. In the spring it was sent down to Salt Lake City and buried there. As that was a prominent point on the overland trail, the tourists did the rest. The saga of Slade as a bad man was widely disseminated.

CHAPTER 11

# The Desperado of the Plains

One pronounced feature of early Western life will have been remarked in the story of the mountain settlements with which we have been concerned, and that is the transient and migratory character of the population. It is astonishing what distances were travelled by the bold men who followed the mining stampedes all over the wilderness of the upper Rockies, in spite of the unspeakable hardships of a region where travel at its best was rude, and travel at its worst well-nigh an impossibility. The West was first peopled by wanderers, nomads, even in its mountain regions, which usually attach their population to themselves and cut off the disposition to roam. This nomad nature of the adventurers made law almost an impossible thing. A town was organised and then abandoned, on the spur of necessity or rumour. Property was unstable, taxes impossible, and any corps of executive officers difficult of maintenance. Before there can be law there must be an attached population.

The lawlessness of the real West was therefore much a matter of conditions after all, rather than of morals. It proved above all things that human nature is very much akin, and that good men may go wrong when sufficiently tempted by great wealth left unguarded. The first and second decades after the close of the civil war found the great placers of the Rockies and Sierras exhausted, and quartz mines taking their place. The same period, as has been shown, marked the advent of the great cattle herds from the South upon the upper ranges of the territories beyond the Missouri River. By this time, the plains began to call to the adventurers as the mines recently had called.

Here, then, was wealth, loose, unattached, apparently almost unowned, nomad wealth, and waiting for a nomad population to share it in one way or another. Once more, the home was lacking, the permanent abode; wherefore, once more the law was also lacking, and man ruled himself after the ancient savage ways. By this time frontiersmen were well armed with repeating weapons, which now used fixed ammunition. There appeared on the plains more and better armed men than were ever known, unorganised, in any land at any period of the earth's history; and the plains took up what the mountains had begun in wild and desperate deeds.

The only property on the arid plains at that time was that of livestock. Agriculture had not come, and it was supposed could never come. The vast herds of cattle from the lower ranges, Texas and Mexico, pushed north to meet the railroads, now springing westward across the plains; but a large proportion of these cattle were used as breeding stock to furnish the upper cow range with horned population. Colorado, Wyoming, Montana, western Nebraska, the Dakotas, discovered that they could raise range cattle as well as the southern ranges, and fatten them far better; so presently thousands upon thousands of cattle were turned loose, without a fence in those thousands of miles, to exist as best they might, and guarded as best might be by a class of men as nomadic as their herds. These cattle were cheap at that time, and they made a general source of food supply much appreciated in a land but just depopulated of its buffalo. For a long time, it was but a venial crime to kill a cow and eat it if one were hungry. A man's horse was sacred, but his cow was not, because there were so many cows, and they were shifting and changing about so much at best.

The ownership of these herds was widely scattered and difficult to trace. A man might live in Texas and have herds in Montana, and *vice versa*. His property right was known only by the brand upon the animal, his being but the tenure of a sign.

"The respect for this sign was the whole creed of the cattle trade. Without a fence, without an atom of actual control, the cattle man held his property absolutely. It mingled with the property of others, but it was never confused therewith. It wandered a hundred miles from him, and he knew not where it was, but it was surely his and sure to find him. To touch it was crime. To appropriate it meant punishment. Common necessity made common custom, common custom made common law, and common law made statutory law." (*The Story of the Cowboy*.)

The old *fierro* or iron mark of the Spanish cattle owner, and his *venta* or sale-brand to another had become common law all over the Southwest when the Anglo-Saxon first struck that region. The Saxon accepted these customs as wise and rational, and soon they were the American law all over the American plains.

The great bands of cattle ran almost free in the Southwest for many years, each carrying the brand of the owner, if the latter had ever seen it or cared to brand it. Many cattle roamed free without any brand whatever, and no one could tell who owned them. When the northern ranges opened, this question of unbranded cattle still remained, and the "maverick" industry was still held matter of sanction, there seeming to be enough for all, and the day being one of glorious freedom and plenty, the baronial day of the great and once unexhausted West.

Now the *venta*, or brand indicating the sale of an animal to another owner, began to complicate matters to a certain extent. A purchaser could put his own *fierro* brand on a cow, and that meant that he now owned it. But then some suspicious soul asked, "How shall we know whence such and such cows came, and how tell whether or not this man did not steal them outright from his neighbour's herd and put his own brand on them?" Here was the origin of the bill of sale, and also of the counter brand or "vent brand," as it is known upon the upper ranges. The owner duplicated his recorded brand upon another recorded part of the animal, and this meant his deed of conveyance, when taken together with the bill of sale over his commercial signature.

Of course, several conveyances would leave the hide much scarred and hard to read; and, as there were "road brands" also used to protect the property while in transit from the South to the North or from the range to the market, the reading of the brands and the determination of ownership of the animal might be, and very often was, a nice matter, and one not always settled without argument; and argument in the West often meant bloodshed in those days. Some hard men started up in trade near the old cattle trails, and made a business of disputing brands with the trail drivers. Sometimes they made good their claims, and sometimes they did not. There were graves almost in line from Texas to Montana.

It is now perfectly easy to see what a wide and fertile field was here offered to men who did not want to observe the law. Here was property to be had without work, and property whose title could easily be called into question; whose ownership was a matter of testimony and record, to be sure, but testimony which could be erased or altered by the same means which once constituted it a record and sign. The brand was made with an iron, and it could be changed with an iron. A large and profitable industry arose in changing these brands. The rustler, brand-burner or brand-blotcher now became one of the new Western characters, and a new sort of bad-manism had its birth.

It is very easy to see how temptation was offered to the cow thief and 'brand blotter.' Here were all these wild cattle running loose over the country. The imprint of a hot iron on a hide made the creature the property of the brander, provided no one else had branded it before. The time of priority was matter of proof. With the handy 'running-iron' or straight rod, which was always attached to his saddle when he rode out, could not the cow thief erase a former brand and put over it one of his own? Could he not, for instance, change a U into an O, or a V into a diamond, or a half-circle into a circle? Could he not, moreover, kill and skin an animal and sell the beef as his own? Between him and the owner was only this little mark. Between him and changing this mark was nothing but his moral principles. The range was very wide. Hardly a figure would show on that unwinking horizon all day long. And what was a heifer here and there?

Such was the temptation and opportunity which led many a man to step over the line between right and wrong. Their excuse lies in the fact that the line was newly drawn and that it was often vague and inexact. It was easy, from killing or rebranding an occasional cow, to see the profits of larger operation. The faithful cowboys who cared for these herds and protected them even with their lives in the interest of absent owners began in time to tire of working on a salary, and settled down into little ranches of their own, starting with a herd of cattle lawfully purchased and branded. An occasional maverick came across their range and they branded it. A brand was faint and not legible, and they put their own iron over it. They learned that pyrography with a hot poker was very profitable. The rest was easy. The first step was the one that counted; but who could tell where that first step was taken?

At any rate, cattle owners began to take notice of their cows as the prices went up, and they had laws made to protect property rapidly enhancing in value. Cow owners were required to have fixed or stencil-irons, and were forbidden to trace a pattern with a straight iron or "running-iron." Each ranch must have its own iron or stencil. Texas as early as the '60's and '70's passed laws forbidding the use of the running-Iron altogether, so that after that it was not safe to be caught riding the range with a straight iron under the saddle flap. Any man so discovered had to do some quick explaining.

The next step after this was the organisation of the cattle associations in the several territories and states which made the home of the cattle trade. These associations banded together in a national association. Detectives were placed at the stockyards in Chicago and Kansas City, charged with the finding of cattle stolen on the range and shipped with or without clean brands. In short, there had now grown up an armed and legal warfare between the cow men themselves—in the first place very large-handed thieves—and the rustlers and "little fellows" who were accused of being too liberal with their brand blotching. The prosecution of these men was undertaken with something of the old vigour that characterized the pursuit of horse thieves, with this difference, that, whereas all the world had hated a horse thief as a common enemy, very much of the world found excuse for the so-called rustler, who was known to be doing only what his accusers had done before him.

There may be a certain interest attaching to the methods of the range riders of this day, and those who care to go into the history of the cattle trade in its early days are referred to the work earlier quoted, where the matter is more fully covered. (The Story of the Cowboy.) Brief reference will suffice here.

The rustler might brand with his own straight running-iron, as it were, writing over again the brand he wished to change; but this was clumsy and apt to be detected, for the new wound would slough and look suspicious. A piece of red-hot hay wire or telegraph wire was a better tool, for this could be twisted into the shape of almost any registered brand, and it would so cunningly connect the edges of both that the whole mark would seem to be one scar of the same date. The fresh burn fitted in with the older one so that it was impossible to swear that it was not a part of the first brand mark. Yet another way of softening a fresh and fraudulent brand was to brand through a wet blanket with a heavy iron, which thus left a wound deep enough, but not apt to slough, and so betray a brand done long after the round-up, and hence subject to scrutiny.

As to the ways in which brands were altered in their lines, these were many and most ingenious. A sample page will be sufficient to show the possibilities of the art by which the rustler set over to his own herds on the free range the cows of his far-away neighbour, whom, perhaps, he did not love as himself. The list following is taken from *The Story of the Cowboy*.

Such, then, was the burglar of the range, the rustler, to whom most of the mysterious and untraceable crimes were ascribed. Such also were the excuses to be offered for some of the men who did what to them did not seem wrong acts. The sudden hostility of the newly-come cow men embittered and inflamed them, and from this it was easy and natural to the arbitrament of arms.

The bad man of the plains dates to this era, and his acts may be attributed to these causes. There were to be found among these men many refugees and outlaws, as well as many better men gone wrong through point of view. Fierce and far were the battles between the rustlers and the cow barons. Commerce had its way at last. The lawless man had to go, and he had to go even before the law had come.

The Vigilantes of the cattle range, organising first in Montana and working southward, made a clean sweep in their work. In one campaign they killed somewhere between sixty and eighty men accused of cattle rustling. They hung thirteen men on one railroad bridge one morning in north-western Nebraska. The statement is believed to be correct that, in the ten years from 1876 to 1886, they executed more men without process of law than have been executed under the law in all the United States since then. These lynchings also were against the law. In short, it may perhaps begin to appear to those who study into the history of our earlier civilization that the term "law" is a very wide and lax and relative one, and one extremely difficult of exact application.

# HOW THE RUSTLER WORKED

1. IO  IOI  7OI  7OL  ЯOB
2. ⊃⊂  O-O  OHO
3. ⊍  ⊙  8
4. V  ◊  ◈    9. ⊍  ⊍  ⊌
5. 999  888    10. ✕  8
6. ⊤  ⊞    11. ⌿H  ⌿B
7. 7O  7OS    12. ∞  ∞-
8. ⋀U  ⋀⊌    13. 21  2b
14. ✷  ⊛

The above plate illustrates the manner in which cow-brands were changed. The original brand appears in each case to the left, and the various alterations follow. It will be noted that with every change there is something added—the rule always adopted by the swindler

CHAPTER 12

# Wild Bill Hickok

As has been shown in preceding chapters, the Western plains were passed over and left unsettled until the advent of the railroads, which began to cross the plains coincident with the arrival of the great cattle herds which came up from the South after a market. This market did not wait for the completion of the railroads, but met the railroads more than half way; indeed, followed them quite across the plains. The frontier sheriff now came upon the Western stage as he had never done before. The bad man also sprang into sudden popular recognition, the more so because he was now accessible to view and within reach of the tourist and tenderfoot investigator of the Western fauna. These were palmy days for the wild West.

Unless it be a placer camp in the mountains, there is no harder collection of human beings to be found than that which gathers in tents and shanties at a temporary railway terminus of the frontier. Yet such were all the capitals of civilization in the earliest days. One town was like another. The history of Wichita and Newton and Fort Dodge was the history of Abilene and Ellsworth and Hays City and all the towns at the head of the advancing rails. The bad men and women of one moved on to the next, just as they did in the stampedes of placer days.

To recount the history of one after another of these wild towns would be endless and perhaps wearisome. But this history has one peculiar feature not yet noted in our investigations. All these cow camps meant to be real towns someday. They meant to take the social compact. There came to each of these camps men bent upon making homes, and these men began to establish a law and order spirit and to set up a government. Indeed, the regular system of American government was there as soon as the railroad was there, and this law was strong on its legislative and executive sides. The frontier sheriff or town marshal was there, the man for the place, as bold and hardy as the bold and hardy men he was to meet and subdue, as skilled with weapons, as willing to die; and upheld, moreover, with that sense of duty and of moral courage which is granted even to the most courageous of men when he feels that he has the sentiment of the majority of good people at his back.

To describe the life of one Western town marshal, himself the best and most picturesque of them all. is to cover all this field sufficiently. There is but one man who can thus be chosen, and that is Wild Bill Hickok, better known for a generation as "Wild Bill," and properly accorded an honourable place in American history.

The real name of Wild Bill was James Butler Hickok, and he was born in May, 1837, in La Salle county, Illinois. This brought his youth into the days of Western exploration and conquest, and the boy read of Carson and Fremont, then popular idols, with the result that he proposed a life of adventure for himself. He was eighteen years of age when he first saw the West as a fighting man under Jim Lane, of Free Soil fame. In the guerrilla days of Kansas before the civil war. He made his mark, and was elected a constable in that dangerous country before he was twenty years of age. He was then a tall, "gangling" youth, six feet one in height, with yellow hair and blue eyes. He later developed into as splendid looking a man as ever trod on leather, muscular, and agile as he was powerful and enduring. His features were clean-cut and expressive, his carriage erect and dignified, and no one ever looked less the conventional part of the bad man assigned in popular imagination.

He was not a quarrelsome man, although a dangerous one, and his voice was low and even, showing a nervous system like that of Daniel Boone—"not agitated." it might have been supposed that he would be a natural master of weapons, and such was the case. The use of rifle and revolver was born in him, and perhaps no man of the frontier ever surpassed him in quick and accurate use of the heavy six-shooter. The religion of the frontier was not to miss, and rarely ever did he shoot except he knew that he would not miss. The tale of his killings in single combat is the longest authentically assigned to any man in American history.

After many experiences with the pro-slavery folk from the border, Bill, or "Shanghai Bill," as he was then known—a nickname which clung for years—went stage driving for the Overland, and incidentally did some effective Indian fighting for his employers, finally, in the year 1861, settling down as station agent for the Overland at Rock Creek station, about fifty miles west of Topeka. He was really there as guard for the horse band, for all that region was full of horse thieves and cutthroats, and robberies and killings were common enough. It was here that there occurred his greatest fight, the greatest fight of one man against odds at close range that is mentioned in any history of any part of the world. There was never a battle like it known, nor is the West apt again to produce one matching it.

The borderland of Kansas was at that time, as may be remembered, ground debated by the anti-slavery and pro-slavery factions, who still waged bitter war against one another, killing, burning, and pillaging without mercy. The civil war was then raging, and Confederates from Missouri were frequent visitors in eastern Kansas under one pretext or another, of which horse lifting was the one most common, it being held legitimate to prey upon the enemy as opportunity offered. Two border outlaws by the name of the McCandlas boys led a gang of hard men in enterprises of this nature, and these intended to run off the stage company's horses when they found they could not seduce Bill to join their number. He told them to come and take the horses if they could; and on the afternoon of December 16, 1861, ten of them, led by the McCandlas brothers, rode up to his dugout to do so. Bill was alone, his stableman being away hunting. He retreated to the dark interior of his dugout and got ready his weapons, a rifle, two six-shooters, and a knife.

The assailants proceeded to batter in the door with a log, and as it fell in, Jim McCandlas, who must have been a brave man to undertake so foolhardy a thing against a man already known as a killer, sprang in at the opening. He, of course, was killed at once. This exhausted the rifle, and Bill picked up the six-shooters from the table and in three quick shots killed three more of the gang as they rushed in at the door. Four men were dead in less than that many seconds; but there were still six others left, all inside the dugout now, and all firing at him at a range of three feet. It was almost a miracle that, under such surroundings, the man was not killed. Bill now was crowded too much to use his firearms, and took to the bowie, thrusting at one man and another as best he might.

It is known among knife-fighters that a man will stand up under a lot of flesh-cutting and blood-letting until the blade strikes a bone. Then he seems to drop quickly if it be a deep and severe thrust. In this chance medley, the knife wounds inflicted on each other by Bill and his swarming foes did not at first drop their men; so that it must

WILD BILL HICKOK'S DESPERATE FIGHT IN THE
DUG-OUT—ONE MAN AGAINST TEN

have been several minutes that all seven of them were mixed in a mass of shooting, thrusting, panting, and gasping humanity. Then Jack McCandlas swung his rifle barrel and struck Bill over the head, springing upon him with his knife as well. Bill got his hand on a six-shooter and killed him just as he would have struck. After that no one knows what happened, not even Bill himself, who got his name then and there. He said, describing it:

> I just got sort of wild, I thought my heart was on fire. I went out to the pump then to get a drink, and I was all cut and shot to pieces.

They called him Wild Bill after that, and he had earned the name. There were six dead men on the floor of the dugout. He had fairly whipped the ten of them, and the four remaining had enough and fled from that awful hole in the ground. Two of these were badly wounded. Bill followed them to the door. His own weapons were exhausted or not at hand by this time, but his stableman came up just then with a rifle in his hands. Bill caught it from him, and, cut up as he was, fired and killed one of the wounded desperadoes as he tried to mount his horse. The other wounded man later died of his wounds. Eight men were killed by the one. The two who got to their horses and escaped were perhaps never in the dugout at all, for it was hardly large enough to hold another man had any wanted to get in. There is no record of any fighting man to equal this.

It took Bill a year to recover from his wounds. The life of the open air and hard work brought many Western men through injuries which would be fatal in the States. The pure air of the plains had much to do with this. Bill now took service as wagon-master under General Fremont and managed to get attacked by a force of Confederates while on his way to Sedalia, the war being now in full swing. He fled and was pursued; but, shooting back with six-shooters, killed four men. It will be seen that he had now in single fight killed twelve men, and he was very young. This tally did not cover Indians, of whom he had slain several.

Although he did not enlist, he went into the army as an independent sharpshooter, just because the fighting was good, and his work at this was very deadly. In four hours at the Pea Ridge battle, where he lay behind a log, on a hill commanding the flat where the Confederates were formed, he is said to have killed thirty-five men, one of them the Confederate General McCullough. It was like shooting buffalo for him. He was charged by a company of the enemy, but was rescued by his own men.

Not yet enlisting, Bill went in as a spy for General Curtis, and took the dangerous work of going into "Pap" Price's lines, among the touch-and-go Missourians and Arkansans, in search of information useful to the Union forces. Bill enlisted for business purposes in a company of Price's mounted rangers, got the knowledge desired, and fled, killing a Confederate sergeant by name of Lawson in his escape. Curtis sent him back again, this time into the forces of Kirby Smith, then in Texas, but reported soon to move up into Arkansas. Bill enlisted again, and again showed his skill in the saddle, killing two men as he fled. Count up all his known victims to this time, and the tally would be at least sixty-two men; and Bill was then but twenty-five.

A third time Curtis sent Bill back into the Confederate lines, this time into another part of Price's army. Here he was detected and arrested as a spy. Bound hand and foot in his death watch, he killed his captor after he had torn his hands free, and once more escaped. After that, he dared not go back again, for he was too well known and too difficult to disguise. He could not keep out of the fighting, however, and went as a scout and free-lance with General Davis, during Price's second Invasion of Missouri. He was not an enlisted man, and seems to have done pretty much as he liked. One day he rode out on his own hook, and was stopped by three men, who ordered him to halt and dismount. All three men had their hands on their revolvers; but, to show the difference between average men and a specialist, Bill killed two of them and fatally shot the other before they could get into action. His tally was now sixty-six men at least.

Curtis now sent Bill out into Kansas to look into a report that some Indians were about to join the Confederate forces. Bill got the news, and also engaged in a knife duel with the Sioux, Conquering Bear, whom he accused of trying to ambush him. It was a fair and desperate fight, with knives, and although Bill finally killed his man, he himself was so badly cut up that he came near dying, his arm being ripped from shoulder to elbow, a wound which it took years to mend. It is doubtful if any man ever survived such Injuries as he did, for by this time he was a mass of scars from pistol and knife wounds. He had probably been in danger of his life more than a hundred times in personal difficulties; for the man with a reputation as a bad man has a reputation which needs continual defending.

After the war. Bill lived from hand to mouth, like most frontier dwellers. It was at Springfield, Missouri, that another duel of his long list occurred, in which he killed Dave Tutt, a fine pistol shot and a man with social ambitions in badness. It was a fair fight in the town square by appointment. Bill killed his man and wheeled so quickly on Tutt's followers that Tutt had not had time to fall before Bill's six-shooter was turned the opposite way, and he was asking Tutt's friends if they wanted any of it themselves. They did not. This fight was forced on Bill, and his quiet attempts to avoid it and his stern way of accepting it, when inevitable, won him high estimation on the border. Indeed, he was now known all over the country, and his like has not since been seen. He was still a splendid looking man, and as cool and quiet and modest as ever he had been.

Bill now went to trapping in the less settled parts of Nebraska, and for a while he lived in peace, until he fell into a saloon row over some trivial matter and invited four of his opponents outside to fight him with pistols; the four were to fire at the word, and Bill to do the same—his pistol against their four. In this fight he killed one man at first fire, but he himself was shot through the shoulder and disabled in his right arm. He killed two more with his left hand and badly wounded the other. This was a fair fight also, and the only wonder is he was not killed; but he seemed never to consider odds, and literally he knew nothing but fight.

His score was now seventy-two men, not counting Indians. He himself never reported how many Indians he and Buffalo Bill killed as scouts in the Black Kettle campaign under Carr and Primrose, but the killing of Black Kettle himself was sometimes attributed to Wild Bill. The latter was badly wounded in the thigh with a lance, and it took a long time for this wound to heal. To give this hurt and others better opportunity for mending, Bill now took a trip back East to his home in Illinois. While East he found that he had a reputation, and he undertook to use it. He found no way of making a living, however, and he returned to the West, where he could better market his qualifications.

At that time Hays City, Kansas, was one of the hardest towns on the frontier. It had more than a hundred gambling dives and saloons to its two thousand population, and murder was an ordinary thing. Hays needed a town marshal, and one who could shoot. Wild Bill was unanimously selected, and in six weeks he was obliged to kill Jack Strawhan for trying to shoot him. This he did by reason of his superior quickness with the six-shooter, for Strawhan was drawing first. Another bad man, Mulvey, started to run Hays, in whose peace and dignity Bill now felt a personal ownership. Covered by Mulvey's two revolvers. Bill found room for the lightning flash of time, which is all that is needed by the real revolver genius, and killed Mulvey on the spot.

His tally was now seventy-five men. He made it seventy-eight in a fight with a bunch of private soldiers, who called him a "long-hair"—a term very accurate, by the way, for Bill was proud of his long, blond hair, as was General Custer and many another man of the West at that time. In this fight. Bill was struck by seven pistol balls and barely escaped alive by flight to a ranch on the prairie nearby. He lay there three weeks, while General Phil Sheridan had details out with orders to get him dead or alive. He later escaped in a box-car to another town, and his days as marshal of Hays were over.

Bill now tried his hand at Wild West theatricals, seeing that already many Easterners were "daffy," as he called it, about the West; but he failed at this, and went back once more to the plains where he belonged. He was chosen marshal of Abilene, then the cow camp par excellence of the middle plains, and as tough a community as Hays had been.

The wild men from the lower plains, fighting men, mad from whiskey and contact with the settlements' possibilities of long-denied indulgence, swarmed in the streets and dives, mingling with desperadoes and toughs from all parts of the frontier. Those who have never lived in such a community will never be able by any description to understand its phenomena. It seems almost unbelievable that sober, steady-going America ever knew such days; but there they were, and not so long ago, for this was only 1870.

Two days after Bill was elected marshal of Abilene, he killed a desperado who was "whooping-up" the town in customary fashion. That same night, he was on the street, in a dim light, when all at once he saw a man whisk around a corner, and saw something shine, as he thought, with the gleam of a weapon. As showing how quick were the hand and eye of the typical gun-man of the day, it may be stated that Bill killed this man in a flash, only to find later that it was a friend, and one of his own deputies. The man was only pulling a handkerchief from his pocket. Bill knew that he was watched every moment by men who wanted to kill him. He had his life in his hands all the time. For instance, he had next to kill the friend of the desperado whom he had shot.

By this time, Abilene respected its new marshal; indeed, was rather proud of him. The reign of the bad man of the plains was at its height, and the professional man-killer, the specialist with firearms, was a figure here and there, over wide regions. Among all these none compared with this unique specimen. He was generous, too, as he was deadly, for even yet he was supporting a McCandlas widow, and he always furnished funerals for his corpses. He had one more to furnish soon. Enemies down the range among the cow men made up a purse of five thousand dollars, and hired eight men to kill the town marshal and bring his heart back South. Bill heard of it, and literally made all of them jump off the railroad train where he met them. One was killed in the jump. His list of homicides was now eighty-one. He had never yet been arrested for murder, and his killing was in fair open fight, his life usually against large odds. He was a strange favourite of fortune, who seemed certainly to shield him roundabout.

Bill now went East for another try at theatricals, in which, happily, he was unsuccessful, and for which he felt a strong distaste. He was scared—on the stage; and when he saw what was expected of him he quit and went back once more to the West. He appeared at Cheyenne, in the Black Hills, wandering thus from one point to another after the fashion of the frontier, where a man did many things and in many places. He had a little brush with a band of Indians, and killed four of them with four shots from his six-shooter, bringing his list in red and white to eighty-five men. He got away alive from the Black Hills with difficulty; but in 1876 he was back again at Deadwood, married now, and, one would have thought, ready to settle down.

But the life of turbulence ends in turbulence. He who lives by the sword dies by the sword. Deadwood was as bad a place as any that could be found in the mining regions, and Bill was not an officer here, as he had been in Kansas towns. As marshal of Hays and Abilene and United States marshal later at Hays City, he had been a national character. He was at Deadwood for the time only plain Wild Bill, handsome, quiet, but ready for anything.

Ready for anything but treachery! He himself had always fought fair and in the open. His men were shot in front. Not such was to be his fate. On the day of August 2, 1876, while he was sitting at a game of cards in a saloon, a hard citizen by name of Jack McCall slipped up behind him, placed a pistol to the back of his head, and shot him dead before he knew he had an enemy near. The ball passed through Bill's head and out at the cheek, lodging in the arm of a man across the table.

Bill had won a little money from McCall earlier in the day, and won it fairly, but the latter had a grudge, and was no doubt one of those disgruntled souls who "had it in" for all the rest of the world. He got away with the killing at the time, for a miners' court let him go. A few days later, he began to boast about his act, seeing what fame was his for ending so famous a life; but at Yankton they arrested him, tried him before a real court, convicted him, and hanged him promptly.

Wild Bill's body was burled at Deadwood, and his grave, surrounded by a neat railing and marked by a monument, long remained one of the features of Deadwood. The monument and fence were disfigured by vandals who sought some memento of the greatest bad man ever in all likelihood seen upon the earth. His tally of eighty-five men seems large, but in fair probability it is not large enough. His main encounters are known historically. He killed a great many Indians at different times, but of these no accurate estimate can be claimed. Nor is his list of victims as a sharpshooter in the army legitimately to be added to his record. Cutting out all doubtful instances, however, there remains no doubt that he killed between twenty and thirty men in personal combat in the open, and that never once was he tried in any court on a charge even of manslaughter.

This record is not approached by that of any other known bad man. Many of them are credited with twenty men, a dozen men, and so forth; but when the records are sifted the list dwindles. It is doubted whether any other bad man in America ever actually killed twenty men in fair personal combat. Bill was not killed in fair fight, nor could McCall have hurt him had Bill suspected his intent.

Hickok was about thirty-nine years old when killed, and he had averaged a little more than two men for each year of his entire life. He was well-known among army officers, and esteemed as a scout and a man, never regarded as a tough in any sense. He was a man of singular personal beauty. Of him General Custer, soon thereafter to fall a victim himself upon the plains, said:

"He was a plainsman in every sense of the word, yet unlike any other of his class. Whether on foot or on horseback, he was one of the most perfect types of physical manhood I ever saw. His manner was entirely free from all bluster and bravado. He never spoke of himself unless requested to do so. His influence among the frontiersmen was unbounded; his word was law. Wild Bill was anything but a quarrelsome man, yet none but himself could enumerate the many conflicts in which he had been engaged."

These are the words of one fighting man about another, and both men are entitled to good rank in the annals of the West. The praise of an army general for a man of no rank or wealth leaves us feeling that, after all, it was a possible thing for a bad man to be a good man, and worthy of respect and admiration, utterly unmingled with maudlin sentiment or weak love for the melodramatic.

CHAPTER 13

# Frontier Wars

The history of the border wars on the American frontier, where the fighting was more like battle than murder, and where the extent of the crimes against law became too large for the law ever to undertake any settlement, would make a long series of bloody volumes. These wars of the frontier were sometimes political, as the Kansas antislavery warfare; or, again, they were fights over town sites, one armed band against another, and both against the law. Wars over cows, as of the cattle men against the rustlers and "little fellows," often took on the phase of large armed bodies of men meeting in bloody encounter; though the bloodiest of these wars are those least known, and the *opera bouffe* wars those most widely advertised.

The state of Kansas, now so calm and peaceful, is difficult to picture as the scene of a general bloodshed; yet wherever you scratch Kansas history you find a fight. No territory of equal size has had so much war over so many different causes. Her story in Indian fighting, gambler fighting, outlaw fighting, town site fighting, and political fighting is one not approached by any other portion of the West; and if at times it was marked with fanaticism or with sordidness. It was none the less bitter and notable.

The border wars of Kansas and Missouri at the time immediately preceding the civil war would be famed in song and story, had not the greater conflict between North and South wiped all that out of memory. Even the North was divided over the great question of the repeal of the Missouri Compromise. Alabama, Arkansas, California, Delaware, Florida, Georgia, Indiana, Iowa, Kentucky, Louisiana, Maryland, Michigan, Missouri, New Hampshire, North Carolina, South Carolina, Tennessee, Texas, and Virginia gave a whole or a majority vote for this repeal of the Compromise. Against the repeal were Connecticut, Maine, Massachusetts, New York, Ohio, Pennsylvania, Rhode Island, Vermont, and Wisconsin. Illinois and New Jersey voted a tie vote. Ohio cast four votes for the repeal measure, seventeen against it.

This vote brought the territories of Kansas and Nebraska into the Union with the option open on whether or not they should have slavery:

> It being the true intent and meaning of this act not to legislate slavery into any territory, nor to exclude it therefrom, but to leave the people thereof perfectly free to form and regulate their own domestic institutions in their own way.

That was very well; but who were "the people" of these debated grounds? Hundreds of abolitionists of the North thought it their duty to flock to Kansas and take up arms. Hundreds of the inhabitants of Missouri thought it incumbent upon them to run across the line and vote in Kansas on the "domestic institutions"; and to shoot in Kansas and to burn and ravage in Kansas. They were met by the anti-slavery legions along the wide frontier, and brother slew brother for years, one series of more or less ignoble and dastardly outrages following another in big or little, murders and arson in big or little, until the whole country at last was drawn into this matter of the domestic institutions of "bleeding Kansas." The animosities formed in those days were bitter and enduring ones, and the more prominent figures on both sides were men marked for later slaughter.

The civil war and the slavery question were fought out all over the West for ten years, even twenty years after the war was over. Some large figures came up out of this internecine strife, and there were many deeds of courage and many romantic adventures; but on the whole, although the result of all this was for the best, and added another state to the list unalterably opposed to human slavery, the story in detail is not a pleasant one, and adds no great glory to either side. It is a chapter of American history which is very well let alone. When the railroads came across the Western plains, they brought a man who has been present on the American frontier ever since the revolutionary war,—the land boomer. He was in Kentucky in time to rob poor old Daniel Boone of all the lands he thought he owned. He founded Marietta, on the Ohio River, on a land steal; and thence, westward, laid out one town after another.

The early settler who came down the Ohio valley in the first and second decades of the past century passed the ruins of abandoned towns far back to the east even in that day. The town-site shark passed across the Mississippi River and the Missouri, and everywhere his record was the same. He was the pioneer of avarice in very many cases, and often he Inaugurated strife where he purported to be establishing law. Each town thought itself the garden spot and centre of the universe—one knows not how many Kansas towns, for instance, contended over the absurd honour of being exactly at the centre of the United States!—and local pride was such that each citizen must unite with others even in arms, if need be, to uphold the merits of his own "city."

This peculiar phase of frontier nature usually came most into evidence over the questions of county seats. Hardly a frontier county seat was ever established without a fight of some kind, and often a bloody one. It has chanced that the author has been in and around a few of these clashes between rival towns, and he may say that the vehemence of the antagonism of such encounters would have been humorous, had it not been so deadly. Two "cities," composed each of a few frame shanties and a set of blue-print maps, one just as barren of delight as the other, and neither worth fighting over at the time, do not seem typical of any great moral purpose; yet at times their citizens fought as stubbornly as did the men who fought for and against slavery in Kansas. One instance of this sort of thing will do, and it is covered in the chapter describing the Stevens County War, one of the most desperate and bloody, as well as one of the most recent feuds of local politicians.

For some reason, perhaps that of remoteness of time, the wars of the cow men of the range seem to have had a bolder, a less sordid and more romantic interest, if these terms be allowable. When the cow man began to fence up the free range, to shut up God's out-of-doors, he intrenched upon more than a local or a political pride. He was now infringing upon the great principle of personal freedom. He was throttling the West itself, which had always been a land of freedom. One does not know whether all one's readers have known it, that unspeakable feeling of freedom, of independence, of rebellion at restraint, which came when one could ride or drive for days across the empire of the plains and never meet a fence to hinder, nor need a road to show the way. To meet one of these new far-flung fences of the rich men who began to take up the West was at that time only to cut it and ride on. The free men of the West would not be fenced in. The range was theirs, so they blindly and lovingly thought. Let those blame them who love this day more than that.

But the fence was the sign of the property-owning man; and the property-owning man has always beaten the nomad and the restless man at last, and set metes and bounds for him to observe. The nesters and rustlers fought out the battle for the free range more fiercely than was ever generally known.

One of the most widely known of these cow wars was the absurd Johnson County War, of Wyoming, which got much newspaper advertising at the time—the summer of 1892—and which was always referred to with a certain contempt among old-timers as the "dude war." Only two men were killed in this war, and the non-resident cattle men who undertook to be ultra-Western and do a little vigilante work for themselves among the rustlers found that they were not fit for the task. They were very glad indeed to get themselves arrested and under cover, more especially in the protection of the military. They found that they had not lost any rustlers when they stirred up a whole valley full and were themselves besieged, surrounded, and well-nigh ready for a general wiping out.

They killed a couple of "little fellows," or, rather, some of their hired Texas cowboys did it for them, but that was all they accomplished, except well-nigh to bankrupt Wyoming in the legal muddle, out of which, of course, nothing came. There were in this party of cattle men a member of the legislature, a member of the stock commission, some two dozen wealthy cattle men, two Harvard graduates, and a young Englishman in search of adventure. They made, on the whole, about the most contemptible and inefficient band of vigilantes that ever went out to regulate things, although their deeds were reported by wire to many journals, and for a time perhaps they felt that they were cutting quite a figure. They had very large property losses to incite them to their action, for the rustlers were then pretty much running things in that part of Wyoming, and the local courts would not convict them. This fiasco scarcely hastened the advent of the day—which came soon enough after the railroads and the farmers—under which the home dweller outweighed the nomad. (*The Story of the Cowboy*.)

Wars between sheep men and cattle men sometimes took on the phase of armed bodies of men meeting in bloody encounter. The sheep were always unwelcome on the range, and are so today, (1905), although the courts now adjust such matters better than they formerly did. The cow baron and his men often took revenge upon the woolly nuisances themselves and killed them in numbers. The author knows of one instance where five thousand sheep were killed in one box canon by irate cow men whose range had been invaded. The sheep eat the grass down to the point of killing It, and cattle will not feed on a country which sheep have crossed. Many wars of this kind have been known all the way from Montana to Mexico.

Again, factional fights might arise over some trivial matter as an immediate cause. In a community or a region where numbers of men fairly equal were separated in self-interest. In a day when life was still wild and free, and when the law was still unknown, these differences of opinion sometimes led to bitter and bloody conflicts between factions.

Chapter 14

# The Lincoln County War

The entire history of the American frontier is one of rebellion against the law, if, indeed, that may be called rebellion whose apostles have not yet recognised any authority of the law. The frontier antedated anarchy. It broke no social compact, for it had never made one. Its population asked no protection save that afforded under the stern suzerainty of the six-shooter. The anarchy of the frontier, if we may call it such, was sometimes little more than self-interest against self-interest. This was the true description of the border conflict now in question.

The Lincoln County War, fully speaking, embraced three wars; the Pecos War of the early '70's, the Harold War of 1874, and the Lincoln County War proper, which may be said to have begun in 1874 and to have ended in 1879. The actors in these different conflicts were all intermingled. There was no blood feud at the bottom of this fighting. It was the war of self-interest against self-interest, each side supported by numbers of fighting men.

At that time Lincoln County, New Mexico, was about as large as the state of Pennsylvania. For judicial purposes it was annexed to Donna Ana County, and its territories included both the present counties of Eddy and Chaves, and part of what is now Donna Ana. It extended west practically as far the Rio Grande River, and embraced a tract of mountains and high tableland nearly two hundred miles square. Out of this mountain chain, to the east and southeast, ran two beautiful mountain streams, the Bonito and the Ruidoso, flowing into the Hondo, which continues on to the flat valley of the Pecos River— once the natural pathway of the Texas cattle herds bound north to Utah and the mountain territories, and hence the natural pathway also for many lawful or lawless citizens from Texas.

At the close of the civil war, Texas was full of unbranded and unowned cattle. Out of the town of Paris, Texas, which was founded by his father, came one John Chisum—one of the most typical cow men that ever lived. Bold, fearless, shrewd, unscrupulous, genial, magnetic, he was the man of all others to occupy a kingdom which had heretofore had no ruler.

John Chisum drove the first herds up the Pecos trail to the territorial market. He held at one time perhaps eighty thousand head of cattle under his brand of the "Long I" and "jinglebob." Moreover, he had powers of attorney from a great many cow men in Texas and lower New Mexico, authorizing him to take up any trail cattle which he found under their respective brands. He carried a tin cylinder, large as a water-spout, that contained, some said, more than a thousand of these powers of attorney.

At least, it is certain he had papers enough to give him a wide authority. Chisum riders combed every north-bound herd. If they found the cattle of any of his "friends," they were cut out and turned on the Chisum range. There were many "little fellows," small cattlemen, nested here and there on the flanks of the Chisum herds. What more natural than that they should steal from him, in case they found a market of their own? That was much easier than raising cows of their own. Now, there was a market up this winding Bonito valley, at Lincoln and Fort Stanton. The soldiers of the latter post, and the Indians of the Mescalero reservation nearby, needed supplies. There were others besides John Chisum who might need a beef contract now and then, and cattle to fill it.

At the end of the civil war, there was in New Mexico, with what was known as the California Column, which joined the forces of New Mexican volunteers, an officer known as Major L. G. Murphy. After the war, a great many men settled near the points where they were mustered out in the South and West. It was thus with Major Murphy, who located as post-trader at the little frontier post known as Fort Stanton, which was founded by Captain Frank Stanton in 1854, in the Indian days. John Chisum located his Bosque Grande ranch about 1865, and Murphy came to Fort Stanton about 1866. In 1875, Chisum dropped down to his South Spring River ranch, and by that time Murphy had been thrown out of the post-tradership by Major Clendenning, commanding officer, who did not like his methods. He had dropped nine miles down the Bonito from Fort Stanton, with two young associates, under the firm name of Murphy, Riley & Dolan,

JOHN SIMPSON CHISUM
A famous cattle king, died December 23, 1884

sometimes spoken of as L. G. Murphy & Co.

Murphy was a hard-drinking man, yet withal something of a student. He was intelligent, generous, bold and shrewd. He "staked" every little cow man in Lincoln County, including a great many who hung on the flanks of John Chisum's herds. These men in turn were in their ethics bound to support him and his methods. Murphy was king of the Bonito country. Chisum was king of the Pecos; not merchant but cow man, and caring for nothing which had not grass and water on it.

Here, then, were two rival kings. Each at times had occasion for a beef contract. The result is obvious to anyone who knows the ways of the remoter West in earlier days. The times were ripe for trouble. Murphy bought stolen beef, and furnished bran Instead of flour on his Indian contracts, as the government records show. His henchmen held the Chisum herds as their legitimate prey. Thus, we now have our stage set and peopled for the grim drama of a bitter border war.

The Pecos war was mostly an indiscriminate killing among cow men and cattle thieves, and it cost many lives, though it had no beginning and no end. The Texas men, hard riders and cheerful shooters for the most part, came pushing up the Pecos and into the Bonito Cañon. Among these, in 1874, were four brothers known as the Harold boys. Bill, Jack, Tom and Bob, who had come from Texas in 1872. Two of them located ranches on the Ruidoso, being "staked" therein by Major Murphy, king for that part of the countryside.

The Harold boys once undertook to run the town of Lincoln, and a foolish justice ordered a constable to arrest them. One Gillam, an ex-sheriff, told the boys to put on their guns. On that night there were killed Gillam, Bill Harold, Dave Warner and Martinez, the Mexican constable. The dead body of Martinez was lying in the street the next morning with a deep cross cut on the forehead. From that time on for the next five years, it was no uncommon thing to see dead men lying in the streets of Lincoln. The Harold boys had sworn revenge.

There was a little dance in an *adobe* one night at Lincoln, when Ben Harold and some Texas men from the Seven Rivers country rode up. They killed four men and one woman that night before they started back to Seven Rivers. From that time on, it was Texas against the law, such as the latter was. No resident places the number of the victims of the Harold war at less than forty or fifty, and it is believed that at least seventy-five would be more correct. These killings proved the weakness of the law, for none of the Harold gang was ever punished. As for the Lincoln County War proper, the magazine was now handsomely laid. Only the spark was needed. What would that naturally be? Either an actual law court, or else—a woman! in due time, both were forthcoming.

The woman in the case still, (1905), lives today in New Mexico, sometimes spoken of as the "Cattle Queen" of New Mexico. She bears now the name of Mrs. Susan E. Barber. Her maiden name was Susan E. Hummer, the name sometimes spelled Homer, and she was born in Gettysburg, Pennsylvania. Susan Hummer was a granddaughter of Anna Maria Spangler-Stauffer. The Spangler family is a noble one of Germany and very old. George Spangler was cup-bearer to Godfrey, Chancellor of Frederick Barbarossa, and was with the latter on the Crusade when Barbarossa was drowned in the Syrian river, Calycadmus, in 1190. The American seat of this old family was in York county, Pennsylvania, where the first Spanglers settled in 1731. It was from this tenacious and courageous ancestry that there sprang this figure of a border warfare in a region wild as Barbarossa's realm centuries ago.

On August 23, 1873, in Atchison, Kansas, Susan Hummer was married to Alexander A. McSween, a young lawyer fresh from the Washington university law school of St. Louis. McSween was born in Charlottetown, Prince Edward Island, and was educated in the first place as a Presbyterian minister. He was a man of good appearance, of intelligence and address, and of rather more polish than the average man. He was an orator, a dreamer, and a visionary; a strange, complex character. He was not a fighting man, and belonged anywhere in the world rather than on the frontier of the bloody Southwest. His health was not good, and he resolved to journey to New Mexico. He and his young bride started overland, with a good team and conveyance, and reached the little *placita* of Lincoln, in the Bonito Cañon, March 15, 1875. Outside of the firm of Murphy, Riley & Dolan, there were at that time but one or two other American families. McSween started up in the practice of law.

There appeared in northern New Mexico at about this time an Englishman by the name of J. H. Tunstall, newly arrived in the West in search of investment. Tunstall was told that there was good open cattle range to be had in Lincoln County. He came to Lincoln, met McSween, formed a partnership with him in the banking and mercantile business, and, moreover, started for himself, and altogether independently, a horse and cattle ranch on the Rio Feliz, a day's journey below Lincoln. Now, King Murphy, of Lincoln County, found a rival

(1) Shot and left for dead, in the Lincoln County War. (2) Leader of a faction in the Lincoln County War. (3) Friend of Kit Carson; the man who carried the news of the big street fight to Ft. Stanton

business growing up directly under his eyes. He liked this no better than King Chisum liked the little cow men on his flanks in the Seven Rivers country. Things were ripening still more rapidly for trouble. Presently, the immediate cause made its appearance.

There had been a former partner and friend of Major Murphy in the post-tradership at Fort Stanton, Colonel Emil Fritz, who established the Fritz ranch, a few miles below Lincoln. Colonel Fritz having amassed a considerable fortune, concluded to return to Germany. He had insured his life in the American Insurance Company for ten thousand dollars, and had made a will leaving this policy, or the greater part of it, to his sister. The latter had married a clerk at Fort Stanton by the name of Scholland, but did not get along well with her husband. Heretofore no such thing as divorce had been known in that part of the world; but courts and lawyers were now present, and it occurred to Mrs. Scholland to have a divorce. She sent to Mr. McSween for legal counsel, and for a time lived in the McSween house.

Now came news of the death, in Germany, of Colonel Emil Fritz. His brother, Charlie Fritz, undertook to look up the estate. He found the will and insurance policy had been left with Major Murphy; but Major Murphy, accustomed to running affairs in his own way, refused to give up the Emil Fritz will, and forced McSween to get a court order appointing Mrs. Scholland administratrix of the Fritz estate. Not even in that capacity would Major Murphy deliver to her the will and insurance policy when they were demanded, and it is claimed that he destroyed the will. Certainly, it was never probated. Murphy was accustomed to keep this will in a tin can, hid in a hole in the *adobe* wall of his store building. There were no safes at that time and place. The policy had been left as security for a loan of nine hundred dollars advanced by a firm known as Spiegelberg Brothers. Few ingredients were now lacking for a typical melodrama. Meantime the plot thickened by the failure of the insurance company!

McSween, in the interest of Mrs. Scholland, now went East to see what could be done in the collection of the Insurance policy. He was able finally, in 1876, to collect the full amount of ten thousand dollars, and this he deposited in his own name in a St. Louis bank then owned by Colonel Hunter. He had been obliged to pay the Spiegelbergs the face of their loan before he could get the policy to take East with him. He wished to be secured against this advancement and reimbursed as well for his expenses, which, together with his fee, amounted to a considerable sum. Moreover, the German Minister enjoined Mc-

Sween from turning over any of this money, as there were other heirs in Germany. Major Murphy owed McSween some money.

Colonel Fritz also died owing McSween thirty-three hundred dollars, fees due on legal work. Yet Murphy demanded the full amount of the Insurance policy from McSween again and again. Murphy, Riley & Dolan now sued out an attachment on McSween's property, and levied on the goods in the Tunstall-McSween store. The "law" was now doing its work; but there was a very liberal interpretation put upon the law's intent. As construed by Sheriff William Brady, the writ applied also to the Englishman Tunstall's property in cattle and horses on the Rio Feliz ranch; which, of course, was high-handed illegality. McSween's statement that he had no interest in the Feliz ranch served no purpose. Brady and Murphy were warm friends.

The lawyer McSween had accused them of being something more than that—allies and conspirators. McSween and Tunstall bought Lincoln county scrip cheap; but when they presented it to the county treasurer. Murphy, it was not paid, and it was charged that he and Brady had made away with the county funds. That was never proved, for, as a matter of fact, no county books were ever kept! McSween started the first set ever known there. At this time there was working for Tunstall on the Feliz ranch the noted desperado, Billy the Kid, who a short time formerly had worked for John Chisum. The latter at this stage of the advancing troubles, appears rather as a third party, or as holding one point of a triangle, whose other two corners were occupied by the Murphy and McSween factions.

Whether or not it was a legal posse which went out to serve the attachment on the Tunstall cattle—or whether or not a posse was necessary for that purpose—the truth is that a band of men, on February 13th, 1878, did go out under some semblance of the law and in the interests of the Murphy people's claim. Some state that William S. Morton, or "Billy" Morton, was chosen by Sheriff Brady as his deputy and as leader of this posse. Others name different men as leaders. Certainly, the band was suited for any desperate occasion. With it was one Tom Hill, who had killed several men at different times, and who had been heard to say that he intended to kill Tunstall. There was also Jesse Evans, just in from the Rio Grande country, and, unless that were Billy the Kid, the most redoubtable fighter in all that country. Evans had formerly worked for John Chisum, and had been the friend of Billy the Kid; but these two had now become enemies. Others of the party were William M. Johnson, Ham Mills, Johnnie Hurley, Frank Baker,

THE McSWEEN STORE AND BANK; PROMINENT IN THE LINCOLN COUNTY WAR several ranchers still living in that country, and two or three Mexicans.

All these rode across the mountains to the Ruidoso valley on their way to the Rio Feliz. They met, coming from the Tunstall ranch, Tunstall himself in company with his foreman, Dick Brewer, John Middleton and Billy the Kid. When the Murphy posse came up with Tunstall, he was alone. His men were at the time chasing a flock of wild turkeys along a distant hillside. When called upon to halt, Tunstall did so, and then came up toward the posse. "You wouldn't hurt me, boys, would you?" he said, as he approached leading his horse.

When within a few yards, Tom Hill said to him, "Why, hello, Tunstall, is that you?" and almost with the words fired upon him with his six-shooter and shot him down.

Some say that Hill shot Tunstall again, and a young Mexican boy called Pantilon beat in his skull with a rock. They put Tunstall's hat under his head and left him lying there beside his horse, which was also killed. His folded coat was found under the horse's head. His body, lashed on a burro's back, was brought over the mountains by his friends that night into Lincoln, twenty miles distant. Fifty men took up the McSween fight that night; for. In truth, the killing of Tunstall was murder and without justification.

That was the beginning of the actual Lincoln County War. Dick Brewer, Tunstall's foreman, was now leader of the McSween fighting men. McSween, of course, supplied him with colour of "legal" authority. He was appointed "special constable." Neither party had difficulty in obtaining all the legal papers required. Each party was presently to have a sheriff of its own. Meantime, there was at Lincoln an accommodating justice of the peace, John P. Wilson, who was ready to give either faction any sort of legal paper it demanded. Dick Brewer, Billy the Kid, and nearly a dozen others of the first McSween posse started to the lower country, where lived a good many of Murphy's friends, small cow men and others.

On the Rio Peñasco, about six miles from the Pecos, they came across a party of five men, two of whom, Billy Morton and Frank Baker, had been present at the killing of Tunstall. Baker and Morton surrendered under promise of safekeeping, and were held for a time at Roswell. On the trail from Roswell to Lincoln, at a point near the Agua Negra, both these men, while kneeling and pleading for their lives, were deliberately shot and killed by Billy the Kid.

There was with the Brewer posse a buffalo-hunter by the name of McClosky, who had promised to take care of these prisoners. Joe

McNab, of the posse, shot and killed McClosky in cold blood. In this McSween posse were "Doc" Skurlock, Charlie Bowdre, Billy the Kid, Hendry Brown, Jim French, John Middleton, with McNab, Wait and Smith, besides McClosky, who seems not to have been loyal enough to them to sanction cold blooded murder. These victims were killed March 7th, 1878.

There had now been deliberate murder committed upon the one side and upon the other. There were many men implicated on each side. These men, in self-interest, now drew apart together. The factions, of necessity, became more firmly established. It may be seen that there was very little principle at stake on either side. The country was now simply going wild again. It meant to take the law into its own hands; and the population was divided into these two factions, to one or the other of which every resident must perforce belong. A choice, and sometimes a quick one, was an Imperative necessity.

The next killing was that of Buckshot Roberts, at Blazer's Mill, near the Mescalero Reservation buildings, an affair described in a later chapter. Thirteen men, later of the Kid's gang, led by Dick Brewer, attacked Roberts, who killed Dick Brewer before he himself died. The death of the latter left the Kid chief of the McSween forces.

A great blood lust now possessed all the population. It wanted no law. There is no doubt about the intention to make away with Judge Warren Bristol of the circuit court. The latter, knowing of these turbulent times in Lincoln, decided not to hold court. He sent word to Sheriff William Brady to open court and then at once to adjourn it. This was on April 1, 1878.

Sheriff Brady, in walking down the street toward the dwelling-house in which court sessions were then held, was obliged to pass the McSween store and residence. Behind the corral wall, there lay ambushed Billy the Kid and at least five others of his gang. Brady was accompanied by Billy Matthews (J. B. Matthews, now dead; postmaster of Roswell, New Mexico, in 1904), by George Hindman, his deputy, and Dad Peppin, later sheriff of Lincoln County. The Kid and his men waited until the victims had gone by. Then a volley was fired.

Sheriff Brady, shot in the back, slowly sank down, his knees weakening under him. "My God! My God! My God!" he exclaimed, as he gradually dropped. He had been struck in the back by five balls. As he sank down, he turned his head to see his murderers, and as he did so received a ball in the eye, and so fell dead.

George Hindman, the deputy, also shot in the back, ran down the street about one hundred and fifty yards before he fell. He lay in the street and few dared to go out to him. A saloon-keeper, Ike Stockton (himself a bad man, and later killed at Durango, Colorado), offered him a drink of water, which he brought in his hat, and Hindman, accepting it, fell back dead.

The murder of Sheriff Brady left the country without even the semblance of law; but each party now took steps to set up a legal machinery of its own, as cover for its own acts. The old justice of the peace, John P. Wilson, would issue a warrant on any pretext for any person; but there must be someone with authority to serve the process. In a quasi-election, the McSween faction Instituted John Copeland as their sheriff. The Murphy faction held that Copeland never qualified as sheriff. He lived with McSween part of the time. It was understood that he was sheriff for the purpose of bothering nobody but the Murphy people.

Meantime, the other party were not thus to be surpassed. In June, 1878, Governor Axtell appointed George W. Peppin as sheriff of Lincoln County. Peppin qualified at Mesilla, came back to Lincoln, and demanded of Copeland the warrants in his possession. He had, on his part, twelve warrants for the arrest of members of the McSween gang. Little lacked now to add confusion in this bloody coil. The country was split into two factions. Each had a sheriff as a figurehead! What and where was the law?

Peppin had to get fighting men to serve his warrants, and he could not always be particular about the social standing of his posses. He had a thankless and dangerous position as the "Murphy sheriff." Most of his posses were recruited from among the small ranchers and cow boys of the lower Pecos. Peppin was sheriff only a few months, and threw up the job $2,800 in debt.

The men of both parties were now scouting about for each other here and there over a district more than a hundred miles square; but presently the war was to take on the dignity of a pitched battle. Early in July, 1878, the Kid and his gang rounded up at the McSween house. There were a dozen white desperadoes in their party. There were about forty Mexicans also identified with the McSween faction. These were quartered in the Montana and Ellis residences, well down the street.

The Murphy forces now surrounded the McSween house, and at once a pitched battle began. The McSween men started the firing from the windows and loopholes of their fortress. The Peppin men replied. The town, divided against itself, held under cover. For three days the two little armies lay here, separated by the distance of the street, perhaps sixty men in all on the McSween side, perhaps thirty or forty in all on the Murphy-Peppin side, of whom nineteen were Americans.

To keep the McSween men inside their fortifications, Peppin had three men posted on the mountain side, whence they could look down directly upon the top of the houses, as the mountain here rises up sharply back of the narrow line of adobe buildings. These pickets were Charlie Crawford, Lucillo Montoye, and another Mexican, and with their long-range buffalo guns they threw a good many heavy slugs of lead into the McSween house. At last, one Fernando Herrera, a McSween Mexican, standing in the back door of the Montana house, fired, at a distance of about nine hundred yards, at Charlie Crawford. The shot cut Crawford down, and he lay, with his back broken, behind a rock on the mountain side in the hot sun nearly all day. Crawford was later brought down to the street. Medical attendance there was none, and few dared to offer sympathy, but Captain Saturnino Baca carried Crawford a drink of water.

★★★★★★

Captain Saturnino Baca was a friend of Kit Carson, an officer in the New Mexican Volunteers, and the second commanding officer of Fort Stanton. He came to Lincoln in 1865, and purchased of J. Trujillo the old stone tower, as part of what was then the Baca property, near the McSween residence. The Bacas were recognised as non-combatants, but were friendly to Major Murphy. Mrs. McSween and Mrs. Baca were bitter enemies, and it was commonly said that, as each side had a sheriff, each side had a woman. Bonifacio J. Baca, son of Captain and Mrs. Baca, was a protege of Major Murphy, who sent him to Notre Dame University, Indiana, to be educated. "Bonnie" Baca was at different times clerk of the probate court, county assessor, deputy sheriff, etc., and was court interpreter under Judge Warren H. Bristol. He was teaching school at the time Sheriff Brady was shot, and from his refuge in the "round tower," a few feet distant, saw Brady fall. Captain Baca, wife and son, were after that closely watched by the men of the McSween faction, but managed to remain neutral and never became involved in the fighting, though Billy the Kid more than once threatened to kill young Baca.

★★★★★★

The death of Crawford ended the second day's fighting. Peppin's party now numbered sixteen men from the Seven Rivers country, or twenty-eight in all. The McSween men besieged in the *adobe* were Billy the Kid, Harvey Norris (killed), Tom O'Folliard, Ighenio Salazar (wounded and left for dead), Ignacio Gonzales, Jose Semora (killed), Francisco Romero (killed), and Alexander A. McSween, leader of the faction (killed). Doc Skurlock, Jack Middleton, and Charlie Bowdre were in the adjoining store building.

At about noon of the third day, old Andy Boyle, ex-soldier of the British Army, said, "We'll have to get a cannon and blow in the doors. I'll go up to the fort and steal a cannon." Half-way up to the fort, he found his cannon—two Catling guns and a troop of coloured cavalry—already on the road to stop what had been reported as firing on women and children. The detachment was under charge of the commanding officer of Fort Stanton, Colonel Dudley, who marched his men past the beleaguered house and drew them up below the place. Colonel Dudley was besought by Mrs. McSween, who came out under fire, to save her husband's life; but he refused to interfere or take side in the matter, saying that the sheriff of the county was there and in charge of his own posse. Mrs. McSween refused to accept protection and go up to the post, but returned to her husband for what she knew must soon be the end.

McSween, ex-minister, lawyer, honest or dishonest instigator, innocent or malicious cause—and one may choose his adjectives in this matter—of all these bloody scenes, now sat in the house, his head bowed in his hands, the picture of foreboding despair. His nerve was absolutely gone. No one paid any attention to him. His wife, the actual leader, was far braver than he. The Kid was the commander. "They'd kill us all if we surrendered," he said. "We'll shoot it out!"

Old Andy Boyle got some sticks and some coal oil, and, under protection of rifles, started a fire against a street door of the house. Jack Long and two others also fired the house in the rear. A keg of powder had been concealed under the floor. The flames reached this powder, and there was an explosion which did more than anything else toward ending the siege.

At about dusk. Bob Beckwith, old man Pierce, and one other man, ran around toward the rear of the house. Beckwith called out to the inmates to surrender. They demanded that the sheriff come for a parley. "I'm a deputy sheriff," replied Beckwith. It was dark or nearly so. Several figures burst out of the rear door of the burning house, among these the unfortunate McSween. Around him, and ahead of him, ran Billy the Kid, Skurlock, French, O'Folliard, Bowdre, and a few others. The flashing of six-shooters at close range ended the three days' battle. McSween, still unarmed, dropped dead. He was found, half sitting, leaning against the corral wall. Bob Beckwith, of the Peppin forces, fell almost at the same time, killed by Billy the Kid. Near McSween's body lay those of Romero and Semora and of Harvey Norris. The latter was a young Kansan, newly arrived in that country, of whom little was known.

With the McSween party, there was one game Mexican, Ighenio Salazar, who is alive today, (1905), by miracle. In the rush from the house, Salazar was shot down, being struck by two bullets. He feigned death. Old Andy Boyle stood over him with his gun cocked. "I guess he's dead," said Andy. "If I thought he wasn't, I shoot him some more." They then jumped on Salazar's body to assure themselves. In the darkness, Salazar rolled over into a ditch, later made his escape, stopped his wounds with some corn husks, and found concealment in a Mexican house until he subsequently recovered.

This fight cost McSween his life just at the point when he thought he had attained success. Four days before he was killed, he had word from the United States Government's commissioner, Angell, that the President had deposed Governor Axtell of New Mexico, on account of his appointment of Dad Peppin as sheriff, and on charges that Axtell was favouring the Murphy faction. General Lew Wallace was now sent out as Governor of New Mexico, invested with "extraordinary powers." He needed them. President Hayes had issued governmental proclamation calling upon these desperate fighting men to lay down their arms, but it was not certain they would easily be persuaded. It was a long way to Washington, and a short way to a six-shooter.

General Wallace assured Mrs. McSween of protection, but he found there was no such thing as getting to the bottom of the Lincoln County War. It would have been necessary to hang the entire population of the county to execute a formal justice. Almost none of the indictments "stuck," and one by one the cases were dismissed. The thing was too big for the law.

The only man ever actually indicted and brought to trial for a killing during the Lincoln County War was Billy the Kid, and there is many a resident of Lincoln today, (1905), who declares that the Kid was made a scapegoat; and many a man even today charges Governor Wallace with bad faith. Governor Wallace met the Kid by appointment at the Ellis House in Lincoln. The Kid came in fully armed, and the old soldier was surprised to see in him a bright-faced and pleasant-talking boy. In the presence of two witnesses now living, Governor Wallace asked the Kid to come in and lay down his arms, and promised to pardon him if he would stand his trial and if he should be convicted in the courts. The Kid declined. "There is no justice for me in the courts of this country now," said he. "I've gone too far." And so, he went back with his little gang of outlaws, to meet a dramatic end, after further incidents in a singular and bloodstained career.

The Lincoln County War now spread wider than even the boundaries of the United States. A United States deputy, Wiederman, had been employed by the father of the murdered J. H. Tunstall to take care of the Tunstall estates and to secure some kind of British revenge for his murder. Wiederman falsely persuaded Tunstall *père* that he had helped kill Frank Baker and Billy Morton, and Tunstall *père* made him rich, Wiederman going to England, where it was safer. The British legation took up the matter of Tunstall's death, and the slow-moving governmental wheels at Washington began to revolve. A United States indemnity was paid for Tunstall's life.

Mrs. McSween, meantime, kept up her work in the local courts. Sometime after her husband's death, she employed a lawyer by the name of Chapman, of Las Vegas, a one-armed man, to undertake the dangerous task of aiding her in her work of revenge. By this time, most of the fighters were disposed to lay down their arms. The whole society of the country had been ruined by the war. Murphy & Co. had long ago mortgaged everything they had, and a good many things, which they did not have, *e. g.*, some of John Chisum's cattle, to Tom Catron, of Sante Fé. A big peace talk was made in the town, and it was agreed that, as there was no longer any advantage of a financial nature in keeping up the war, all parties concerned might as well quit organised fighting, and engage in individual pillage instead. Murphy & Co. were ruined. Murphy and McSween were both dead. Chisum could be depended upon to pay some of the debts to the warriors through stolen cattle, if not through signed checks. Why, then, should good, game men go on killing each other for nothing? This was the argument used.

In this conference there were, on the Murphy side, Jesse Evans, Jimmie Dolan and Bill Campbell. On the other side were Billy the Kid, Tom O'Folliard and the game Mexican, Salazar. Each of these men had a .45 Colt at his belt, and a cocked Winchester in his hand.

The "women in the case" in the Lincoln County War. Mrs. Susan E. Barber was known as the "Cattle Queen of the West"

1. MRS. SATURNINO BACA (in early life)   2. MRS. SUSAN E. BARBER   3. MRS. SATURNINO BACA (Mother)

At last, however, the six men shook hands. They agreed to end the war. Then, frontier fashion, they set off for the nearest saloon.

The Las Vegas lawyer, Chapman, happened to cross the street as these desperate fighting men, used to killing, now well drunken, came out, all armed, and all swearing friendship.

"Halt, you, there!" cried Bill Campbell to Chapman; and the latter paused. "Damn you," said Campbell to Chapman; "you are the —— of a —— that has come down here to stir up trouble among us fellows. We're peaceful. It's all settled, and we're friends now. Now, damn you, just to show you're peaceable too, you dance."

"I'm a gentleman," said Chapman, "and I'll dance for no ruffian." An instant later, shot through the heart by Campbell's six-shooter, as is alleged, he lay dead in the roadway. No one dared disturb his body. He was shot at such close range that some papers in his coat pocket took fire from the powder flash, and his body was partially consumed as it lay there in the road.

For this killing, Jimmie Dolan, Billy Matthews and Bill Campbell were indicted and tried. Dolan and Matthews were acquitted. Campbell, in default of a better jail, was kept in the guard-house at Fort Stanton. One night he disappeared, in company with his guard and some United States cavalry horses. Since then nothing has been heard of him. His real name was not Campbell, but Ed Richardson.

Billy the Kid did not kill John Chisum, though all the country wondered at that fact. There was a story that he forced Chisum to sign a bill of sale for eight hundred head of cattle. He claimed that Chisum owed money to the McSween fighting men, to whom he had promised salaries which were never paid; but no evidence exists that Chisum ever made such a promise, although he sometimes sent a wagonload of supplies to the McSween fighting men.

John Chisum died of cancer at Eureka Springs, Missouri, December 26, 1884, and his great holdings as a cattle king afterward became somewhat involved. He could once have sold out for $600,000, but later mortgaged his holdings for $250,000. He was concerned in a packing plant at Kansas City, a business into which he was drawn by others, and of which he knew nothing.

Major Murphy died at Sante Fe before the big fight at Lincoln. Jimmie Dolan died a few years later, and lies buried in the little graveyard near the Fritz ranch. Riley, the other member of the firm, went to Colorado, and was last heard of at Rocky Ford, where he was prosperous. The heritage of hatred was about all that McSween left to his widow, who presently married George L. Barber, at Lincoln, and later proved herself to be a good business woman—good enough to make a fortune in the cattle business from the four hundred head of cattle John Chisum gave her to settle a debt he had owed McSween. She afterward established a fine ranch near Three Rivers, New Mexico.

Dad Peppin, known as the "Murphy sheriff" by the McSween faction, lived out his life on his little holding at the edge of Lincoln *placita*. He died in 1905. His rival, John Copeland, died in 1902. The street of Lincoln, one of the bloodiest of its size in the world, is silent. Another generation is growing up. William Brady, Major Brady's eldest son, and Josefina Brady-Chavez, a daughter, live in Lincoln; and Bob Brady, another son of the murdered sheriff, was long jailer at Lincoln jail. The law has arisen over the ruin wrought by lawlessness. It is a noteworthy fact that, although the law never punished the participants in this border conflict, the lawlessness was never ended by any vigilante movement. The fighting was so desperate and prolonged that it came to be held as warfare and not as murder. There is no doubt that, barring the border fighting of Kansas and Missouri, this was the greatest of American border wars.

## Chapter 15

# The Stevens County War

In the month of May, 1886, the writer was one of a party of buffalo-hunters bound for the Neutral Strip and the Panhandle of Texas, where a small number of buffalo still remained at that time. We travelled across the entire southwestern part of Kansas, below the Santa Fé railroad, at a time when the great land boom of 1886 and 1887 was at its height. Town-site schemes in western Kansas were at that time innumerable, and a steady stream of immigration was pouring westward by rail and wagon into the high and dry plains of the country, where at that time farming remained a doubtful experiment.

In the course of our travels, we saw one morning, rising before us in the mirage of the plains, what seemed to be a series of crenelated turrets, castles peaked and bastioned. We knew this was but the mirage, and knew that it must have some physical cause. But what was a town doing in that part of the world? We drove on and, in a few hours, found the town—a little, raw boom town of unpainted boards and tents, which had sprung up almost overnight in that far-off region. The population was that of the typical frontier town, and the pronounced belief of all was that this settlement was to be the commercial metropolis of the Southwest. This little town was later known as Woodsdale, Kansas. It offered then no hint of the bloody scenes in which it was soon to figure; but within a few weeks it was so deeply embroiled in war with the rival town of Hugoton as to make history notable even on that turbulent frontier.

Mr. Herbert M. Tonney, now a prosperous citizen of Flora, Illinois, was a resident of that portion of the country in the stirring days of the land boom, and became involved to an extent beyond his own seeking in this county seat fight. While serving as an officer of the peace, he was shot and left for dead. No story can serve so well as his personal narrative to convey a clear idea of the causes, methods and results of a typical county seat war in the West. His recountal follows:

> I do not need to swear to the truthfulness of my story, for I have already done so in many courts and under the cross-examination of some of the ablest lawyers in the country. I have repeated the story on the stand in a criminal case which cost the United States Government more money than it has ever expended in any similar trial, unless perhaps that having to do with the assassination of President Lincoln. I can say that I know what it is to be murdered.
>
> In March, 1886, I moved out into southwestern Kansas, in what was later to be known as Stevens county, then a remote and apparently unattractive region. In 1885 a syndicate of citizens of McPherson, Kansas, had been formed for the purpose of starting a new town in southwestern Kansas. The members were leading bankers, lawyers, and merchants. These sent out an exploration party, among which were such men as Colonel C. E. Cook, former postmaster of McPherson; his brother, Orrin Cook, a lawyer; John Pancoast, J. B. Chamberlain, J. W. Calvert, John Robertson, and others. They located a section of school lands, in what was later known as Stevens County, as near the centre of the proposed county as the range of sand dunes along the Cimarron River would permit.
>
> Others of the party located lands as close to the town site as possible. On August 3, 1886, Governor Martin issued a proclamation for the organisation of Stevens county. It appeared upon the records of the State of Kansas that the new county had 2,662 *bona-fide* inhabitants, of whom 868 were householders. These claimed a taxable property, in excess of legal exemptions, amounting to $313,035, including railroad property of $140,380. I need not state that the organisation was wholly based upon fraud. An election was called for September 9, and the town of Hugoton—at first called Hugo—was chosen.
>
> There can be competition in the town-site business, however. At Mead Centre, Kansas, there resided an old-time Kansas man, Colonel S. N. Wood, who also wanted a town site in the new county. Wood's partner, Captain I. C. Price, went down on July 3 to look over the situation. He was not known to the Hugoton men, and he was invited by Calvert, the census taker, to

register his name as a citizen. He protested that he was only a visitor, but was informed that this made no possible difference; whereupon, Price proceeded to register his own name, that of his partner, those of many of his friends, and many purely imaginary persons. He also registered the families of these persons, and finally—in a burst of good American humour—went so far as to credit certain single men of his acquaintance with large families, including twenty or thirty pairs of twins! This cheerful imagination on his part caused trouble afterwards; but certain it is that these fictitious names, twins and all, went into the sworn records of Hugoton—an unborn population of a defunct town, whose own conception was in iniquity!

Price located a section of government land on the north side of the sand hills, eight miles from Hugoton, and this was duly platted for a town site. Corner lots were selling at Hugoton for $1,000 apiece, and people were flocking to that town. The new town was called Woodsdale, and Colonel Wood offered lots free to any who would come and build upon them. Settlers now streamed to Woodsdale. Tents, white-topped wagons and frail shanties sprung up as though by magic. The Woodsdale boom attracted even homesteaders who had cast in their lot with Hugoton. Many of these forgot their oaths in the land office, pulled up and filed on new quarter sections nearer to Woodsdale. The latter town was jubilant. Colonel Wood and Captain Price, in the month of August, held a big ratification meeting, taunting the men of Hugoton with those thirty pairs of twins that never were on land or sea. A great deal of bad blood was engendered at this time.

Soon after this Wood and Price started together for Garden City. They were followed by a band of Hugoton men and captured in a dugout on the Cimarron river. Brought back to Hugoton, a mock trial was held upon them and they were released on a mock bond, being later taken out of town under guard. A report was printed in the Hugoton paper that certain gentlemen of that town had gone south with Colonel Wood and Captain Price, 'for the purpose of a friendly buffalo hunt.' it was the intention to take these two prisoners into the wild and lawless region of No Man's Land, or the Panhandle of Texas, there to kill them, and to bring back the report that they were accidentally killed in the buffalo chase.

This strange hunting party did go south, across No Man's Land and into the desert region lying around the headwaters of the Beaver. The prisoners knew what they were to expect, but, as it chanced, their captors did not dare kill them. Meantime, Woodsdale had organised a 'posse' of twenty-four men, under Captain S. O. Aubrey, the noted frontier trailer, formerly an Indian scout. This band, taking up the trail below Hugoton, followed and rescued Wood and Price, and took prisoners the entire Hugoton 'posse.' The latter were taken to Garden City, and here the law was in turn set at defiance by the Woodsdale men, the horses, wagons, arms, etc., of the Hugoton party being put up and sold in the court to pay the board of the teams, expenses of publication, etc. Colonel Wood bought these effects in at public auction.

By this time, Stevens County had been organised and the Hugoton 'pull' was in the ascendency. A continuance had been taken at Garden City by the Hugoton prisoners, who were charged with kidnapping. The papers in this case were sent down from Finney county to the first session of the District Court of Stevens County. The result was foregone. Tried by their friends, the prisoners were promptly discharged.

The feeling between the two towns was all the time growing more bitter. Cases had been brought against Calvert, the census-taker, for perjury, and action was taken looking toward the setting aside of the organisation of the county. The Kansas legislature, however, now met, and the political 'pull' of Hugoton was still strong enough to secure a special act legalizing the organisation of Stevens county. It was now the legislature against the Supreme Court; for a little later the Supreme Court declared that the organisation had been made through open fraud and by means of perjury.

Naturally, trouble might have been expected at the fall election. There were two centres of population, two sets of leaders, two clans, separated by only eight miles of sand hills. There could be but one county seat and one set of officers. Here Woodsdale began to suffer, for her forces were divided among themselves. Colonel Wood, the leader of this community, had slated John M. Cross as his candidate for sheriff. A rival for the nomination was Sam Robinson, who owned the hotel at Woodsdale, and had invested considerable money there. Robinson was about forty years of age, and was known to be a bad man, credited with two or three killings elsewhere. Wood had always been able to flatter him and handle him; but when Cross was declared as the nominee for sheriff, Robinson became so embittered that he moved over to Hugoton, where he was later chosen town marshal and township constable. Hugoton men bought his hotel, leaving Robinson in the position of holding real estate in Woodsdale without owning the improvements on it.

Hence when the town-site commissioners began to issue deeds, Robinson was debarred from claiming a deed by reason of the hotel property having been sold. Bert Nobel, a friend of Robinson's, sold his drug store and moved over with Robinson to Hugoton. Hugoton bought other property of Woodsdale malcontents, leaving the buildings standing at Woodsdale and taking the citizens to themselves. The Hugoton men put up as their candidate one Dalton, and declared him elected. Wood contested the election, and finally succeeded in getting his man Cross declared as sheriff of Stevens County.

It was now proposed to issue bonds for a double line of railroad across this county, such bonds amounting to eight thousand dollars per mile. At this time, the population was largely one of adventurers, and there was hardly a foot of deeded land in the entire county. In the discussion over this bond election, Robinson got into trouble with the new sheriff, in which Robinson was clearly in the wrong, as he had no county jurisdiction, being at the time of the altercation outside of his own township and town. Later on, a warrant for Robinson's arrest was issued and placed in the hands of Ed Short, town marshal of Woodsdale. Short was known as a killer, and hence as a fit man to go after Robinson.

★★★★★★

This man, Ed. Short, later came to a tragic end. A man of courage, as has been intimated, he had assisted in the capture of a member of the famous Dalton gang, one Dave Bryant, who had robbed a Rock Island express train, and was taking him to Wichita, Kansas, to jail. On the way Short had occasion to go into the smoker of the train, leaving the prisoner in charge of the express messenger, whom Short had furnished with a revolver. By some means Bryant became possessed of this revolver, held up the messenger, and was in the act of jumping from the swiftly moving train, when Short came out of the smoker. Catching sight of Short, Bryant fired and struck him. Short returning the fire, and both falling from the train together, dead.

★★★★★★

He went to Hugoton to arrest Robinson, and there was a shooting affair, in which the citizens of Hugoton protected their man. The Woodsdale town marshal, however, still retained his warrant and cherished his purpose of arresting his man.

On July 22 of this year, 1888, Short learned that Sam Robinson, the two Cooks, and a man by the name of Donald, together with some women and children, had gone on a picnic down in the Neutral Strip, south of the Stevens county line. Short raised a 'posse' of four or five men and started after Robinson, who was surprised in camp near Goff creek. There was a parley, which resulted in Robinson escaping on a fast horse, which was tied near the shack where he was stopping with his wife and children. Short, meantime, had sent back word to Woodsdale, stating that he needed help to take Robinson. Meantime, also, the Hugoton men, learning that Short had started down after Robinson, had sent out two strong parties to rescue the latter. A battle was imminent.

It was at this time that I myself appeared upon the scene of this turbulent and lawless drama, although, in my own case, I went as a somewhat unwilling participant and as a servant of the law, not anticipating consequences so grave as those which followed.

The sheriff of the county, John M. Cross, on receiving the message from Short, called for volunteers, which was equivalent to summoning a 'posse.' He knew there was going to be trouble, and left his money and watch behind him, stating that he feared for the result of his errand. His 'posse' was made up of Ted Eaton, Bob Hubbard, Holland Wilcox, and myself. At that time, I was only a boy, about nineteen years of age.

We had a long and hard ride to Reed's camp, on Goff Creek, whence Short had sent up his message. Arriving there, we found Reed, who was catching wild horses, together with a man by the name of Patterson and another man, but Short was not in sight. From Reed we learned that Robinson had gotten away from Short, who had started back, leaving word for Mr. Cross, should he arrive, to return home. A band of men from

Hugoton, we learned later, had overtaken Short and his men and chased them for twenty-five miles, but the latter reached Springfield, Seward county, unharmed.

Robinson, who had made his escape to a cow camp and thence to Hugoton upon a fresh horse, now met and led down into the Strip one of the first Hugoton 'posses.' Among them were Orrin Cook, Charles Cook, J. W. Calvert, J. B. Chamberlain, John Jackson, John A. Rutter, Fred Brewer, William Clark, and a few others. Robinson was, of course, the leader of this band.

After Sheriff Cross asked me to go down with him to see what had become of Ed Short, I went over and got Wilcox and we rode down to the settlement of Voorhees. Thence we rode to Goff Creek, and all reached Reed's camp about seven or eight o'clock on Wednesday morning, July 25, 1888. Here we remained until about five o'clock of that afternoon, when we started for home. Our horses gave out, and we got off and led them until well on into the night.

At about moonrise, we came to a place in the Neutral Strip known as the 'Hay Meadows,' where there was a sort of pool of standing water, at which settlers cut a kind of coarse hay. There was in camp there, making hay, an old man by the name of A. B. Haas, of Voorhees, and with him were his sons, C. and Keen Haas, as well as Dave Scott, a Hugoton partisan. When we met these people here, we concluded to stop for a while. Eaton and Wilcox got into the wagon-box and lay down. My horse got loose and I was a few minutes in repicketing him.

I had not been lying down more than twenty minutes, when we were surprised by the Hugoton 'posse' under Robinson. The latter had left the trail, which came down from the northeast, and were close upon us. They had evidently been watching us during the evening with field-glasses, as they seemed to know where we had stopped, and had completely surrounded us before we knew of their being near us.

The first I heard was Cross exclaiming, 'They have got us!' At that time there was shooting, and Robinson called out, 'Boys, close in!' He called out to Cross, 'Surrender, and hold up your hands!' Our arms were mostly against the haystacks. Not one of us fired a shot, or could have done so at that moment.

Sheriff Cross, Hubbard, and myself got up and stood together. We held up our hands. They did not seem to notice Wilcox and

Eaton, who were lying in the wagon. Robinson called out to Cross, 'Give up your arms!'

'I have no arms,' replied Cross. He explained that his Winchester was on his saddle and that he had no revolver.

'I know better than that,' said Robinson. 'Search him!' Some one of the Hugoton party then went over Cross after weapons, and told Robinson that he had no arms.

'I know better,' reiterated Robinson. The others stood free at that moment, and Robinson exclaimed, 'Sheriff Cross, you are my first man.' He raised his Winchester and fired at Cross, a distance of a few feet, and I saw Cross fall dead at my side. It was all a sort of trance or dream to me. I did not seem to realise what was going on, but knew that I could make no resistance. My gun was not within reach. I knew that I, too, would be shot down.

Hubbard had now been disarmed, if indeed he had on any weapon. Robinson remarked to him, 'I want you, too!' and as he spoke he raised his Winchester and shot him dead, Hubbard also falling close to where I stood, his murderer being but a few feet from him.

I knew that my turn must come pretty soon. It was Chamberlain who was to be my executioner, J. B. Chamberlain, chairman of the board of county commissioners of Stevens county, and always prominent in Hugoton matters. Chamberlain was about eight feet from me, or perhaps less, when he raised his rifle deliberately to kill me. There were powder burns on my neck and face from the shot, as the woman who cared for me on the following day testified in court.

I saw the rifle levelled, and realised that I was going to be killed. Instinctively, I flinched to one side of the line of the rifle. That saved my life. The ball entered the left side of my neck, about three-quarters of an inch from the carotid artery and about half an inch above the left clavicle, coming out through the left shoulder. I felt no pain at the time, and, indeed, did not feel pain until the next day. The shock of the shot knocked me down and numbed me, and I suppose I lay a minute or two before I recovered sensation or knew anything about my condition. It was supposed by all that I was killed, and, in a vague way, I agreed that I must be killed; that my spirit was simply present listening and seeing.

Eaton had now got out of the wagon, and he started to run towards the horses. Robinson and one or two others now turned and pursued him, and I heard a shot or so. Robinson came back and I heard him say, 'I have shot the —— —— —— who drew a gun on me!'

Then I heard the Hugoton men talking and declaring that they must have the fifth man of our party, whom they had not yet found. At this time, old man Haas and his sons came and stood near where I was and saw me looking up. The former, seeing that I was not dead, asked me where I had been shot. 'They have shot my arm off,' I answered him. At this moment I heard the Hugoton men starting toward me, and I dropped back and feigned death. Haas did not betray me. The Hugoton men now lit matches and peered into the faces of their victims to see if they were dead. I kept my eyes shut when the matches were held to my face, and held my breath.

They finally found Wilcox, I do not know just where, but they stood him up within fifteen feet of where I was lying feigning death. They asked Wilcox what he had been doing there, and he replied that he had just been down on the Strip looking around.

'That's a damned lie!' replied Robinson, the head executioner. As he spoke, he raised his Winchester and fired. Wilcox fell, and as he lay he moaned a little bit, as I heard:

'Put the fellow out of his misery,' remarked Robinson, carelessly. Someone then apparently fired a revolver shot and Wilcox became silent.

Someone came to me, took hold of my foot, and began to pull me around to see whether I was dead. Robinson wanted it made sure. Chamberlain, my executioner, said, 'He's dead; I gave him a centre shot. I don't need shoot a man twice at that distance.' Either Chamberlain or someone else took me by the legs, dragged me about, and kicked me in the side, leaving bruises which were visible for many days afterwards. I feigned death so well that they did not shoot me again. They did shoot a second time each of the others who lay near me. We found seven cartridges on the ground near where the killing was done. Eaton was shot at a little distance from us, and I do not know whether he was shot more than once or not.

The haymakers were now in trouble, and said that they could

not go on putting up their hay with the corpses lying around. Robinson told them to hitch up and follow the Hugoton party away. They did this, and after a while I was left lying there in the half-moonlight, with the dead bodies of my friends for company.

After the party had been gone about twenty minutes, I found I could get on my feet, although I was very weak. At first, I went and examined Wilcox, Cross, and Hubbard, and found they were quite dead. Their belts and guns were gone. Then I went to get my horse. It was hard for me to get into the saddle, and it has always seemed to me providential that I could do so at all. My horse was very wild and difficult to mount under ordinary circumstances. Now, it seemed to me that he knew my plight. It is certain that at that time and afterwards he was perfectly quiet and gentle, even when I laboriously tried to get into the saddle. At a little distance, there was a buffalo wallow, with some filthy water in it. I led my horse here, lay down in the water, and drank a little of it. After that I rode about fifteen or sixteen miles along a trail, not fully knowing where I was going. In the morning, I met constable Herman Cann, of Voorhees, who had been told by the Haas party of the foregoing facts. Of course, we might expect a Hugoton 'posse' at any time. As a matter of fact, the same crowd who did the killing (fifteen of them, as I afterwards learned), after taking the haymakers back toward the State of Kansas, returned on their hunt for one of Short's men, who they supposed was still in that locality. It was probably not later than one or two o'clock in the morning when they found me gone.

Our butchers now again sat down on the ground near the bodies of their victims, and they seem to have enjoyed themselves. There was talk that some beer bottles were emptied and left near the heads of their victims as markers, but whether this was deliberately done I cannot say.

Constable Cann later hid me in the middle of a cornfield. This, no doubt, saved my life, for the Hugoton scouts were soon down there the next morning, having discovered that one of the victims had come to life. Woodsdale had sent out two wagons with ice to bring in the bodies of the dead men, but these Hugoton scouts met them and made them ride through Hugoton, so that the assembled citizens of that town might see the corpses. The county attorney, William O'Connor, made a speech, demanding that Hugoton march on Woodsdale and kill Wood and Ed Short.

By this time, of course, all Woodsdale was also under arms. My friends gathered from all over the countryside, a large body of them, heavily armed. Mr. Cann, the constable, had tried to take me to Liberal, but I could not stand the ride. I was then taken to the house of a doctor in the settlement at LaFayette. On the second night after the massacre I was taken to Woodsdale by about twenty of the Woodsdale boys, who came after me. We arrived at Woodsdale about daybreak next morning. In our night trip we could see the skyrocket signals used by the Robinson-Cook gang.

After my arrival at Woodsdale, it might have been supposed that all the country was in a state of war, instead of living in a time of modern civilization. Entrenchments were thrown up, rifle pits were dug, and stands established for sharp-shooters. Guards were thrown out all around the town, and mounted scouts continued to scour the country. Hugoton, expecting that Woodsdale would make an organised attack in retaliation, was quite as fully fortified in every way. Had there been a determined leader, the bloodshed would have been much greater. Of course, the result of this state of hostilities was that the governor sent out the militia, and there were Investigations, and, later on, arrests and trials. The two towns literally fought each other to the death.

The murder of Sheriff Cross occurred in 1888. The militia were withdrawn within about thirty days thereafter. Both towns continued to break the law—in short, agreed jointly to break the law. They drew up a stipulation, it is said, under which Colonel Wood was to have all the charges against the Hugoton men dismissed. In return, Wood was to have all the charges against him in Hugoton dismissed, and was to have safe conduct when he came up to court. Not even this compounding of felony was kept as a pact between these treacherous communities.

The trial lagged. Wood was once more under bond to appear at Hugoton, before the court of his enemy, Judge Botkin, and among many other of his Hugoton enemies. On the day that Colonel Wood was to go for his trial, June 23, 1891, he drove up in a buggy. In the vehicle with him were his wife and a Mrs.

Perry Carpenter. Court was held in the Methodist church. At the time of Wood's arrival, the docket had been called and a number of cases set for trial, including one against Wood for arson—there was no crime in the calendar of which one town did not accuse the other, and, indeed, of which the citizens of either were not guilty.

Wood left the two ladies sitting in the buggy, near the door, and stepped up to the clerk's desk to look over some papers. As he went in, he passed, leaning against the door, one Jim Brennan, a deputy of Hugoton, who did not seem to notice him. Brennan was a friend of C. E. Cook, then under conviction for the Hay Meadows massacre. Brennan stood talking to Mrs. Wood and Mrs. Carpenter, smiling and apparently pleasant. Colonel Wood turned and came down towards the door, again passing close to Brennan but not speaking to him. He was almost upon the point of climbing to his seat in the buggy, when Brennan, without a word and without any sort of warning, drew a revolver and shot him in the back.

Wood wheeled around, and Brennan shot him the second time, through the right side. Not a word had been spoken by any one. Wood now started to run around the corner of the house. His wife, realising now what was happening, sprang from the buggy-seat and followed to protect him. Brennan fired a third time, but missed. Mrs. Wood, reaching her husband's side, threw her arms around his neck. Brennan coming close up, fired a fourth shot, this time through Wood's head. The murdered man fell heavily, literally in his wife's arms, and for the moment it was thought both were killed. Brennan drew a second revolver, and so stood over Wood's corpse, refusing to surrender to anyone but the sheriff of Morton County.

The presiding judge at this trial was Theodosius Botkin, a figure of peculiar eminence in Kansas at that time. Botkin gave Brennan into the custody of the sheriff of Morton County. He was removed from the county, and it need hardly be stated that when he was at last brought back for trial it was found impossible to empanel a jury, and he was set free. No one was ever punished for this cold-blooded murder.

Colonel S. N. Wood was an Ohio man, but moved to Kansas in the early Free Soil days. He was a friend and champion of old John Brown and a colonel of volunteers in the civil war. He had served in the legislature of Kansas, and was a good type of the early and adventurous pioneer.

Whether or not suspicion attached to Judge Botkin for his conduct in this matter, he himself seems to have feared revenge, for he held court with a Winchester at his hand and a brace of revolvers on the desk in front of him, his court-house always surrounded with an armed guard. He offended men in Seward County, and there was a plot made to kill him. A party lay in wait along the road to intercept Botkin on his journey from his homestead—everyone in Kansas at that time had a 'claim'—but Botkin was warned by some friend. He sent out Sam Dunn, sheriff of Seward County, to discover the truth of the rumour. Dunn went on down the trail and, in a rough part of the country, was fired upon and killed, instead of Botkin. Arrests were made in this matter also, but the sham trials resulted much as had that of Brennan. The records of these trials may be seen in Seward County. It was murder for murder, anarchy for anarchy, evasion for evasion, in this portion of the frontier. Judge Botkin soon after this resigned his seat upon the bench and went to lecturing upon the virtues of the Keeley cure. Afterwards he went to the legislature—the same legislature which had once tried him on charges of impeachment as a judge!

These events all became known in time, and lawlessness proved its own Inability to endure. The towns were abandoned. Where in 1889 there were perhaps 4,000 people, there remained not 100. The best of the farms were abandoned or sold for taxes, the late inhabitants of the two warring settlements wandering out over the world. The legislature, hoodwinked or cajoled heretofore, at length disorganised the county, and anarchy gave back its own to the wilderness.

I have indicated that the trial of the men guilty of assassinating my friends and of attempting to kill myself in the Hay Meadow butchery was one which reached a considerable importance at the time. The crimes were committed in that strange portion of the country called No Man's Land or the Neutral Strip. The accused were tried in the United States court at Paris, Texas. I myself drew the indictments against them. There were tried the Cooks, Chamberlain, Robinson and others of the Hugoton party, and of these six were convicted and sentenced to be hung. These men were defended by Colonel George R. Peck, later chief counsel of the Chicago, Milwaukee & St. Paul Railway. With him were associated Judge John F. Dillon, of New York; W. H. Rossington, of St. Louis; Senator Manderson, of Nebraska; Colonel Robert G. Ingersoll, and others. The Knights of Pythias raised a fund to defend the prisoners, and spent perhaps a hundred thousand dollars in all in this undertaking.

A vast political 'pull' was exercised at Topeka and Washington. After the sentence had been passed, the case was taken up to the United States Supreme Court, on the ground that the Texas court had no jurisdiction in the premises, and on the further grounds of errors in the trial. The United States Supreme Court, in 1891, reversed the Texas court, on an error on the admission of evidence, and remanded the cases. The men were never put on trial again, except that, in 1898, Sam Robinson, meantime pardoned out of the penitentiary in Colorado, where he had been sent for robbing the United States mails at Florissant, Colorado, returned to Texas, and was arrested on the old charge. The men convicted were C. E. Cook, Orrin Cook, Cyrus C. Freese, John Lawrence and John Jackson.

The Illinois legislature petitioned Congress to extend United States jurisdiction over No Man's Land, and so did the state of Indiana; and it was attached to the East District of Texas for the purposes of jurisdiction. Congressman Springer held up this bill for a time, using it as a club for the passage of a measure of his own upon which he was intent. Thus, it may be seen that the tawdry little tragedy in that land which indeed was 'No Man's Land' in time attained a national prominence.

The collecting of the witnesses for this trial cost the United States government over one hundred thousand dollars. The trial was long and bitterly fought. It resulted, as did every attempt to convict those concerned in the bloody doings of Stevens county, in an absolute failure of the ends of justice. Of all the murders committed in that bitter fighting, not one murderer has ever been punished! Never was greater political or judicial mockery.

I had the singular experience, once in my life, of eating dinner at the same table with the man who brutally shot me down and left me for dead. J. B. Chamberlain, the man who shot me, and who thought he had killed me, came in with a friend and sat down at the same table in a Leavenworth, Kansas, restaurant, where I was eating. My opportunity for revenge was there. I did not take it. Chamberlain and his friend did not know who I was. I left the matter to the law, with what results the records of the law's failure in these matters has shown.

Of those who were tried for these murders, J. B. Chamberlain is now dead. C. E. Cook, who was much alarmed lest the cases might be reinstated in the year 1898, claims Quincy, Illinois, as his home, but has interests in Florida. O. J. Cook is dead. Jack Lawrence is dead. John Kelley is dead. Other actors in the drama, unconvicted, are also dead or nameless wanderers. As the indictments were all quashed in 1898, Sam Robinson, whose whereabouts is unknown, will never be brought to trial for his deeds in the Hay Meadow butchery. He was not tried at Paris, being then in the Colorado penitentiary.

His friend and partner, Bert Nobel, who was sent to the penitentiary for seven years for participating in the post-office robbery, was pardoned out, and later killed a policeman at Trinidad, Colorado. He was tried there and hanged. So far as I know, this is the only legal punishment ever inflicted upon any of the Hugoton or Woodsdale men, who outvied each other in a lawlessness for which anarchy would be a mild name.

CHAPTER 16

# Biographies of Bad Men

The desert regions of the West seemed always to breed truculence and touchiness. Some of the most desperate outlaws have been those of western Texas, New Mexico, and Arizona. These have sometimes been Mexicans, sometimes half-breed Indians, very rarely full-blood or half-blood negroes. The latter race breeds criminals, but lacks in the initiative required in the character of the desperado. Texas and the great arid regions west of Texas produced rather more than their full quota of bad white men who took naturally to the gun.

By all means the most prominent figure in the general fighting along the Southwestern border, which found climax in the Lincoln County War, was that historic and somewhat romantic character known as Billy the Kid, who had more than a score of killings to his credit at the time of his death at the age of twenty-one. His character may not be chosen as an exemplar for youth, but he affords an instance hardly to be surpassed of the typical bad man.

The true name of Billy the Kid was William H. Bonney, and he was born in New York City, November 23, 1859. His father removed to Coffeyville, on the border of the Indian Nations, in 1862, where soon after he died, leaving a widow and two sons. Mrs. Bonney again moved, this time to Colorado, where she married again, her second husband being named Antrim. All the time clinging to what was the wild border, these two now moved down to Santa Fé, New Mexico, where they remained until Billy was eight years of age. In 1868, the family made their home at Silver City, New Mexico, where they lived until 1871, when Billy was twelve years of age. His life until then had been one of shifting about. In poverty or at best rude comfort. His mother seems to have been a wholesome Irishwoman, of no great education, but of good instincts. Of the boy's father nothing is known;

and of his stepfather little more, except that he was abusive to the stepchildren. Antrim survived his wife, who died about 1870. The Kid always said that his stepfather was the cause of his "getting off wrong."

The Kid was only twelve years old when, in a saloon row in which a friend of his was being beaten, he killed with a pocket-knife a man who had previously insulted him. Some say that this was an insult offered to his mother; others deny it and say that the man had attempted to horsewhip Billy. The boy turned up with a companion at Fort Bowie, Pima County, Arizona, and was around the reservation for a while. At last he and his associate, who appears to have been as well saturated with border doctrine as himself at tender years, stole some horses from a band of Apaches, and incidentally killed three of the latter in a night attack. They made their first step at easy living in this enterprise, and, young as they were, got means in this way to travel about over Arizona.

They presently turned up at Tucson, where Billy began to employ his precocious skill at cards; and where, presently, in the inevitable gambler's quarrel, he killed another man. He fled across the line now into old Mexico, where, in the state of Sonora, he set up as a youthful gambler. Here he killed a gambler, Jose Martinez, over a *monte* game, on an "even break," being the fraction of a second the quicker on the draw. He was already beginning to show his natural fitness as a handler of weapons. He kept up his record by appearing next at Chihuahua and robbing a few monte dealers there, killing one whom he waylaid with a new companion by the name of Segura.

The Kid was now old enough to be dangerous, and his life had been one of irresponsibility and lawlessness. He was nearly at his physical growth at this time, possibly five feet seven and a half inches in height, and weighing a hundred and thirty-five pounds. He was always slight and lean, a hard rider all his life, and never old enough to begin to take on flesh. His hair was light or light brown, and his eyes blue or blue-grey, with curious red hazel spots in them. His face was rather long, his chin narrow but long, and his front teeth were a trifle prominent. He was always a pleasant mannered youth, hopeful and buoyant, never glum or grim, and he nearly always smiled when talking.

The Southwestern border at this time offered but few opportunities for making an honest living. There were the mines and there were the cow ranches. It was natural that the half-wild life of the cow punchers would sooner or later appeal to the Kid. He and Jesse Evans met somewhere along the lower border a party of punchers, among

BILLY THE KID
Said to have slain twenty-two men in his short career. Killed when twenty-one years old by Sheriff Pat F. Garrett

whom were Billy Morton and Frank Baker, as well as James McDaniels; the last named being the man who gave Billy his name of "The Kid," which hung to him all his life.

The Kid arrived in the Seven Rivers country on foot. In his course east over the mountains from Mesilla to the Pecos valley he had been mixed up with a companion, Tom O'Keefe, in a fight with some more Apaches, of whom the Kid is reported to have killed one or more. There is no doubt that the Guadalupe mountains, which he crossed, were at that time a dangerous Indian country. That the Kid worked for a time for John Chisum, on his ranch near Roswell, is well known, as is the fact that he cherished a grudge against Chisum for years, and was more than once upon the point of killing him for a real or fancied grievance. He left Chisum and took service with J. H. Tunstall on his Feliz ranch late in the winter of 1877, animated by what reason we may not know.

In doing this, he may have acted from pique or spite or hatred. There was some quarrel between him and his late associates. Tunstall was killed by the Murphy faction on February 18, 1878. From that time, the path of the Kid is very plain and his acts well known and authenticated. He had by this time killed several men, certainly at least two white men; and how many Mexicans and Indians he had killed by fair means or foul will never be really known. His reputation as a gun fighter was well established.

Dick Brewer, Tunstall's foreman, was now sworn in as a "special deputy" by McSween, and a war of reprisal was now on. The Kid was soon in the saddle with Brewer and after his former friends, all Murphy allies. There were about a dozen in this posse. On March 6, 1878, these men discovered and captured a band of five men, including Frank Baker and Billy Morton, both old friends of the Kid, at the lower crossing of the Rio Peñasco, some six miles from the Pecos. The prisoners were kept overnight at Chisum's ranch, and then the posse started with them for Lincoln, not taking the Hondo-Bonito trail, but one *via* the Agua Negra, on the east side of the Capitans; proof enough that something bloody was in contemplation, for that was far from any settlements.

Apologists of the Kid say that Morton and Baker "tried to escape," and that the Kid followed and killed them. The truth in all probability is that the party, sullen and bloody-minded, rode on, waiting until wrath or whiskey should inflame them so as to give resolution for the act they all along intended. The Kid, youngest but most determined of the band, no doubt did the killing of Billy Morton and Frank Baker; and in all likelihood there is truth in the assertion that they were on their knees and begging for their lives when he shot them. McClosky was killed by McNab, on the principle that dead men tell no tales. This killing was on March 9, 1878. The murder of Sheriff William Brady and George Hindman by the Kid and his half-dozen companions occurred April 1, 1878, and it is another act which can have no palliation whatever.

The Kid was now assuming prominence as a gun fighter and leader, young as he was. After the big fight in Lincoln was over, and the McSween house in flames, the Kid was leader of the sortie which took him and a few of his companions to safety. The list of killings back of him was now steadily lengthening, and, indeed, one murder followed another so fast all over that country that it was hard to keep track of them all.

The killing of the Indian agency clerk, Bernstein, August 5, 1878, on a horse-stealing expedition, was the next act of the Kid and his men, who thereafter fled northeast, out through the Capitan Gap, to certain old haunts around Fort Sumner, some ninety miles north of Roswell, up the Pecos valley. Here a little band of outlaws, led by the Kid, lived for a time as they could by stealing horses along the Bonito and around the Capitans, and running them off north and east. There were in this band at the time the Kid, Charlie Bowdre, Doc Skurlock, Wayt, Tom O'Folliard, Hendry Brown and Jack Middleton.

Some or all of these were in the march with stolen horses which the Kid engineered that fall, going as far east as Atacosa, on the Canadian, before the stock was all gotten rid of. Middleton, Wayt, and Hendry Brown there left the Kid's gang, telling him that he would get killed before long; but the latter laughed at them and returned to his old grounds, alternating between Lincoln and Fort Sumner, and now and then stealing some cows from the Chisum herd.

In January, 1880, the Kid enlarged his list of victims by killing, in a very justifiable encounter, a bad man from the Panhandle by the name of Grant, who had been loafing around in his country, and who, no doubt, intended to kill the Kid for the glory of it. The Kid had, a few moments before he shot Grant, taken the precaution to set the hammer of the latter's revolver on an "empty," as he whirled it over in examination. They were apparently friends, but the Kid knew that Grant was drunk and bloodthirsty. He shot Grant twice through the throat, as Grant snapped his pistol in his face. Nothing was done with the Kid for this, of course.

Birds of a feather now began to appear in the neighbourhood of Fort Sumner, and the Kid's gang was increased by the addition of Tom Pickett, and later by Billy Wilson, Dave Rudabaugh. Buck Edwards, and one or two others. These men stole cattle now from ranges as far east as the Canadian, and sold them to obliging butcher-shops at the new mining camp of White Oaks, just coming into prominence; or, again, they took cattle from the lower Pecos herds and sold them north at Las Vegas; or perhaps they stole horses at the Indian reservation and distributed them along the Pecos valley. Their operations covered a country, more than two hundred miles across in either direction.

They had accomplices and friends in nearly every little *placita* of the country. Sometimes they gave a man a horse as a present. If he took it, it meant that they could depend upon him to keep silent. Partly by friendliness and partly by terrorising, their influence was extended until they became a power in all that portion of the country; and their self-confidence had now arisen to the point that they thought none dared to molest them, while in general they behaved in the high-handed fashion of true border bandits. This was the heyday of the Kid's career.

It was on November 27, 1880, that the Kid next added to his list of killings. The men of White Oaks, headed by deputy sheriff William Hudgens, saloon-keeper of White Oaks, formed a posse, after the fashion of the day, and started out after the Kid, who had passed all bounds in impudence of late. In this posse were Hudgens and his brother, Johnny Hudgens, Jim Watts, John Mosby, Jim Brent, J. P. Langston, Ed. Bonnell, W. G. Dorsey, J. W. Bell, J. P. Eaker, Charles Kelly, and Jimmy Carlyle. They bayed up the Kid and his gang in the Greathouse ranch, forty miles from White Oaks, and laid siege, although the weather was bitterly cold and the party had not supplies or blankets for a long stay.

Hudgens demanded the surrender of the Kid, and the latter said he could not be taken alive. Hudgens then sent word for Billy Wilson to come out and have a talk. The latter refused, but said he would talk with Jimmy Carlyle, if the latter would come into the house. Carlyle, against the advice of all, took off his pistol belt and stepped into the house. He was kept there for hours. About two o'clock in the afternoon they heard the window glass crash and saw Carlyle break through the window and start to run. Several shots followed, and Carlyle fell dead, the bullets that killed him cutting dust in the faces of Hudgens' men, as they lay across the road from the house.

This murder was a nail in the Kid's coffin, for Carlyle was well liked at White Oaks. By this time the toils began to tighten in all directions. The United States Government had a detective, Azariah F. Wild, in Lincoln county. Pat Garrett had now just been elected sheriff, and was after the outlaws. Frank Stewart, a cattle detective, with a party of several men, was also in from the Canadian country looking for the Kid and his gang for thefts committed over to the east of Lincoln county, across the lines of Texas and the Neutral Strip.

The Kid at this time wrote to Captain J. C. Lea, at Roswell, that if the officers would leave him alone for a time, until he could get his stuff together, he would pull up and leave the country, going to old Mexico, but that if he was crowded by Garrett or anyone else, he surely would start in and do some more killing. This did not deter Garrett, who, with a posse made up of Chambers, Barney Mason, Frank Stewart, Juan Roibal, Lee Halls, Jim East, "Poker Tom," "Tenderfoot Bob," and "The Animal," with others, all more or less game, or at least game enough to go as far as Fort Sumner, at length rounded up the Kid, and took him, Billy Wilson, Tom Pickett and Dave Rudabaugh; Garrett killing O'Folliard and Bowdre.

Pickett was left at Las Vegas, as there was no United States warrant out against him. Rudabaugh was tried later for robbing the United States mails, later tried for killing his jailer, and was convicted and sentenced to be hung; but once more escaped from the Las Vegas jail and got away for good. The Kid was not so fortunate. He was tried at Mesilla, before Judge Warren H. Bristol, the same man whose life he was charged with attempting in 1879. Judge Bristol appointed Judge Ira E. Leonard, of Lincoln, to defend the prisoner, and Leonard got him acquitted of the charge of killing Bernstein on the reservation. He was next tried, at the same term of court, for the killing of Sheriff William Brady, and in March, 1881, he was convicted under this charge and sentenced to be hanged at Lincoln on May 13, 1881. He was first placed under guard of Deputies Bob Ollinger and Dave Woods, and taken across the mountains in the custody of Sheriff Garrett, who received his prisoner at Fort Stanton on April 21.

Lincoln County was just beginning to emerge from savagery. There was no jail worth the name, and all the county could claim as a place for the house of law and order was the big store building lately owned by Murphy, Riley & Dolan. It was necessary to keep the Kid under guard for the three weeks or so before his execution, and Sheriff Garrett chose as the best available material Bob Ollinger and J. W. Bell, a good, quiet man from White Oaks, to act as the death watch over this dangerous man, who seemed now to be nearly at the end of his day. Against Bob Ollinger the Kid cherished an undying hatred, and longed to kill him. Ollinger hated him as much, and wanted nothing so much as to kill the Kid. He was a friend of Bob Beckwith, whom the Kid had killed, and the two had always been on the opposite sides of the Lincoln county fighting. Ollinger taunted the Kid with his deeds, and showed his own hatred in every way.

There are many stories about what now took place in this old building at the side of bloody little Lincoln street. A common report is that in the evening of April 28, 1881, the Kid was left alone in the room with Bell, Ollinger having gone across the street for supper; that the Kid slipped his hands out of his irons—as he was able to do when he liked, his hands being very small—struck Bell over the head with his shackles while Bell was reading or was looking out of the window, later drawing Bell's revolver from its scabbard and killing him with it. This story is not correct. The truth is that Bell took the Kid, at his request, into the yard back of the jail; returning, the Kid sprang quickly up the stairs to the guard-room door, as Bell turned to say something to old man Goss, a cook, who was standing in the yard.

The Kid pushed open the door, caught up a revolver from a table, and sprang to the head of the stairs just as Bell turned the angle and started up. He fired at Bell and missed him, the ball striking the left-hand side of the staircase. It glanced, however, and passed through Bell's body, lodging in the wall at the angle of the stair. Bell staggered out into the yard and fell dead. This story is borne out by the reports of Goss and the Kid, and by the bullet marks. The place is very familiar to the author, who at about that time practiced law in the same building, when it was used as the Court House, and who has also talked with many men about the circumstances.

The Kid now sprang into the next room and caught up Ollinger's heavy shotgun, loaded with the very shells Ollinger had charged for him. He saw Ollinger coming across the street, and just as he got below the window at the corner of the building the Kid leaned over and said, coolly and pleasantly, "Hello, old fellow!" The next instant he fired and shot Ollinger dead. He then walked around through the room and out upon the porch, which at that time extended the full length of the building, and, coming again in view of Ollinger's body, took a second deliberate shot at it. Then he broke the gun across the railing and threw the pieces down on Ollinger's body.

"Take that to hell with you," he said coolly. Then, seeing himself free and once more king of Lincoln street, he warned away all who would approach, and, with a file which he compelled Goss to bring to him, started to file off one of his leg irons. He got one free, ordered a bystander to bring him a horse, and at length, mounting, rode away for the Capitans, and so to a country with which he had long been familiar. At Las Tablas he forced a Mexican blacksmith to free him of his irons. He sent the horse, which belonged to Billy Burt, back by some unknown friend the following night.

He was now again on his native heath, a desperado and an outlaw indeed, and obliged to fight for his life at every turn; for now, he knew the country would turn against him, and, as he had been captured through information furnished through supposed friends, he knew that treachery was what he might expect. He knew also that sheriff Garrett would never give him up now, and that one or the other of the two must die.

Yet, knowing all these things, the Kid, by means of stolen horses, broke back once more to his old stamping grounds around Fort Sumner. Garrett again got on his trail, and as the Kid, with Incredible fatuity, still hung around his old haunts, he was at length able to close with him once more. With his deputies, John Poe and Thomas P. McKinney, he located the Kid in Sumner, although no one seemed to be explicit as to his whereabouts. He went to Pete Maxwell's house himself, and there, as his two deputies were sitting at the edge of the gallery in the moonlight, he killed the Kid at Maxwell's bedside.

Billy the Kid had very many actual friends, whom he won by his pleasant and cheerful manners and his liberality, when he had anything with which to be liberal, although that was not often. He was very popular among the Mexicans of the Pecos valley. As to the men the Kid killed in his short twenty-one years, that is a matter of disagreement. The usual story is twenty-one, and the Kid is said to have declared he wanted to kill two more—Bob Ollinger and "Bonnie" Baca—before he died, to make it twenty-three in all. Pat Garrett says the Kid had killed eleven men. Others say he had killed nine. A very few say that the Kid never killed any man without full justification and in self-defence. They regard the Kid as a scapegoat for the sins of others. Indeed, he was less fortunate than some others, but his deeds brought him his deserts at last, even as they left him an enduring reputation as one of the most desperate desperadoes ever known in the West.

"THE NEXT INSTANT HE FIRED AND SHOT OLLINGER DEAD"

Central and eastern New Mexico, from 1860 to 1880, probably held more desperate and dangerous men than any other corner of the West ever did. It was a region then more remote and less known than Africa is today, and no record exists of more than a small portion of its deeds of blood. Nowhere in the world was human life ever held cheaper, and never was any population more lawless. There were no courts and no officers, and most of the scattered inhabitants of that time had come thither to escape courts and officers. This environment which produced Billy the Kid brought out others scarcely less dangerous, and of a few of these there may be made passing mention.

Joel Fowler was long considered a dangerous man. He was a ranch owner and cow man, but he came into the settlements often, and nearly always for the immediate purpose of getting drunk. In the latter condition he was always bloodthirsty and quarrelsome, and none could tell what or whom he might make the object of his attack. He was very insulting and overbearing, very noisy and obnoxious, the sort of desperado who makes unarmed men beg and compels "tenderfeet" to dance for his amusement. His birth and earlier life seem hidden by his later career, when, at about middle life, he lived in central New Mexico. He was accredited with killing about twenty men, but there may have been the usual exaggeration regarding this.

His end came in 1884, at Socorro. He was arrested for killing his own ranch foreman. Jack Cale, a man who had befriended him and taken care of him in many a drunken orgy. He stabbed Cale as they stood at the bar in a saloon, and while everyone thought he was unarmed. The law against carrying arms while in the settlements was then just beginning to be enforced; and, although it was recognised as necessary for men to go armed while journeying across those wild and little settled plains, the danger of allowing six-shooters and whiskey to operate at the same time was generally recognised as well. If a man did not lay aside his guns on reaching a town, he was apt to be invited to do so by the sheriff or town marshal, as Joel had already been asked that evening.

Fowler's victim staggered to the door after he was stabbed and fell dead at the street, the act being seen by many. The law was allowed to take its course, and Fowler was tried and sentenced to be hanged. His lawyers took an appeal on a technicality and sent the case to the supreme court, where a long delay seemed inevitable. The jail was so bad that an expensive guard had to be maintained. At length, some of the citizens concluded that to hang Fowler was best for all concerned.

They took him, mounted, to a spot some distance up the railroad, and there hanged him.

Bill Howard, a negro section hand, was permitted by his section boss to make a coffin and bury Fowler, a matter which the Committee had neglected; and he says that he knows Fowler was buried there and left there for several years, near the railway tracks. The usual story says that Fowler was hanged to a telegraph pole in town. At any rate, he was hanged, and a very wise and seemly thing it was.

Jesse Evans was another bad man of this date, a young fellow in his early twenties when he first came to the Pecos country, but good enough at gun work to make his services desirable. He was one of the very few men who did not fear Billy the Kid. He always said that the Kid might beat him with the Winchester, but that he feared no man living with the six-shooter. Evans came very near meeting an Inglorious death. He and the notorious Tom Hill once held up an old German in a sheep camp near what is now Alamagordo, New Mexico. The old man did not know that they were bad men, and while they were looting his wagon, looking for the money he had in a box under the wagon seat, he slipped up and killed Tom Hill with his own gun, which had been left resting against a bush nearby, nearly shooting Hill's spine out. Then he opened fire on Jesse, who was close by, shooting him twice, through the arm and through the lungs.

The latter managed to get on his horse, bareback, and rode that night, wounded as he was, and partly trailed by the blood from his lungs, sixty miles or more to the San Augustine mountains, where he holed up at a friendly ranch, later to be arrested by Constable Dave Wood, from the railway settlements. In default of better jurisdiction, he was taken to Fort Stanton, where he lay in the hospital until he got ready to escape, when he seems to have walked away.

Evans and his brother, who was known as George Davis—the latter being the true name of both—then went down toward Pecos City and got into a fight with some rangers, who killed his brother on the spot and captured Jesse, who was confined in the Texas penitentiary for twenty years. He escaped and was returned; yet in the year 1882, when he should have been in the Texas prison, he is said to have been seen and recognised on the streets of Lincoln. Evans, or Davis, is said to have been a Texarkana man, and to have returned to his home soon after this, only to find his wife living with another man, and supposing her first husband dead. He did not tell the new husband of his presence, but took away with him his boy, whom he found now well grown. It was stated that he went to Arizona, and nothing more is known of him.

Tom Hill, the man above mentioned as killed by the sheep man, was a typical rough, dark, swarthy, low-browed, as loud-mouthed as he was ignorant. He was a braggart, but none the less a killer.

Charlie Bowdre is supposed to have been a Texas boy, as was Tom Hill. Bowdre had a little ranch on the Rio Ruidoso, twenty miles or so from Lincoln; but few of these restless characters did much farming. It was easier to steal cattle, and to eat beef free if one were hungry. Bowdre joined Billy the Kid's gang and turned outlaw for a trade. It was all over with his chances of settling down after that. He was a man who liked to talk of what he could do, and a very steady practicer with the six-shooter, with which weapon he was a good shot, or just good enough to get himself killed by sheriff Pat Garrett.

Frank Baker, murdered by his former friend, Billy the Kid, at Agua Negra, near the Capitans, was part Cherokee in blood, a well-spoken and pleasant man and a good cow hand. He was drawn into this fighting through his work for Chisum as a hired man. Baker was said to be connected with a good family in Virginia, who looked up the facts of his death.

Billy Morton, killed with Baker by the Kid, was a similar instance of a young man loving the saddle and six-shooter and finally getting tangled up with matters outside his proper sphere as a cow hand. He had often ridden with the Kid on the cow range. He was said to have been with the posse that killed Tunstall.

Hendry Brown was a crack gun fighter, whose services were valued in the posse fighting. He went to Kansas and long served as marshal of Caldwell. He could not stand it to be good, and was killed after robbing the bank and killing the cashier.

Johnny Hurley was a brave young man, as brave as a Hon. Hurley was acting as deputy for sheriff John Poe, together with Jim Brent, when the desperado Arragon was holed up in an *adobe* and refused to surrender. The Mexican shot Hurley as he carelessly crossed an open space directly in front of the door. Hurley was brown-haired and blue-eyed; a very pleasant fellow.

Andy Boyle, one of the rough and ruthless sort of warriors, was an ex-British soldier, a drunkard, and a good deal of a ruffian. He drank himself to death after a decidedly mixed record.

John McKinney had a certain fame from the fact that in the fight at the McSween house the Kid shot off half his moustache for him at close range, when the latter broke out of cover and ran.

The tough buffalo hunter, Bill Campbell, who figured largely in bloody deeds in New Mexico, was arrested, but escaped from Fort Stanton, and was never heard from afterward. He came from Texas, but little is known of him. His name, as earlier stated, is thought to have been Ed. Richardson.

Captain Joseph C. Lea, the staunch friend of Pat Garrett, and the man who first brought him forward as a candidate for sheriff of Lincoln county, died February 8, 1904, at Roswell, where he lived for a long time. Lea was said to have been a Quantrell man in the Lawrence massacre. Much of the population of that region had a history that was never written. Lea was a good man and much respected, peaceable, courteous and generous.

One more southwestern bad man found Texas congenial after the close of his active fighting, and his is a striking story. Billy Wilson was a gentlemanly and good-looking young fellow, who ran with Billy the Kid's gang.

Wilson was arrested on a United States warrant, charged with passing counterfeit money; but he later escaped and disappeared. Several years after all these events had happened, and after the country had settled down into quiet, a certain ex-sheriff of Lincoln county chanced to be near Uvalde, Texas, for several months. There came to him without invitation, a former merchant of White Oaks, New Mexico, who told the officer that Billy Wilson, under another name, was living below Uvalde, towards the Mexican frontier. He stated that Wilson had been a cow hand, a ranch foreman and cow man, was now doing well, had resigned all his bad habits, and was a good citizen. He stated that Wilson had heard of the officer's presence and asked whether the latter would not forego following up a reformed man on the old charges of another and different day.

The officer replied at once that if Wilson was indeed leading a right life, and did not intend to go bad again, he would not only leave him alone, but would endeavour to secure for him a pardon from the president of the United States. Less than six months from that time, this pardon, signed by President Grover Cleveland, was in the possession of this officer. In his office in a Rio Grande town of New Mexico. A telegram was sent to Billy Wilson, and he was brave man enough to come and take his chances. The officer, without much speech, went over to his safe, took out the signed pardon from the president, and handed it to Wilson. The latter trembled and broke into tears as he took the paper.

"If you ever need my life," said he, "count on me. And I'll never go back on this!" as he touched the executive pardon. He went back to Texas, and is living there today,(1905), a good citizen. It would be wrong to mention names in an incident like this.

Tom O'Folliard was another noted character. He was something of a gun expert, in his own belief, at least. He was a man of medium height and dark complexion, and of no very great amount of mental capacity. He came into the lower range from somewhere east, probably from Texas, and little is known of him except that he was in some fighting, and that he is buried at Sumner with Bowdre and the Kid. He got away with one or two bluffs and encounters, and came to think that he was as good as the best of men, or rather as bad as the worst; for he was one of those who wanted a reputation as a bad man.

Tom Pickett was another not far from the O'Folliard class, ambitious to be thought wild and woolly and hard to curry; which he was not, when it came to the real currying, as events proved. He was a very pretty handler of a gun, and took pride in his skill with it. He seems to have behaved well after the arrest of the Kid's gang near Sumner, and is not known in connection with any further criminal acts, though he still for a long time wore two guns in the settlements. Once a well-known sheriff happened, by mere chance, to be in his town, not knowing Pickett was there.

The latter literally took to the woods, thinking something was on foot in which he was concerned. Being reminded that he had lost an opportunity to show how bad he was he explained: "I don't want anything to do with that long-legs." Pickett, no doubt, settled down and became a useful man. Indeed, although it seems a strange thing to say. It is the truth that much of the old wildness of that border was a matter of general custom, one might also say of habit. The surroundings were wild, and men got to running wild. When times changed, some of them also changed, and frequently showed that after all they could settle down to work and lead decent lives. Lawlessness is sometimes less a matter of temperament than of surroundings.

CHAPTER 17

# The Fight of Buckshot Roberts

Next to the fight of Wild Bill with the McCandlas gang, the fight of Buckshot Roberts at Blazer's Mill, on the Mescalero Indian reservation, is perhaps the most remarkable combat of one man against odds ever known in the West. The latter affair is little known, but deserves its record.

Buckshot Roberts was one of those men who appeared on the frontier and gave little history of their own past. He came West from Texas, but it is thought that he was born farther East than the Lone Star state. He was long in the United States Army, where he reached the rank of sergeant before his discharge; after which he lingered on the frontier, as did very many soldiers of that day. He was at one time a member of the famous Texas rangers, and had reputation as an Indian fighter. He had been badly shot by the Comanches. Again, he was on the other side, against the rangers, and once stood off twenty-five of them, although nearly killed in this encounter. From these wounds he was so badly crippled in his right arm that he could not lift a rifle to his shoulder. He was usually known as "Buckshot" Roberts because of the nature of his wounds.

Roberts took up a little ranch in the beautiful Ruidoso valley of central New Mexico, one of the most charming spots in the world; and all he asked was to be let alone, for he seemed able to get along, and not afraid of work. When the Lincoln County War broke out, he was recognised as a friend of Major Murphy, one of the local faction leaders; but when the fighting men curtly told him it was about time for him to choose his side, he as curtly replied that he intended to take neither side; that he had seen fighting enough in his time, and would fight no man's battle for him. This for the time and place was treason, and punishable with death. Roberts' friends told him that Billy the

Kid and Dick Brewer Intended to kill him, and advised him to leave the country.

It is said that Roberts had closed out his affairs and was preparing to leave the country, when he heard that the gang was looking for him, and that he then gave them opportunity to find him. Others say that he went up to Blazer's Mill to meet there a friend of his by the name of Kitts, who, he heard, had been shot and badly wounded. There is other rumour that he went up to Blazer's Mill to have a personal encounter with Major Godfroy, with whom there had been some altercation. There is a further absurd story that he went for the purpose of killing Billy the Kid, and getting the reward which was offered for him. These latter things are unlikely. The probable truth is that he, being a brave man, though fully determined to leave the country, simply found it written in his creed to go up to Blazer's Mill to see his supposedly wounded friend, and also to see what there was in the threats which he had heard.

There are living three eye-witnesses of what happened at that time: Frank and George Coe, ranchers on the Ruidoso today, (1905), and Johnnie Patten, cook on Carrizzo ranch. Patten was an ex-soldier of H Troop, Third Cavalry, and was mustered out at Fort Stanton in 1869. At the time of the Roberts fight, he was running the sawmill for Dr. Blazer. Frank Coe says that he himself was attempting to act as peacemaker, and that he tried to get Roberts to give up his arms and not make any fight. Patten says that he himself, at the peril of his life, had warned Roberts that Dick Brewer, the Kid, and his gang intended to kill him. It is certain that when Roberts came riding up on a mule, still wet from the fording of the Tularosa River, he met there Dick Brewer, Billy the Kid, George Coe, Frank Coe, Charlie Bowdre, Doc Middleton, one Scroggins, and Dirty Steve (Stephen Stevens), with others, to the number of thirteen in all. These men still claimed to be a posse, and were under Dick Brewer, "special constable."

The Brewer party withdrew to the rear of the house. Frank Coe parleyed with Roberts at one side. Kate Godfroy, daughter of Major Godfroy, protested at what she knew was the purpose of Brewer and his gang. Dick Brewer said to his men, "Don't do anything to him now. Coax him up the road a way."

Roberts declined to give up his weapons to Frank Coe. He stood near the door, outside the house. Then, as it is told by Johnnie Patten, who saw it all, there suddenly came around upon him from behind the house the gang of the Kid, all gun fighters, each opening fire as he came. The gritty little man gave back not a step toward the open door. Crippled by his old wounds so that he could not raise his rifle to his shoulder, he worked the lever from his hip. Here were a dozen men, the best fighting men of all that wild country, shooting at him at a distance of not a dozen feet; yet he shot Jack Middleton through the lungs, though failing to kill him. He shot a finger off the hand of George Coe, who then left the fight. Roberts then half stepped forward and pushed his gun against the stomach of Billy the Kid.

For some reason the piece failed to fire, and the Kid was saved by the narrowest escape he ever had in his life. Charlie Bowdre now appeared around the corner of the house, and Roberts fired at him next. His bullet struck Bowdre in the belt, and cut the belt off from him. Almost at the same time, Bowdre fired at him and shot him through the body. He did not drop, but staggered back against the wall; and so, he stood there, crippled of old and now wounded to death, but so fierce a human tiger that his very looks struck dismay into this gang of professional fighters. They actually withdrew around the house and left him there!

Each claimed the credit for having shot the victim. "No," said Charlie Bowdre, "I shot him myself. I dusted him on both sides. I saw the dust fly out on both sides of his coat, where my bullet went clean through him." They argued, but they did not go around the house again.

Roberts now staggered back into the house. He threw down his own Winchester and picked up a heavy Sharps' rifle which belonged to Dr. Appel, and which he found there, in Dr. Blazer's room. Brewer told Dr. Blazer to bring Roberts out, but, like a man, Blazer refused. Roberts pulled a mattress off the bed to the floor and threw himself down upon it near an open window in the front of the house. The gang had scattered, surrounding the house. Dick Brewer had taken refuge behind a thirty-inch sawlog near the mill, just one hundred and forty steps from the window near which this fierce little fighting man was lying, wounded to death. Brewer raised his head just above the top of the sawlog, so that he could see what Roberts was doing. His eyes were barely visible above the top of the log, yet at that distance the heavy bullet from Roberts' buffalo gun struck him in the eye and blew off the top of his head.

Billy the Kid was now leader of the posse. His first act was to call his men together and ride away from the spot, his whole outfit whipped by a single man! There was a corpse behind them, and wounded men with them.

Thirty-six hours later there was another corpse at Blazer's Mill. The doctor, brought over from Fort Stanton, could do nothing for Roberts, and he died in agony. Johnnie Patten, sawyer and rough carpenter, made one big coffin, and in this the two, Brewer and Roberts, were buried side by side. "I couldn't make a very good coffin," says Patten, "so I built it in the shape of a big V, with no end piece at the foot. We just put them both in together." And there they lie today, (1905), grim grave-company, according to the report of this eye-witness, who would seem to be in a position indicating accuracy. Emil Blazer, a son of Dr. Blazer, still, (1905), lives on the site of this fierce little battle, and he says that the two dead men were buried separately, but side by side, Brewer to the right of Roberts. The little graveyard holds a few other graves, none with headboards or records, and grass now grows above them all.

The building where Roberts stood at bay is now gone, and another *adobe* is erected a little farther back from the raceway that once fed the old mountain sawmill, but which now is not used as of yore. The old flume still exists where the water ran over onto the wheel, and the site of the old mill, which is now also torn down, is easily traceable. When the author visited the spot in the fall of 1905, all these points were verified and the distances measured. It was a long shot that Roberts made, and downhill. The vitality of the man who made it, his courage, and his tenacity alike of life and of purpose against such odds make Roberts a man remembered with admiration even today in that once bloody region.

CHAPTER 18

# The Man Hunt

The deeds of the Western sheriff have for the most part gone unchronicled, or have luridly been set forth in fiction as incidents of blood, Interesting only because of their bloodiness. The frontier officer himself, usually not a man to boast of his own acts, has quietly stepped into the background of the past, and has been replaced by others who more loudly proclaim their prominence in the advancement of civilization. Yet the typical frontier sheriff, the good man who went after bad men, and made it safe for men to live and own property and to establish homes and to build up a society and a country and a government, is a historical character of great interest. Among very many good ones, we shall perhaps best get at the type of all by giving the story of one; and we shall also learn something of the dangerous business of man hunting in a region filled with men who must be hunted down.

Patrick Floyd Garrett, better known as Pat Garrett, was a Southerner by birth. He was born in Chambers County, Alabama, June 5, 1850. In 1856, his parents moved to Claiborne parish, Louisiana, where his father was a large landowner, and of course at that time and place, a slave owner, and among the bitter opponents of the new regime which followed the civil war. When young Garrett's father died, the large estates dwindled under bad management; and when within a short time the mother followed her husband to the grave, the family resources, affected by the war, became involved, although the two Garrett plantations embraced nearly three thousand acres of rich Louisiana soil. On January 25, 1869, Pat Garrett, a tall and slender youth of eighteen, set out to seek his fortunes in the wild West, with no resources but such as lay in his brains and body.

He went to Lancaster, in Dallas County, Texas. A big ranch owner

PAT F. GARRETT
The most famous peace officer of the Southwest

in southern Texas wanted men, and Pat Garrett packed up and went home with him. The world was new to him, however, and he went off with the northbound cows, like many another youngster of the time. His herd was made up at Eagle Lake, and he only accompanied the drive as far north as Denison. There he began to get uneasy, hearing of the delights of the still wilder life of the buffalo hunters on the great plains which lay to the west, in the Panhandle of Texas. For three winters, 1875 to 1877, he was in and out between the buffalo range and the settlements, by this time well wedded to frontier life.

In the fall of 1877, he went West once more, and this time kept on going west. With two hardy companions, he pushed on entirely across the wild and unknown Panhandle country, leaving the wagons near what was known as the "Yellow Houses," and never returning to them. His blankets, personal belongings, etc., he never saw again. He and his friends had their heavy Sharps' rifles, plenty of powder and lead, and their reloading tools, and they had nothing else. Their beds they made of their saddle blankets, and their food they killed from the wild herds. For their love of adventure, they rode on across an unknown country, until finally they arrived at the little Mexican settlement of Fort Sumner, on the Pecos River, in the month of February, 1878.

Pat and his friends were hungry, but all the cash they could find was just one dollar and a half between them. They gave it to Pat and sent him over to the store to see about eating. He asked the price of meals, and they told him fifty cents per meal. They would permit them to eat but once. He concluded to buy a dollar and a half's worth of flour and bacon, which would last for two or three meals. He joined his friends, and they went into camp on the river bank, where they cooked and ate, perfectly happy and quite careless about the future.

As they finished their breakfast, they saw up the river the dust of a cattle herd, and noted that a party were working a herd, cutting out cattle for some purpose or other.

"Go up there and get a job," said Pat to one of the boys. The latter did go up, but came back reporting that the boss did not want any help.

"Well, he's got to have help," said Pat. So saying, he arose and started up stream himself.

Garrett was at that time, as has been said, of very great height, six feet four and one-half inches, and very slender. Unable to get trousers long enough for his legs, he had pieced down his best pair with about three feet of buffalo leggins with the hair out. Gaunt, dusty, and unshaven, he looked hard, and when he approached the herd owner and asked for work, the other was as much alarmed as pleased. He declined again, but Pat firmly told him he had come to go to work, and was sorry, but it could not be helped. Something in the quiet voice of Garrett seemed to arrest the attention of the cow man. "What can you do, Lengthy?" he asked.

"Ride anything with hair, and rope better than any man you've got here," answered Garrett, casting a critical glance at the other men.

The cow man hesitated a moment and then said, "Get in." Pat got in. He stayed in. Two years later he was still at Fort Sumner, and married.

Garrett moved down from Fort Sumner soon after his marriage, and settled a mile east of what is now the flourishing city of Roswell, at a spring on the bank of the Hondo, and in the middle of what was then the virgin plains. Here he picked up land, until he had in all more than twelve hundred and fifty acres. If he owned it now, (1905), he would be worth a half million dollars.

He was not, however, to live the steady life of the frontier farmer. His friend. Captain J. C. Lea, of Roswell, came to him and asked if he would run as sheriff of Lincoln County. Garrett consented and was elected. He was warned not to take this office, and word was sent to him by the bands of hard-riding outlaws of that region that if he attempted to serve any processes on them he would be killed. He paid no attention to this, and, as he was still an unknown quantity in the country, which was new and thinly settled, he seemed sure to be killed. He won the absolute confidence of the governor, who told him to go ahead, not to stand on technicalities, but to break up the gang that had been rendering life and property unsafe for years and making the territory a mockery of civilization.

If the truth were known, it might perhaps be found that sometimes Garrett arrested a bad man and got his warrant for it later, when he went to the settlements. He found a straight six-shooter the best sort of warrant, and in effect he took the matter of establishing a government in southwestern New Mexico in his own hands, and did it in his own way. He was the whole machinery of the law. Sometimes he boarded his prisoners out of his own pocket. He himself was the state! His word was good, even to the worst cutthroat that ever he captured. Often, he had in his care prisoners whom, under the law, he could not legally have held, had they been demanded of him; but he held them in spite of any demand; and the worst prisoner on that border knew that he was safe in Pat Garrett's hands, no matter what happened, and that if Pat said he would take him through to any given point, he would take him through.

After he had finished his first season of work as sheriff and as United States marshal, Garrett ranched it for a time. In 1884, his reputation as a criminal-taker being now a wide one, he organised and took charge of a company of Texas rangers in Wheeler county, Texas, and made Atacosa and thereabouts headquarters for a year and a half. So great became his fame now as a man-taker that he was employed to manage the affairs of a cattle detective agency; it being now so far along in civilization that men were beginning to be careful about their cows. He was offered ten thousand dollars to break up a certain band of raiders working in upper Texas, and he did it; but he found that he was really being paid to kill one or two men, and not to capture them; and, being unwilling to act as the agent of any man's revenge, he quit this work and went into the employment of the "V" ranch in the White mountains.

He then moved down to Roswell again, in the spring of 1887. Here he organised the Pecos Valley Irrigation Company. He was the first man to suspect the presence of artesian water in this country, where the great Spring rivers push up from the ground; and through his efforts wells were bored which revolutionized all that valley. He ran for sheriff of Chaves County, and was defeated. Angry at his first reverse in politics, he pulled up at Roswell, and sacrificed his land for what he could get for it. Today, (1905), it is covered with crops and fruits and worth sixty to one hundred dollars an acre.

Garrett now went back to Texas, and settled near Uvalde, where he engaged once more in an irrigation enterprise. He was here five years, ranching and losing money. W. T. Thornton, the governor of New Mexico, sent for him and asked him if he would take the office of sheriff of Donna Ana county, to fill the unexpired term of Numa Raymond. He was elected to serve two subsequent terms as sheriff of Donna Ana county, and no frontier officer has a better record for bravery.

In the month of December, 1901, President Theodore Roosevelt, who had heard of Garrett, met him and liked him, and without any ado or consultation appointed him collector of customs at El Paso, Texas. Here for the next four years Garrett made a popular collector, and an honest and fearless one.

The main reputation gained by Garrett was through his killing the desperado, Billy the Kid. It is proper to set down here the chronicle of that undertaking, because that will best serve to show the manner in which a frontier sheriff gets a bad man.

When the Kid and his gang killed the agency clerk, Bernstein, on the Mescalero reservation, they committed a murder on United States Government ground and an offense against the United States law. A United States warrant was placed in the hands of Pat Garrett, then deputy United States marshal and sheriff-elect, and he took up the trail, locating the men near Fort Sumner, at the ranch of one Brazil, about nine miles east of the settlement. With the Kid were Charlie Bowdre, Tom O'Folliard, Tom Pickett and Dave Rudabaugh, fellows of like kidney. Rudabaugh had just broken jail at Las Vegas, and had killed his jailer. Not a man of the band had ever hesitated at murder. They were now eager to kill Garrett and kept watch, as best they could, on all his movements.

One day Garrett and some of his improvised posse were riding eastward of the town when they jumped Tom O'Folliard, who was mounted on a horse that proved too good for them in a chase of several miles. Garrett at last was left alone following O'Folliard, and fired at him twice. The latter later admitted that he fired twenty times at Garrett with his Winchester; but it was hard to do good shooting from the saddle at two or three hundred yards range, so neither man was hit. O'Folliard did not learn his lesson. A few nights later, in company with Tom Pickett, he rode into town. Warned of his approach, Garrett with another man was waiting, hidden in the shadow of a building.

As O'Folliard rode up, he was ordered to throw up his hands, but went after his gun instead, and on the instant Garrett shot him through the body. "You never heard a man scream the way he did," said Garrett. "He dropped his gun when he was hit, but we did not know that, and as we ran up to catch his horse, we ordered him again to throw up his hands. He said he couldn't, that he was killed. We helped him down then, and took him in the house. He died about forty-five minutes later. He said it was all his own fault, and that he didn't blame anybody. I'd have killed Tom Pickett right there, too," concluded Garrett, "but one of my men shot right past my face and blinded me for the moment, so Pickett got away."

The remainder of the Kid's gang were now located in the stone house above mentioned, and their whereabouts reported by the ranchman whose house they had just vacated. The manhunt therefore proceeded methodically, and Garrett and his men, of whom he had

A TYPICAL WESTERN MAN HUNT
Pat F. Garrett chasing Tom O'Folliard

only two or three upon whom he relied as thoroughly game, surrounded the house just before dawn. Garrett, with Jim East and Tom Emory, crept up to the head of the ravine which made up to the ridge on which the fortress of the outlaws stood.

The early morning is always the best time for a surprise of this sort. It was Charlie Bowdre who first came out in the morning, and as he stepped out of the door his career as a bad man ended. Three bullets passed through his body. He stepped back into the house, but only lived about twenty minutes. The Kid said to him, "Charlie, you're killed anyhow. Take your gun and go out and kill that long-legged —— before you die." He pulled Bowdre's pistol around in front of him and pushed him out of the door. Bowdre staggered feebly toward the spot where the sheriff was lying. "I wish—I wish—" he began, and motioned toward the house; but he could not tell what it was that he wished. He died on Garrett's blankets, which were laid down on the snow.

Previous to this Garrett had killed one horse at the door beam where it was tied, and with a remarkable shot had cut the other free, shooting off the rope that held it. These two shots he thought about the best he ever made; and this is saying much, for he was a phenomenal shot with rifle or revolver. There were two horses inside, but the dead horse blocked the door. Pickett now told the gang to surrender. "That fellow will kill every man that shows outside that door," said he, "that's all about it. He's killed O'Folliard, and he's killed Charlie, and he'll kill us. Let's surrender and take a chance at getting out again." They listened to this, for the shooting they had seen had pretty well broken their hearts.

Garrett now sent over to the ranch house for food for his men, and the cooking was too much for the hungry outlaws, who had had nothing to eat. They put up a dirty white rag on a gun barrel and offered to give up. One by one, they came out and were disarmed. That night was spent at the Brazil ranch, the prisoners under guard and the body of Charlie Bowdre, rolled in its blankets, outside in the wagon. The next morning, Bowdre was buried in the little cemetery next to Tom O'Folliard. The Kid did not know that he was to make the next in the row.

These men surrendered on condition that they should all be taken through to Santa Fé, and Garrett, at the risk of his life, took them through Las Vegas, where Rudabaugh was wanted. Half the town surrounded the train in the depot yards. Garrett told the Kid that if the mob rushed in the door of the car he would toss back a six-shooter to him and ask him to help fight.

"All right, Pat," said the Kid, cheerfully. "You and I can whip the whole gang of them, and after we've done it I'll go back to my seat and you can put the irons on again. You've kept your word." There is little doubt that he would have done this, but as it chanced there was no need, since at the last moment deputy Malloy, of Las Vegas, jumped on the engine and pulled the train out of the yard.

Billy the Kid was tried and condemned to be executed. He had been promised pardon by Governor Lew Wallace, but the pardon did not come. A few days before the day set for his execution, the Kid, as elsewhere described, killed the two deputies who were guarding him, and got back once more to his old stamping grounds around Fort Sumner.

Garrett said to the writer, speaking reminiscently of the bloody scenes as we lately visited that country together:

> I knew now that I would have to kill the Kid. We both knew that it must be one or the other of us If we ever met. I followed him up here to Sumner, as you know, with two deputies, John Poe and 'Tip' McKinney, and I killed him in a room up there at the edge of the old cottonwood avenue.

He spoke of events now long gone by. It had been only with difficulty that we located the site of the building where the Kid's gang had been taken prisoners. The structure itself had been torn down and removed. As to the old military post, once a famous one, it offered now nothing better than a scene of desolation. There was no longer a single human inhabitant there. The old avenue of cottonwoods, once four miles long, was now ragged and unwatered, and the great parade ground had gone back to sand and sage brush. We were obliged to search for some time before we could find the site of the old Maxwell house, in which was ended a long and dangerous man hunt of the frontier. Garrett finally located the place, now only a rough quadrangle of crumbled earthen walls.

He said, pointing to one corner of the grass-grown oblong:

> This is the place, Pete Maxwell's bed was right in this corner of the room, and I was sitting in the dark and talking to Pete, who was in bed. The Kid passed Poe and McKinney right over there, on what was then the gallery, and came through the door right here.

We paused for a time and looked with a certain gravity at this wind-swept, desolate spot, around which lay the wide, unwinking desert. About us were the ruins of what had been a notable settlement in its day, but which now had passed with the old frontier.

Garrett at length resumed:

I got word of the Kid up here in much the way I had once before, and I followed him, resolved to get him or to have him get me. We rode over into the edge of the town and learned that the Kid was there, but of course we did not know which house he was in. Poe went in to inquire around, as he was not known there like myself. He did not know the Kid when he saw him, nor did the Kid know him.

It was a glorious moonlight night; I can remember it perfectly well. Poe and McKinney and I all met a little way out from the edge of the place. We decided that the Kid was not far away. We went down to the houses, and I put Poe and McKinney outside of Pete Maxwell's house and I went inside. Right here was the door. We did not know it at that time, but just about then the Kid was lying with his boots off in the house of an old Mexican just across there, not very far away from Maxwell's door.

He told the Mexican, when he came in, to cook something for him to eat. Maxwell had killed a beef not long before, and there was a quarter hanging up under the porch out in front. After a while, the Kid got up, got a butcher knife from the old Mexican, and concluded to go over and cut himself off a piece of meat from the quarter at Maxwell's house. This is how the story arose that he came into the house with his boots in his hand to keep an appointment with a Mexican girl.

The usual story is that I was down close to the wall behind Maxwell's bed. This was not the case, for the bed was close against the wall. Pete Maxwell was lying in bed, right here in this corner, as I said. I was sitting in a chair and leaning over toward him, as I talked in a low tone. My right side was toward him, and my revolver was on that side. I did not know that the Kid was so close at hand, or, indeed, know for sure that he was there in the settlement at all.

Maxwell did not want to talk very much. He knew the Kid was there, and knew his own danger. I was talking to him in Spanish, in a low tone of voice, as I say, when the Kid came over here, just as I have told you. He saw Poe and McKinney sitting right out there in the moonlight, but did not suspect anything. '*Quien es?*'—'Who is it?'—he asked, as he passed them. I heard him speak and saw him come backing into the room, facing toward Poe and McKinney. He could not see me, as it was dark in the room, but he came up to the bed where Maxwell was lying and where I was sitting. He seemed to think something might not be quite right. He had in his hand his revolver, a self-cocking .41. He could not see my face, and he had not heard my voice, or he would have known me.

The Kid stepped up to the bedside and laid his left hand on the bed and bent over Maxwell. He saw me sitting there in the half darkness, but did not recognise me, as I was sitting down. My height would have betrayed me had I been standing. 'Pete, *Quien es?* he asked in a low tone of voice; and he half motioned toward me with his six-shooter. That was when I looked across into eternity. It wasn't far to go.

That was exactly how the thing was. I gave neither Maxwell nor the Kid time for anything farther. There flashed over my mind at once one thought, and it was that I had to shoot and shoot at once, and that my shot must go to the mark the first time. I knew the Kid would kill me in a flash if I did not kill him.

Just as he spoke and motioned toward me, I dropped over to the left and rather down, going after my gun with my right hand as I did so. As I fired, the Kid dropped back. I had caught him just about the heart. His pistol, already pointed toward me, went off as he fell, but he fired high. As I sprang up, I fired once more, but did not hit him, and did not need to, for he was dead.

I don't know that he ever knew who it was that killed him. He could not see me in the darkness. He may have seen me stoop over and pull. If he had had the least suspicion who it was, he would have shot as soon as he saw me. When he came to the bed, I knew who he was. The rest happened as I have told you. There is no other story about the killing of Billy the Kid which is the truth. It is also untrue that his body was ever removed from Fort Sumner. It lies there today,(1905), and I'll show you where we buried him. I laid him out myself, in this house here, and I ought to know.

Twenty-five years of time had done their work in all that country, as we learned when we entered the little barbed-wire enclosure of the cemetery where the Kid and his fellows were buried. There are no headstones in this cemetery, and no sacristan holds its records. Again, Garrett had to search in the salt grass and greasewood. "Here is the place," said he, at length. "We buried them all in a row. The first grave is the Kid's, and next to him is Bowdre, and then O'Folliard."

Here was the sole remaining record of the manhunt's end. So, passes the glory of the world! in this desolate resting-place, in a windswept and forgotten graveyard, rests all the remaining fame of certain bad men who in their time were bandit kings, who ruled by terror over half a Western territory. Even the headboard which once stood at the Kid's grave—and which was once riddled with bullets by cowards who would not have dared to shoot that close to him had he been alive—was gone. It is not likely that the graves will be visited again by anyone who knows their locality. Garrett looked at them in silence for a time, then, turning, went to the buckboard for a drink at the canteen. "Well," said he, quietly, "here's to the boys, anyway. If there is any other life, I hope they'll make better use of it than they did of the one I put them out of."

CHAPTER 19

# Bad Men of Texas

A review of the story of the American desperado will show that he has always been most numerous at the edge of things, where there was a frontier, a debatable ground between civilization and lawlessness, or a border between opposing nations or sections. He does not wholly pass away with the coming of the law, but his home is essentially in a new and undeveloped condition of society. The edge between East and West, between North and South, made the territory of the bad man of the American interior.

The far Southwest was the oldest of all American frontiers, and the stubbornest. We have never, as a nation, been at war with any other nation whose territory has adjoined our own except in the case of Mexico; and long before we went to war as a people against Mexico, Texas had been at war with her as a state, or rather as a population and a race against another race. The frontier of the Rio Grande is one of the bloodiest of the world, and was such long before Texas was finally admitted to the union. There was never any new territory settled by so vigorous and belligerent a population as that which first found and defended the great empire of the Lone Star. Her early men were, without exception, fighters, and she has bred fighters ever since.

The allurement which the unsettled lands of the Southwest had for the young men of the early part of the last century lay largely in the appeal of excitement and adventure, with a large possibility of worldly gain as well. The men of the South who drifted down the old River Road across Mississippi and Louisiana were shrewd in their day and generation. They knew that eventually Texas would be taken away from Mexico, and taken by force. Her vast riches would belong to those who had earned them. Men of the South were even then hunting for another West, and here was a mighty one. The call came back that the fighting was good all along the line; and the fighting men of all the South, from Virginia to Louisiana, fathers and sons of the boldest and bravest of Southern families, pressed on and out to take a hand. They were scattered and far from numerous when they united and demanded a government of their own, independent of the far-off and inefficient head of the Mexican law. They did not want Coahuila as their country, but Texas, and asked a government of their own. Lawless as they were, they wanted a real law, a law of Saxon right and justice.

Men like Crockett, Fannin, Travers and Bowie were influenced half by political ambition and half by love of adventure when they moved across the plains of eastern Texas and took up their abode on the firing line of the Mexican border. If you seek a historic band of bad men, fighting men of the bitterest Baresark type, look at the immortal defenders of the Alamo. Some of them were, in the light of calm analysis, little better than guerrillas; but every man was a hero. They all had a chance to escape, to go out and join Sam Houston farther to the east; but they refused to a man, and, plying the border weapons as none but such as themselves might, they died, full of the glory of battle; not in ranks and shoulder to shoulder, with banners and music to cheer them, but each for himself and hand to hand with his enemy, a desperate fighting man.

The early men of Texas for generations fought Mexicans and Indians in turn. The country was too vast for any system of law. Each man had learned to depend upon himself. Each cabin kept a rifle and pistol for each male old enough to bear them, and each boy, as he grew up, was skilled in weapons and used to the thought that the only arbitrament among men was that of weapons. Part of the population, appreciating the exemptions here to be found, was, without doubt, criminal; made up of men who had fled, for reasons of their own, from older regions. These in time required the attention of the law; and the armed bodies of hard-riding Texas rangers, a remedy born of necessity, appeared as the executives of the law.

The cattle days saw the wild times of the border prolonged. The buffalo range caught its quota of hard riders and hard shooters. And always the apparently exhaustless empires of new and unsettled lands— an enormous, untracked empire of the wild—beckoned on and on; so that men in the most densely settled sections were very far apart, and so that the law as a guardian could not be depended upon. It was not to be wondered at that the name of Texas became the synonym for savagery. That was for a long time the wildest region within our national confines. Many men who attained fame as fighters along the Pecos and Rio Grande and Gila and Colorado came across the borders from Texas. Others slipped north into the Indian Nations, and left their mark there. Some went to the mines of the Rockies, or the cattle ranges from Montana to Arizona. Many stayed at home, and finished their eventful lives there in the usual fashion—killing now and again, then oftener, until at length they killed once too often and got hanged; or not often enough once, and so got shot.

To undertake to give even the most superficial study to a field so vast as this would require a dozen times the space we may afford, and would lead us far into matters of history other than those intended. We can only point out that the men of the Lone Star state left their stamp as horsemen and weapon-bearers clear on to the north, and as far as the foot of the Arctic circle. Their language and their methods mark the entire cattle business of the plains from the Rio Grande to the Selkirks. Theirs was a great school for frontiersmen, and its graduates gave full account of themselves wherever they went. Among them were bad men, as bad as the worst of any land, and in numbers not capable of compass even in a broad estimate.

Some citizens of Montgomery County, Texas, were not long ago sitting in a store of an evening, and they fell to counting up the homicides which had fallen under their notice in that county within recent memory. They counted up seventy-five authenticated cases, and could not claim comprehensiveness for their tally. Many a county of Texas could do as well or better, and there are many counties. It takes you two days to ride across Texas by railway. A review of the bad man field of Texas pauses for obvious reasons!

So many bad men of Texas have attained reputation far wider than their state that it became a proverb upon the frontier that any man born on Texas soil would shoot, just as any horse born there would "buck." There is truth back of most proverbs, although today both horses and men of Texas are losing something of their erstwhile bronco character. That out of such conditions, out of this hardy and indomitable population, the great state could bring order and quiet so soon and so permanently over vast unsettled regions, is proof alike of the fundamental sternness and justness of the American character and the value of the American fighting man.

Yet, though peace hath her victories not less than war, it is to be doubted whether in her own heart Texas is more proud of her statesmen and commercial kings than of her stalwart fighting men, bred to the use of arms. The beautiful city of San Antonio is today, (1905), busy and prosperous; yet today you tread there ground which has been stained red over and over again. The names of Crockett, Milam, Travis, Bowie, endure where those of captains of Industry are forgotten. Out of history such as this, covering a half century of border fighting, of frontier travel and merchandising, of cattle trade and railroad building, it is impossible—In view of the many competitors of equal claims—to select an example of bad eminence fit to bear the title of the leading bad man of Texas.

There was one somewhat noted Texas character, however, whose life comes down to modern times, and hence is susceptible of fairly accurate review—a thing always desirable, though not often practical, for no history is more distorted, not to say more garbled, than that dealing with the somewhat mythical exploits of noted gun fighters. Ben Thompson, of Austin, killer of more than twenty men, and a very perfect exemplar of the creed of the six-shooter, will serve as instance good enough for a generic application. Thompson was not a hero. He did no deeds of war. He led no forlorn hope into the imminent deadly breach. His name is preserved in no history of his great commonwealth. He was in the opinion of certain peace officers, all that a citizen should not be.

Yet in his way he reached distinction; and so striking was his life that even today he does not lack apologists, even as he never lacked friends. Ben Thompson was of English descent, and was born near Lockhart, Texas, according to general belief, though it is stated that he was born in Yorkshire, England. Later his home was in Austin, where he spent the greater part of his life, though roaming from place to place. Known as a bold and skilful gunman, he was looked on as good material for a hunter of bad men, and at the time of his death was marshal of police at Austin.

In personal appearance Thompson looked the part of the typical gambler and gun fighter. His height was about five feet eight inches, and his figure was muscular and compact. His hair was dark and waving; his eyes grey. He was very neat in dress, and always took particular pains with his footwear, his small feet being always clad in well-fitting boots of light material, a common form of foppery in a land where other details of dress were apt to be carelessly regarded. He wore a dark moustache which, in his early years, he was wont to keep waxed to points. In speech he was quiet and unobtrusive, unless excited by drink. With the six-shooter he was a peerless shot, an absolute genius, none in all his wide surrounding claiming to be his superior; and he had a ferocity of disposition which grew with years until he had, as one of his friends put it, "a craving to kill people."

Each killing seemed to make him desirous of another. He thus came to exercise that curious fascination which such characters have always commanded. Fear he did not know, or at least no test arising in his somewhat varied life ever caused him to show fear. He passed through life as a wild animal, ungoverned by the law, rejoicing in blood; yet withal he was held as a faithful friend and a good companion. To this day many men repel the accusation that he was bad, and maintain that each of his twenty killings was done in self-defence. The brutal phase of his nature was no doubt dominant, even although it was not always in evidence. He was usually spoken of as a "good fellow," and those who palliate or deny most of his wild deeds declare that local history has never been as fair to him as he deserved.

Thompson's first killing was while he was a young man at New Orleans, and according to the story, arose out of his notions of chivalry. He was passing down the street in a public conveyance, in company of several young Creoles, who were going home from a dance in a somewhat exhilarated condition. One or two of the strangers made remarks to an unescorted girl, which Thompson construed to be offensive, and he took it upon himself to avenge the insult to womanhood. In the affray that followed he killed one of the young men.

For this he was obliged to flee to old Mexico, taking one of the boats down the river. He returned presently to Galveston, where he set up as a gambler, and began to extend his reputation as a fighting man. Most of his encounters were over cards or drink or women, the history of many or most of the border killings.

Thompson's list grew steadily, and by the time he was forty years of age he had a reputation far wider than his state. In all the main cities of Texas he was a figure more or less familiar, and always dreaded. His skill with his favourite weapon was a proverb in a state full of men skilled with weapons. Moreover, his disposition now began to grow more ugly, sullen and bloodthirsty. He needed small pretext to kill a man if, for the slightest cause, he took a dislike to him. To illustrate the ferocity of the man, and his readiness to provoke a quarrel, the following story is told of him:

A gambler by the name of Jim Burdette was badly whipped by the proprietor of a variety show, Mark Wilson, who, after the fight, told Burdette that he had enough of men like him, who only came to his theatre to raise trouble and interfere with his business, and that if either he or any of his gang ever again attempted to disturb his audiences that they would have him (Wilson) to deal with. The next day Ben Thompson, seated in a barber shop, heard about the row and said to a negro standing by: "Mack, d—n your nigger soul, you go down to that place this evening and when the house is full and everybody is seated, you just raise hell and we'll see what that —— is made of."

The program was carried out. The negro arose in the midst of the audience and delivered himself of a few bloodcurdling yells. Instantly the proprietor came out of the place, but caught sight of Thompson, who had drawn a pair of guns and stood ready to kill Wilson. The latter was too quick for him, and quickly disappeared behind the scenery, after his shotgun. There was too much excitement that night, and the matter passed off without a killing. A few nights thereafter, Thompson procured some lamp-black, which he gave the gambler Burdette, with instructions to go to the theatre, watch his chance, and dash the stuff in Wilson's face. This was done and when the ill-fated proprietor, who immediately went for his shotgun, came out with that weapon, Thompson fell to the ground, and the contents of the gun, badly fired at the hands of Wilson, his face full of lamp-black, passed over Thompson's head. Thompson then arose and filled Wilson full of holes, killing him instantly.

The bartender, seeing his employer's life in danger, fired at Thompson wildly, and as Thompson turned on him he dodged behind the bar to receive his death wound through the counter and in his back. Thompson at the court of last resort managed to have a lot of testimony brought to bear, and, with a half-dozen gamblers to swear to anything he needed, he was admitted to bail and later freed.

He is said to have killed these two men for no reason in the world except to show that he could "run" a place where others had failed. A variation of the story is that a saloon keeper fired at Thompson as he was walking down the street in Austin, and missing him, sprang back behind the bar, Thompson shooting him through the head, through the bar front. Another man's life now meant little to him. He desired to be king, to be "chief," just as the leaders of the desperadoes in the mining regions of California and Montana sought to be "chief." it meant recognition of their courage, their skill, their willingness to take human life easily and carelessly and quickly, a singular ambition which has been so evidenced in no other part of the world than the American West. It is certain that the worst bad men all over Texas were afraid of Ben Thompson. He was "chief."

Ben Thompson left the staid paths of life in civilized communities. He did not rob, and he did not commit theft or burglary or any highway crimes; yet toiling and spinning were not for him. He was, for the most part, a gambler, and after a while he ceased even to follow that calling as a means of livelihood. Forgetting the etiquette of his chosen profession, he insisted on winning no manner how and no matter what the game. He would go into a gambling resort in some town, and sit in at a game. If he won, very well. If he lost, he would become enraged, and usually ended by reaching out and raking in the money on the table, no matter what the decision of the cards. He bought drinks for the crowd with the money he thus took, and scattered it right and left, so that his acts found a certain sanction among those who had not been despoiled.

To know what nerve it required to perform these acts of audacity, one must know something of the frontier life, which at no corner of the world was wilder and touchier than in the very part of the country where Thompson held forth. There were hundreds of men quick with the gun all about him, men of nerve, but he did not hesitate to take all manner of chances in that sort of population. The madness of the bad man was upon him. He must have known what alone could be his fate at last, but he went on, defying and courting his own destruction, as the finished desperado always does, under the strange creed of self-reliance which he established as his code of life.

Thus, at a banquet of stockmen in Austin, and while the dinner was in progress, Thompson, alone, stampeded every man of them, and at that time nearly all stockmen were game. The fear of Thompson's pistol was such that no one would stand for a fight with him. Once Thompson went to the worst place in Texas, the town of Luling, where Rowdy Joe was running the toughest dance house in America. He ran all the bad men out of the place, confiscated what cash he needed from the gaming tables and raised trouble generally. He showed that he was "chief."

In the early eighties. In the quiet, sleepy, bloody old town of San Antonio, there was a dance hall, gambling resort and vaudeville theatre, in which the main proprietor was one Jack Harris, commonly known as Pegleg Harris.

Thompson frequently patronised this place on his visits to San Antonio, and received treatment which left him with a grudge against Harris, whom he resolved to kill. He followed his man into the bar-room one day and killed Harris as he stood in the semi-darkness. It was only another case of "self-defence" for Thompson, who was well used to being cleared of criminal charges or left unaccused altogether; and no doubt Harris would have killed him if he could. After killing Harris, Thompson declared that he proposed to kill Harris' partners, Foster and Simms. He had an especial grudge against Billy Simms, then a young man not yet nineteen years of age, because, so it is stated, he fancied that Simms supplanted him in the affections of a woman in Austin; and he carried also his grudge against the gambling house, where Simms now was the manager.

Every time Thompson got drunk, he declared his intention of killing Billy Simms, and as the latter was young and inexperienced, he trembled in his boots at this talk which seemed surely to spell his doom. Simms, to escape Thompson's wrath, removed to Chicago, and remained there for a time, but before long was summoned home to Austin, where his mother was very ill.

Thompson knew of his presence in Austin, but with magnanimity declined to kill Simms while he was visiting his sick mother. "Wait till he goes over to Santone," he said, "then I'll step over and kill the little ———." Simms, presently called to San Antonio to settle some debt of Jack Harris' estate, of which as friend and partner of the widow he had been appointed administrator, went to the latter city with a heavy heart, supposing that he would never leave it alive. He was told there that Thompson had been threatening him many times; and Simms received many telegrams to that effect. Some say that Thompson himself telegraphed Simms that he was coming down that day to kill him. Certainly, a friend of Simms on the same day wired him warning: "Party who wants to destroy you on train this day bound for San Antonio."

Friends of Thompson deny that he made such threats, and insist that he went to San Antonio on a wholly peaceful errand. In any case, this guarded but perfectly plain message set Simms half distracted. He went to the city marshal and showed his telegram, asking the marshal for protection, but the latter told him nothing could be done until Thompson had committed some "overt act." The sheriff and all the other officers said the same thing, not caring to meet Thompson if they could avoid it. Simms later in telling his story would sob at the memory of his feeling of helplessness at that time. The law gave him no protection. He was obliged to take matters in his own hands. He went to a judge of the court, and asked him what he should do.

The judge pondered for a time, and said: "Under the circumstances, I should advise a shotgun."

Simms went to one of the *faro* dealers of the house, a man who was known as bad, and who never sat down to deal *faro* without a brace of big revolvers on the table; but this dealer advised him to go and "make friends with Thompson." He went to Foster, Harris' old partner, and laid the matter before him. Foster said, slowly, "Well, Billy, when he comes we'll do the best we can." Simms thought that he too was weakening.

There was a big policeman, a Mexican by name of Coy, who was considered a brave man and a fighter, and Simms now went to him and asked for aid, saying that he expected trouble that night, and wanted Coy to do his duty. Coy did not become enthusiastic, though as a matter of fact neither he nor Foster made any attempt to leave the place. Simms turned away, feeling that his end was near. In desperation he got a shotgun, and for a time stationed himself near the top of the stair up which Thompson would probably come when entering the place. The theatre was up one flight of stairs, and at the right was the customary bar, from which "ladies" in short skirts served drinks to the crowd during the variety performance, which was one of the attractions of the place.

It was nervous work, waiting for the killer to come, and Simms could not stand it. He walked down the stairway, and took a turn around the block before he again ascended the stairs to the hall. Meantime, Ben Thompson, accompanied by another character. King Fisher, a man with several notches on his gun, had ascended the stairs, and had taken a seat on the right-hand side and beyond the bar, in the row nearest the door. When Simms stepped to the foot of the stairs on his return, he met the barkeeper, who was livid with terror. He pointed trembling up the stair and whispered, "He's there!" Ben Thompson and King Fisher had as yet made no sort of demonstration.

It is said that King Fisher had decoyed Thompson into the theatre, knowing that a trap was laid to kill him. It is also declared that Thompson went in merely for amusement. A friend of the author, a New Mexican sheriff who happened to be in San Antonio, saw and talked with both men that afternoon. They were both quiet and sober then.

Simms' heart was in his mouth, but he made up his mind to die game, if he had to die. Slowly he walked up the stairway. Such was Thompson's vigilance, that he quickly arose and advanced toward

THE OLD CHISUM RANCH BELOW ROSWELL, NEW MEXICO

Simms, who stood at the top of the stairs petrified and unable to move a muscle. Before Simms could think, his partner, Foster, appeared on the scene, and as he stood up, Thompson saw him and walked toward him and said: "Hello, Foster, how are you?" Slowly and deliberately Foster spoke: "Ben, this world is not big enough for us both. You killed poor Jack Harris like a dog, and you didn't as much as give him a chance for his life. You and I can never be friends anymore."

Quick as a flash and with a face like a demon, Thompson drew his pistol and jammed it into Foster's mouth, cruelly tearing his lips and sending him reeling backward. While this was going on, Simms had retreated to the next step, and there drew his pistol, not having his shotgun in hand then. He stepped forward as he saw Foster reel from the blow Thompson gave him, and with sudden courage opened fire. His first shot must have taken effect, and perhaps it decided the conflict. Thompson's gun did not get into action. Simms kept on firing. Thompson reeled back against King Fisher, and the two were unable to fire. Meantime the big Mexican, Coy, showed up from somewhere, just as Foster had. Both Foster and Coy rushed in front of the line of fire of Simms' pistol; and then without doubt, Simms killed his own friend and preserver. Foster got his death wound in such position that Simms admitted he must have shot him.

None the less Foster ran into Thompson as the latter reeled backwards upon Fisher, and, with the fury of a tiger, shoved his own pistol barrel into Thompson's mouth in turn, and fired twice, completing the work Simms had begun. The giant Coy hurled his bulk into the struggling mass now crowded into the corner of the room, and some say he held Ben Thompson's arms, though in the melee it was hard to tell what happened. He called out to Simms, "Don't mind me," meaning that Simms should keep on firing. "Kill the —— of ——!" he cried.

Coy no doubt was a factor in saving Simms' life, for one or the other of these two worst men in the Southwest would have got a man before he fell, had he been able to get his hands free in the struggling. Coy was shot in the leg, possibly by Simms, but did not drop. Simms took care of Coy to the end of his life, Coy dying but recently.

One of the men engaged in this desperate fight says that Coy did not hold Thompson, and that at first no one was shot to the floor. Thompson was staggered by Simms' first shot, which prevented a quick return of fire. It was Foster who killed Thompson and very likely King Fisher, the latter being hemmed in in the corner with

Thompson in front of him. Coy rushed into the two and handled them so roughly that they never got their guns into action so far as known.

Leaving the fallen men at the rear of the theatre, Simms now went down stairs, carrying Foster's pistol, with two chambers empty (the shots that killed Thompson) and his own gun. He saw Thompson's brother Bill coming at him. He raised the gun to kill him, when Phil Shardein, then city marshal, jumped on Thompson and shielded him with his body, calling out, "Don't shoot, Billy, I've got him." This saved Bill Thompson's life. Then several shots were heard upstairs, and upon investigation, it was found that Coy had emptied his pistol into the dead body of Thompson. He also shot Fisher, to "make sure the —— were dead."

Thus, they died at last, two of the most notorious men of Texas, both with their boots on. There were no tears. Many told what they would or could have done had Ben Thompson threatened them. This closing act in the career of Ben Thompson came in the late spring of 1882. He was then about forty-three years of age.

King Fisher, who met death at the same time with Thompson, was a good disciple of desperadoism. He was a dark-haired, slender young man from Goliad County—which county seems to have produced far more than its share of bad men. He had killed six men and stolen a great many horses in his time. Had he lived longer, he would have killed more. He was not of the calibre sufficient to undertake the running of a large city, but there was much relief felt over his death. He had many friends, of course, and some of these deny that he had any intention of making trouble when he went into the theatre with Ben Thompson, just as friends of the latter accuse King Fisher of treachery. There are never lacking men who regard dead desperadoes as martyrs; and indeed, it is usually the case that there are mixed circumstances arid frequently extenuating ones, to be found in the history of any killer's life.

Another Goliad County man well known around San Antonio was Alfred Y. Allee, who was a rancher a short distance back from the railway. Allee was decent when sober, but when drunk was very dangerous, and was recognised as bad and well worth watching. Liquor seemed to transform him and to make him a bloodthirsty fiend. He had killed several men, one or two under no provocation whatever and when they were defenceless, including a porter on a railway train. It was his habit to come to town and get drunk, then to invite everyone to drink with him and take offense at any refusal. He liked to be "chief" of the drinking place which he honoured with his presence. He once ordered a peaceful citizen of San Antonio, a friend of the writer, up to drink with him, and when the latter declined came near shooting him. The man took his drink, then slipped away and got his shotgun. Perhaps his second thought was wiser. "What's the use?" he argued with himself. "Somebody'll kill Allee before long anyhow."

This came quite true, for within the week Allee had run his course. He dropped down to Laredo and began to 'hurrah' that town also. The town marshal, Joe Bartelow, was a Mexican, but something of a killer himself, and he resolved to end the Allee disturbances, once for all. It is said that Allee was not armed when at length they met in a saloon, and it is said that Bartelow offered his hand in greeting. At once Bartelow threw his arm around Alee's neck, and with his free hand cut him to death with a knife. Whether justifiable or not, that was the fashion of the homicide.

Any man who has killed more than twenty men is in most countries considered fit to qualify as bad. This test would include the little human tiger, Tumlinson, of South Texas, who was part of the time an officer of the law and part of the time an independent killer in Texas. He had many more than twenty men to his credit, it was said, and his Mexican wife, smilingly, always said that "Tumlinson never counted Mexicans." He was a genius with the revolver, and as good a rifle shot as would often be found. It made no difference to him whether or not a man was running, for part of his pistol practice was in shooting at a bottle swinging in the wind from the bough of a tree. Legend goes that Tumlinson killed his wife and then shot himself dead, taking many secrets with him. He was bad.

Sam Bass was a noted outlaw and killer in West Texas, accustomed to ride into town and to take charge of things when he pleased. He had many thefts and robberies to his credit, and not a few murders. His finish was one not infrequent in that country. The citizens got wind of his coming one day, just before he rode into Round Rock for a little raid. The city marshal and several others opened fire on Bass and his party, and killed them to a man.

It was of such stuff as this that most of the bad men and indeed many of the peace officers were composed, along a wide frontier in the early troublous days following the civil war, when all the border was a seething mass of armed men for whom the law had as yet gained no meaning. To tell the story of more individuals would be to depart from the purpose of this work. Were these men wrong, and were they wholly and unreservedly bad? Ignorance and bigotry will be the first to give the answer, the first to apply to them the standards of these later days.

CHAPTER 20

# Modern Bad Men

Outlawry of the early border, in days before any pretence at establishment of a system of law and government, and before the holding of property had assumed any very stable form, may have retained a certain glamour of romance. The loose gold of the mountains, the loose cattle of the plains, before society had fallen into any strict way of living, and while plenty seemed to exist for any and all, made a temptation easily accepted and easily excused. The ruffians of those early days had a largeness in their methods which gives some of them at least a colour of interest. If any excuse may be offered for lawlessness, any palliation for acts committed without countenance of the law, that excuse and palliation may be pleaded for these men if for any. But for the man who is bad and mean as well, who kills for gain, and who adds cruelty and cunning to his acts instead of boldness and courage, little can be said. Such characters afford us horror, but it is horror unmingled with any manner of admiration.

Yet, if we reconcile ourselves to tarry a moment with the cheap and gruesome, the brutal and ignorant side of mere crime, we shall be obliged to take into consideration some of the bloodiest characters ever known in our history; who operated well within the day of established law; who made a trade of robbery, and whose capital consisted of disregard for the life and property of others. That men like this should live for years at the very door of large cities, in an old settled country, and known familiarly in their actual character to thousands of good citizens, is a strange commentary on the American character; yet such are the facts.

It has been shown that a widely extended war always has the effect of cheapening human life in and out of the ranks of the fighting armies. The early wars of England, in the days of the longbow and buckler, brought on her palmiest days of cutpurses and cutthroats. The days following our own civil war were fearful ones for the entire country from Montana to Texas; and nowhere more so than along the dividing line between North and South, where feeling far bitterer than soldierly antagonism marked a large population on both sides of that contest. We may further restrict the field by saying that nowhere on any border was animosity so fierce as in western Missouri and eastern Kansas, where jayhawker and border ruffian waged a guerrilla war for years before the nation was arrayed against itself in ordered ranks. If mere blood be matter of our record here, assuredly, is a field of interest. The deeds of Lane and Brown, of Quantrell and Hamilton, are not surpassed in terror in the history of any land. Osceola, Marais du Cygne, Lawrence—these names warrant a shudder even today, (1905).

This locality—say that part of Kansas and Missouri near the towns of Independence and Westport, and more especially the counties of Jackson and Clay in the latter state—was always turbulent, and had reason to be. Here was the halting place of the westbound civilization, at the edge of the plains, at the line long dividing the whites from the Indians.

Here settled, like the gravel along the cleats of a sluice, the daring men who had pushed west from Kentucky, Tennessee, lower Ohio, eastern Missouri—the Boones, Carsons, Crocketts, and Kentons of their day. Here came the Mormons to found their towns, and later to meet the armed resistance which drove them across the plains. Here, at these very towns, was the outfitting place and departing point of the caravans of the early Santa Fé trade; here the Oregon Trail left for the far Northwest; and here the Forty-niners paused a moment in their mad rush to the golden coast of the Pacific. Here, too, adding the bitterness of fanaticism to the courage of the frontier, came the bold men of the North who Insisted that Kansas should be free for the expansion of the northern population and Institutions.

This corner of Missouri-Kansas was a focus of recklessness and daring for more than a whole generation. The children born there had an inheritance of indifference to death such as has been surpassed nowhere in our frontier unless that were in the bloody Southwest. The men of this country, at the outbreak of the civil war, made as high an average in desperate fighting as any that ever lived. Too restless to fight under the ensign of any but their own Ilk, they set up a banner of their own. The black flags of Quantrell and of Lane, of border ruffian and jayhawker, were guidons under which quarter was unknown, and mercy a forgotten thing. Warfare became murder, and murder became assassination. Ambushing, surprise, pillage and arson went with murder; and women and children were killed as well as fighting men. Is it any wonder that in such a school there grew up those figures which a certain class of writers have been wont to call bandit kings; the bank robbers and train robbers of modern days, the James and Younger type of bad men?

The most notorious of these border fighters was the bloody leader, Charles William Quantrell, leader at the sacking of Lawrence, and as dangerous a partisan leader as ever threw leg into saddle. He was born in Hagerstown, Maryland, July 20, 1836, and as a boy lived for a time in the Ohio city of Cleveland. At twenty years of age, he joined his brother for a trip to California, via the great plains. This was in 1856, and Kansas was full of Free Sellers, whose political principles were not always untempered by a large-minded willingness to rob. A party of these men surprised the Quantrell party on the Cottonwood river, and killed the older brother. Charles William Quantrell swore an undying revenge; and he kept his oath.

It is not necessary to mention in detail the deeds of this border leader. They might have had commendation for their daring had it not been for their brutality and treachery.

Quantrell had a band of sworn men, held under solemn oath to stand by each other and to keep their secrets. These men were well armed and well mounted, were all fearless and all good shots, the revolver being their especial arm, as it was of Mosby's men in the civil war. The tactics of this force comprised surprise, ambush, and a determined rush, in turn; and time and again they defeated Federal forces many times their number, being thoroughly well acquainted with the country, and scrupling at nothing in the way of treachery, just as they considered little the odds against which they fought. Their victims were sometimes paroled, but not often, and a massacre usually followed a defeat—almost invariably so if the number of prisoners was small.

Cold-blooded and unhesitating murder was part of their everyday life. Thus Jesse James, on the march to the Lawrence massacre, had in charge three men, one of them an old man, whom they took along as guides from the little town of Aubrey, Kansas. They used these men until they found themselves within a few miles of Lawrence, and then, as is alleged, members of the band took them aside and killed them, the old man begging for his life and pleading that he never had done them any wrong. His murderers were no more than boys. This act may have been that of bad men, but not of the sort of bad men that leaves us any sort of respect, such as that which may be given Wild Bill, even Billy the Kid, or any of a dozen other big-minded desperadoes.

This assassination was but one of scores or hundreds. A neighbour suspected of Federal sympathies was visited in the night and shot or hanged, his property destroyed, his family killed. The climax of the Lawrence massacre was simply the working out of principles of blood and revenge. In that fight, or, more properly, that massacre, women and children went down as well as men. The James boys were Quantrell riders, Jesse a new recruit, and that day they maintained that they had killed sixty-five persons between them, and wounded twenty more! What was the total record of these two men alone in all this period of guerrilla fighting? it cannot be told. Probably they themselves could not remember. The four Younger boys had records almost or quite as bad.

There, indeed, was a border soaked in blood, a country torn with intestinal warfare. Quantrell was beaten now and then, meeting fighting men in blue or in jeans, as well as leading fighting men; and at times he was forced to disband his men, later to recruit again, and to go on with his marauding up and down the border. His career attracted the attention of leaders on both sides of the opposing armies, and at one time it was nearly planned that Confederates should join the Unionists and make common cause against these guerrillas, who had made the name of Missouri one of reproach and contempt. The matter finally adjusted itself by the death of Quantrell in a fight at Smiley, Kentucky, in January, 1865.

With a birth and training such as this, what could be expected for the surviving Quantrell men? They scattered over all the frontier, from Texas to Minnesota, and most of them lived in terror of their lives thereafter, with the name of Quantrell as a term of loathing attached to them where their earlier record was known. Many and many a border killing years later and far removed in locality arose from the implacable hatred descended from those days.

As for the James boys, the Younger boys, what could they do? The days of war were gone. There were no longer any armed banners arrayed one against the other. The soldiers who had fought bravely and openly on both sides had laid down their arms and fraternized. The Union grew, strong and indissoluble. Men settled down to farming, to artisanship, to merchandising, and their wounds were healed. Amnesty was extended to those who wished it and deserved it. These men could have found a living easy to them, for the farming lands still lay rich and ready for them. But they did not want this life of toil. They preferred the ways of robbery and blood in which they had begun. They cherished animosity now, not against the Federals, but against mankind. The social world was their field of harvest; and they reaped It, weapon in hand.

The James family originally came from Kentucky, where Frank was born, in Scott County, in 1846. The father, Robert James, was a Baptist minister of the Gospel. He removed to Clay County, Missouri, in 1849, Jesse was born there in 1850. Reverend Robert James left for California in 1851 and never returned. The mother, a woman of great strength of character, later married a Doctor Samuels. She was much embittered by the persecution of her family, as she considered it. She herself lost an arm in an attack by detectives upon her home, in which a young son was killed. The family had many friends and confederates throughout the country; else the James boys must have found an end long before they were brought to justice.

From precisely the same surroundings came the Younger boys, Thomas Coleman, or "Cole," Younger, and his brothers, John, Bruce, James, and Robert. Their father was Henry W. Younger, who settled in Jackson County, Missouri, in 1825, and was known as a man of ability and worth. For eight years he was county judge, and was twice elected to the state legislature. He had fourteen children, of whom five certainly were bad. At one time he owned large bodies of land, and he was a prosperous merchant in Harrisonville for some time.

Cole Younger was born January 15, 1844, John in 1846, Bruce in 1848, James in 1850, and Bob in 1853. As these boys grew old enough, they joined the Quantrell bands, and their careers were precisely the same as those of the James boys. The cause of their choice of sides was the same. Jennison, the Kansas jayhawker leader, in one of his raids into Missouri, burned the houses of Younger and confiscated the horses in his livery stables. After that the boys of the family swore revenge.

At the close of the war, the Younger and James boys worked together very often, and were leaders of a band which had a cave in Clay county and numberless farm houses where they could expect shelter in need. With them, part of the time, were George and Ollie Shepherd; other members of their band were Bud Singleton, Bob Moore, Clel Miller and his brother, Arthur McCoy; others who came and went from time to time were regularly connected with the bigger operations. It would be wearisome to recount the long list of crimes these men committed for ten or fifteen years after the war. They certainly brought notoriety to their country. They had the entire press of America reproaching the State of Missouri; they had the governors of that state and two or three others at their wits' end; they had the best forces of the large city detective agencies completely baffled. They killed two detectives—one of whom, however, killed John Younger before he died—and executed another in cold blood under circumstances of repellent brutality.

They raided over Missouri, Kansas, Kentucky, Tennessee, even as far east as West Virginia, as far north as Minnesota, as far south as Texas and even old Mexico. They looted dozens of banks, and held up as many railway passenger trains and as many stage coaches and travellers as they liked. The James boys alone are known to have taken in their robberies $275,000, and, including the unlawful gains of their colleagues, the Youngers, no doubt they could have accounted for over half a million dollars. They laughed at the law, defied the state and county governments, and rode as they liked, here, there, and everywhere, until the name of law in the West was a mockery. If magnitude in crime be claim to distinction, they might ask the title, for surely their exploits were unrivalled, and perhaps cannot again be equalled. And they did all of these unbelievable things in the heart of the Mississippi valley, in a country thickly settled, in the face of a long reputation for criminal deeds, and in a country fully warned against them! Surely, it seems sometimes that American law is weak.

It was much the same story in all the long list of robberies of small country banks. A member of the gang would locate the bank and get an idea of the interior arrangements. Two or three of the gang would step in and ask to have a bill changed; then they would cover the cashier with revolvers and force him to open the safe. If he resisted, he was killed; sometimes killed no matter what he did, as was cashier Sheets in the Gallatin bank robbery. The guard outside kept the citizens terrified until the booty was secured; then flight on good horses followed.

After that ensued the frantic and unorganised pursuit by citizens and officers, possibly another killing or two *en route*, and a return to their lurking place in Clay County, Missouri, where they never had any difficulty in proving all the *alibis* they needed. None of these men ever confessed to a full list of these robberies, and, even years later, they all denied complicity; but the facts are too well known to warrant any attention to their denials, founded upon a very natural reticence. Of course, their safety lay in the sympathy of a large number of neighbours of something the same kidney; and fear of retaliation supplied the only remaining motive needed to enforce secrecy.

Some of the most noted bank robberies in which the above mentioned men, or some of them, were known to have been engaged were as follows: The Clay County Savings Association, of Liberty, Missouri, February 14, 1866, in which a little boy by name of Wymore was shot to pieces because he obeyed the orders of the bank cashier and gave the alarm; the bank of Alexander Mitchell & Co., Lexington, Missouri, October 30, 1860; the McLain Bank, of Savannah, Missouri, March 2, 1867, in which Judge McLain was shot and nearly killed; the Hughes & Mason Bank, of Richmond, Missouri, May 23, 1867, and the later attack on the jail, in which Mayor Shaw, Sheriff J. B. Griffin, and his brave fifteen-year-old boy were all killed; the bank of Russellville, Kentucky, March 20, 1868, in which cashier Long was badly beaten; the Daviess County Savings Bank, of Gallatin, Missouri, December 7, 1869, in which cashier John Sheets was brutally killed; the bank of Obocock Brothers, Corydon, Iowa, June 3, 1871, in which forty thousand dollars was taken, although no one was killed; the Deposit Bank, of Columbia, Missouri, April 29, 1872, in which cashier R. A. C. Martin was killed; the Savings Association, of Ste. Genevieve, Missouri; the Bank of Huntington, West Virginia, September 1, 1875, in which one of the bandits, McDaniels, was killed; the Bank of Northfield, Minnesota, September 7, 1876, in which cashier J. L. Haywood was killed, A. E. Bunker wounded, and several of the bandits killed and captured as later described.

These same men or some of them also robbed a stage coach now and then; near Hot Springs, Arkansas, for example, January 15, 1874, where they picked up four thousand dollars, and included ex-Governor Burbank, of Dakota, among their victims, taking from him alone fifteen hundred dollars; the San Antonio-Austin coach, in Texas, May 12, 1875, in which John Breckenridge, president of the First National Bank of San Antonio, was relieved of one thousand dollars; and the Mammoth Cave, Kentucky, stage, September 3, 1880, where they took nearly two thousand dollars in cash and jewellery from passengers of distinction.

The most daring of their work, however, and that which brought them into contact with the United States government for tampering with the mails, was their repeated robbery of railway mail trains, which became a matter of simplicity and certainty in their hands. To flag a train or to stop it with an obstruction; or to get aboard and mingle with the train crew, then to halt the train, kill anyone who opposed them, and force the opening of the express agent's safe, became a matter of routine with them in time, and the amount of cash they thus obtained was staggering in the total.

The most noted train robberies in which members of the James-Younger bands were engaged were the Rock Island train robbery near Council Bluffs, Iowa, July 21, 1873, in which engineer Rafferty was killed in the wreck, and but small booty secured; the Gad's Hill, Missouri, robbery of the Iron Mountain train, January 28, 1874, in which about five thousand dollars was secured from the express agent, mail bags and passengers; the Kansas-Pacific train robbery near Muncie, Kansas, December 12, 1874, in which they secured more than fifty-five thousand dollars in cash and gold dust, with much jewellery; the Missouri-Pacific train robbery at Rocky Cut, July 7, 1876, where they held the train for an hour and a quarter and secured about fifteen thousand dollars in all; the robbery of the Chicago & Alton train near Glendale, Missouri, October 7, 1879, in which the James boys' gang secured between thirty-five and fifty thousand dollars in currency; the robbery of the Rock Island train near Winston, Missouri, July 15, 1881, by the James boys' gang, in which conductor Westfall was killed, messenger Murray badly beaten, and a passenger named MacMillan killed, little booty being obtained; the Blue Cut robbery of the Alton train, September 7, 1881, in which the James boys and eight others searched every passenger and took away a two-bushel sack full of cash, watches, and jewellery, beating the express messenger badly because they got so little from the safe. This last robbery caused the resolution of Governor Crittenden, of Missouri, to take the bandits dead or alive, a reward of thirty thousand dollars being arranged by different railways and express companies, a price of ten thousand dollars each being put on the heads of Frank and Jesse James.

Outside of this long list of the bandit gang's deeds of outlawry, they were continually in smaller undertakings of a similar nature. Once they took away ten thousand dollars in cash at the box office of the Kansas City Fair, this happening September 26, 1872, in a crowded city, with all the modern machinery of the law to guard its citizens. Many acts at widely separated parts of the country were accredited to the Younger or the James boys, and although they cannot have been guilty of all of them, and, although many of the adventures accredited to them in Texas, Mexico, California, the Indian Nations, etc., bear earmarks of apocryphal origin, there is no doubt that for twenty years after the close of the civil war they made a living in this way, their gang being made up of perhaps a score of different men in all, and usually consisting of about six to ten men, according to the size of the undertaking on hand.

Meantime, all these years, the list of homicides for each of them was growing. Jesse James killed three men out of six who attacked his house one night, and not long after Frank and he are alleged to have killed six men in a gambling fight in California. John and Jim Younger killed the Pinkerton detectives Lull and Daniels, John being himself killed at that time by Daniels. A little later, Frank and Jesse James and Clel Miller killed Detective Wicher, of the same agency, torturing him for some time before his death in the attempt to make him divulge the Pinkerton plans. The James boys killed Daniel Askew in revenge; and Jesse James and Jim Anderson killed Ike Flannery for motives of robbery. This last set the gang into hostile camps, for Flannery was a nephew of George Shepherd. Shepherd later killed Anderson in Texas for his share in that act; he also shot Jesse James and for a long time supposed he had killed him.

The full record of these outlaws will never be known. Their career came to an end soon after the heavy rewards were put upon their heads, and it came in the usual way, through treachery. Allured by the prospect of gaining ten thousand dollars, two cousins of Jesse James, Bob and Charlie Ford, pretending to join his gang for another robbery, became members of Jesse James' household while he was living *incognito* as Thomas Howard. On the morning of April 3, 1882, Bob Ford, a mere boy, not yet twenty years of age, stepped behind Jesse James as he was standing on a chair dusting off a picture frame, and, firing at close range, shot him through the head and killed him. Bob Ford never got much respect for his act, and his money was soon gone. He himself was killed in February, 1892, at Creede, Colorado, by a man named Kelly.

Jesse James was about five feet ten inches in height, and weighed about one hundred and sixty-five pounds. His hair and eyes were brown. He had, during his life, been shot twice through the lungs, once through the leg, and had lost a finger of the left hand from a bullet wound. Frank James was slighter than his brother, with light hair and blue eyes, and a ragged, reddish moustache. Frank surrendered to Governor Crittenden himself at Jefferson City, in October, 1882,

THE OLD FRITZ RANCH

A BORDER FORTRESS

taking off his revolvers and saying that no man had touched them but himself since 1861. He was sentenced to the penitentiary for life, but later pardoned, as he was thought to be dying of consumption.

At this writing, he is still alive, somewhat old and bent now, but leading a quiet and steady life, and showing no disposition to return to his old ways. He is sometimes seen around the race tracks, where he does but little talking. Frank James has had many apologists, and his life should be considered in connection with the environments in which he grew up. He killed many men, but he was never as cold and cruel as Jesse, and of the two he was the braver man, men say who knew them both. He never was known to back down under any circumstances.

The fate of the Younger boys was much mingled with that of the James boys, but the end of the careers of the former came in more dramatic fashion. The wonder is that both parties should have clung together so long, for it is certain that Cole Younger once intended to kill Jesse James, and one night he came near killing George Shepherd through malicious statements Jesse James had made to him about the latter. Shepherd met Cole at the house of a friend named Hudspeth, in Jackson County, and their host put them in the same bed that night for want of better accommodations.

Shepherd said later, in describing this:

> After we lay down, I saw Cole reach up under his pillow and draw out a pistol, which he put beside him under the cover. Not to be taken unawares, I at once grasped my own pistol and shoved it down under the covers beside me. Were it to save my life, I couldn't tell what reason Cole had for becoming my enemy. We talked very little, but just lay there watching each other. He was behind and I on the front side of the bed, and during the entire night we looked into each other's eyes and never moved. It was the most wretched night I ever passed in my life.

So much may at times be the price of being "bad." By good fortune, they did not kill each other, and the next day Cole told Shepherd that he had expected him to shoot on sight, as Jesse James had said he would. Explanations then followed. It nearly came to a collision between Cole Younger and Jesse James later, for Cole challenged him to fight, and it was only with difficulty that their friends accommodated the matter.

The history of the Younger boys is tragic all the way through. Their father was assassinated, their mother was forced to set fire to her own house and destroy it under penalty of death; three sisters were arrested and confined in a barracks at Kansas City, which during a high wind fell in, killed two of the girls and crippled the other. John Younger was a murderer at the age of fourteen, and how many times Cole Younger was a murderer, with or without his wish, will never be known. He was shot three times in one fight in guerrilla days, and probably few bad men ever carried off more lead than he.

The story of the Northfield bank robbery in Minnesota, which ended so disastrously to the bandits who undertook it, is interesting as showing what brute courage, and, indeed, what fidelity and fortitude may at times be shown by dangerous specimens of bad men. The purpose of the robbery was criminal, its carrying out was attended with murder, and the revenge for it came sharp and swift. In all the annals of desperadoes, there is not a battle more striking than this which occurred in a sleepy and contented little village in the quiet northern farming country, where no one for a moment dreamed that the bandits of the rumoured bloody lands along the Missouri would ever trouble themselves to come. The events immediately connected with this tragedy, the result of which was the ending of the Younger gang, were as hereinafter described.

Bill Chadwell, *alias* Styles, a member of the James boys gang, had formerly lived in Minnesota. He drew a pleasing picture of the wealth of that country, and the ease with which it could be obtained by bandit methods. Cole Younger was opposed to going so far from home, but was overruled. He finally joined the others—Frank and Jesse James, Clel Miller, Jim and Bob Younger, Charlie Pitts and Chadwell. They went to Minnesota by rail, and, after looking over the country, purchased good horses, and prepared to raid the little town of Northfield, in Rice County. They carried their enterprise into effect on September 7, 1876, using methods with which earlier experience had made them familiar. They rode into the middle of the town and opened fire, ordering every one off the streets.

Jesse James, Charlie Pitts and Bob Younger entered the bank, where they found cashier J. L. Haywood, with two clerks, Frank Wilcox and A. E. Bunker. Bunker started to run, and Bob Younger shot him through the shoulder. They ordered Haywood to open the safe, but he bluntly refused, even though they slightly cut him in the throat to enforce obedience. Firing now began from the citizens on the street, and the bandits in the bank hurried in their work, contenting themselves with such loose cash as they found in the drawers and on the counter. As they started to leave the bank, Haywood made a motion toward a drawer as if to find a weapon. Jesse James turned and shot him through the head, killing him instantly.

These three of the bandits then sprang out into the street. They were met by the fire of Doctor Wheeler and several other citizens. Hide, Stacey, Manning and Bates. Doctor Wheeler was across the street in an upstairs room, and as Bill Chadwell undertook to mount his horse, Wheeler fired and shot him dead. Manning fired at Clel Miller, who had mounted, and shot him from his horse. Cole Younger was by this time ready to retreat, but he rode up to Miller, and removed from his body his belt and pistols. Manning fired again, and killed the horse behind which Bob Younger was hiding, and an instant later a shot from Wheeler struck Bob in the right elbow. Although this arm was disabled Bob shifted his pistol to his left hand and fired at Bates, cutting a furrow through his cheek, but not killing him. About this time a Norwegian by the name of Gustavson appeared on the street, and not halting at the order to do so, he was shot through the head by one of the bandits, receiving a wound from which he died a few days later. The gang then began to scatter and retreat. Jim Younger was on foot and was wounded. Cole rode back up the street, and took the wounded man on his horse behind him. The entire party then rode out of town to the west, not one of them escaping without severe wounds.

As soon as the bandits had departed, news was sent by telegraph, notifying the surrounding country of the robbery. Sheriffs, policemen and detectives rallied in such numbers that the robbers were hard put to it to escape alive. A state reward of $1,000 for each was published, and all lower Minnesota organised Itself into a determined man hunt. The gang undertook to get over the Iowa line, and they managed to keep away from their pursuers until the morning of the 13th, a week after the robbery. The six survivors were surrounded on that day in a strip of timber. Frank and Jesse James broke through, riding the same horse. They were fired upon, a bullet striking Frank James in the right knee, and passing through into Jesse's right thigh. None the less, the two got away, stole a horse apiece that night, and passed on to the Southwest. They rode bareback, and now and again enforced a horse trade with a farmer or livery-stable man. They got down near Sioux Falls, and there met Doctor Mosher, whom they compelled to dress their wounds, and to furnish them horses and clothing. Later on, their horses gave out, and they hired a wagon and kept on. Their escape seems incomprehensible, yet it is the case that they got quite clear, finally reaching Missouri.

Of the other bandits there were left Cole, Jim and Bob Younger and Charlie Pitts; and after these a large number of citizens followed close. In spite of the determined pursuit, they kept out of reach for another week. On the morning of September 21st, two weeks after the robbery, they were located in the woods along the Watonwan River, not far from Madelia. Sheriff Glispin hurriedly got together a posse and surrounded them in a patch of timber not over five acres in extent. In a short time, more than one hundred and fifty men, were about this cover; but although they kept up firing, they could not drive out the concealed bandits. Sheriff Glispin called for volunteers; and with Colonel Vaught, Ben Rice, George Bradford, James Severson, Charles Pomeroy and Captain Murphy moved into the cover.

As they advanced, Charlie Pitts sprang out from the brush, and fired point blank at Glispin. At the same Instant the latter also fired and shot Pitts, who ran a short distance and fell dead. Then Cole, Bob and Jim Younger stood up and opened fire as best they could, all of the men of the storming party returning their fire. Murphy was struck in the body by a bullet, and his life was saved by his pipe, which he carried in his vest pocket. Another member of the posse had his watch blown to pieces by a bullet. The Younger boys gave back a little, but this brought them within sight of those surrounding the thicket, so they retreated again close to the line of the volunteers. Cole and Jim Younger were now badly shot. Bob, with his broken right arm, stood his ground, the only one able to continue the fight, and kept his revolver going with his left hand. The others handed him their revolvers after his own was empty.

The firing from the posse still continued, and at last Bob called out to them to stop, as his brothers were all shot to pieces. He threw down his pistol, and walked forward to the sheriff, to whom he surrendered. Bob always spoke with respect of Sheriff Glispin both as a fighter and as a peace officer. One of the farmers drew up his gun to kill Bob after he had surrendered, but Glispin told him to drop his gun or he would kill him.

It is doubtful if any set of men ever showed more determination and more ability to stand punishment than these misled outlaws. Bob Younger was hurt less than any of the others. His arm had been broken at Northfield two weeks before, but he was wounded but once, slightly in the body, out of all the shots fired at him while in the thicket. Cole Younger had a rifle bullet in the right cheek, which paralyzed his right eye. He had received a .45 revolver bullet through the body, and also had been shot through the thigh at Northfield. He received eleven different wounds in the fight, or thirteen bad wounds in all, enough to have killed a half dozen men. Jim's case seemed even worse, for he had in his body eight buckshot and a rifle bullet. He had been shot through the shoulder at Northfield, and nearly half his lower jaw had been carried away by a heavy bullet, a wound which caused him intense suffering. Bob was the only one able to stand on his feet.

Of the two men killed in town, Clel Miller and Bill Chadwell, the former had a long record in bank robberies; the latter, guide in the ill-fated expedition to Minnesota, was a horse thief of considerable note at one time in lower Minnesota.

The prisoners were placed in jail at Faribault, the county seat of Rice County, and in a short time the Grand Jury returned true bills against them, charging them with murder and robbery. Court convened November 7th, Judge Lord being on the bench. All of the prisoners pleaded guilty, and the order of the court was that each should be confined in the state penitentiary for the period of his natural life.

The later fate of the Younger boys may be read in the succinct records of the Minnesota State Prison at Stillwater:

> Thos. Coleman Younger, sentenced Nov. 20, 1876, from Rice County under a life sentence for the crime of Murder in the first degree. Paroled July 14, 1901. Pardoned Feb. 4, 1903, on condition that he leave the State of Minnesota, and that he never exhibit himself in public in any way.
>
> James Younger, sentenced Nov. 20, 1876, from Rice County under a life sentence for the crime of Murder in the first degree. Paroled July 13, 1901. Shot himself with a revolver in the city of St. Paul, Minn., and died at once from the wound inflicted on Oct. 19, 1902.
>
> Robt. Younger, sentenced Nov. 20, 1876, from Rice County under a life sentence for the crime of Murder in the first degree. He died Sept. 16, 1889, of phthisis.

The James boys almost miraculously escaped, travelled clear across the State of Iowa and got back to their old haunts. They did not stop, but kept on going until they got to Mexico, where they remained for some time. They did not take their warning, however, and some of their most desperate train robberies were committed long after the Younger boys were in the penitentiary.

In view of the bloody careers of all these men, it is to be said that the law has been singularly lenient with them. Yet the Northfield Incident was conclusive, and was the worst back-set ever received by any gang of bad men; unless, perhaps, that was the defeat of the Dalton gang at Coffeyville, Kansas, some years later, the story of which is given in the following chapter.

(*The James and Younger Brothers: the Story of One the Most Notorious and Legendary Outlaw Gangs of the American West*, by J. A. Dacus is also published by Leonaur.)

CHAPTER 21

# Bad Men of the Indian Nations

What is true for Texas, in the record of desperadoism, is equally applicable to the country adjoining Texas upon the north, long known under the general title of the Indian Nations; although it is now rapidly being divided and allotted under the increasing demands of an ever-advancing civilization.

The great breeding ground of outlaws has ever been along the line of demarcation between the savage and the civilized. Here in the Indian country, as though in a hotbed especially contrived, the desperado has flourished for generations. The Indians themselves retained much their old savage standards after they had been placed in this supposedly perpetual haven of refuge by the government. They have been followed, ever since the first movement of the tribes into these reservations, by numbers of unscrupulous whites such as hang on the outskirts of the settlements and rebel at the requirements of civilization.

Many white men of certain type married among the Indians, and the half-breed is reputed as a product inheriting the bad traits of both races and the good ones of neither—a sweeping statement not always wholly true. Among these also was a large infusion of negro blood, emanating from the slaves brought in by the Cherokees, and added to later by negroes moving in and marrying among the tribes. These mixed bloods seem to have been little disposed toward the ways of law and order. Moreover, the system of law was here, of course, altogether different from that of the States. The freedom from restraint, the exemption from law, which always marked the border, here found their last abiding place.

The Indians were not adherents to the white man's creed, save as to the worst features, and they kept their own creed of blood. No man will ever know how many murders have been committed in these fair and pleasant *savannahs*, among these rough hills or upon these rolling grassy plains from the time William Clark, the "Red Head Chief," began the government work of settling the tribes in these lands, then supposed to be far beyond the possible demands of the white population of America.

Life could be lived here with small exertion. The easy gifts of the soil and the chase, coupled with the easy gifts of the government, unsettled the minds of all from those habits of steady industry and thrift which go with the observance of the law. If one coveted his neighbour's possessions, the ready arbitrament of firearms told whose were the spoils. Human life has been cheap here for more than half a hundred years; and this condition has endured directly up to and into the days of white civilization. The writer remembers very well that in his hunting expeditions of twenty years ago it was always held dangerous to go into the Nations; and this was true whether parties went in across the Neutral Strip, or farther east among the Osages or the Creeks.

The country below Coffeyville was wild and remote as we saw it then, although now it is settling up, is traversed by railroads, and is slowly passing into the hands of white men in severalty, as fast as the negroes release their lands, or as fast as the government allows the Indians to give individual titles. In those days it was a matter of small concern if a traveller never returned from a journey among the timber clad mountains, or the black jack thickets along the rivers; and many was the murder committed thereabouts that never came to light.

In and around the Indian Nations there have also always been refugees from the upper frontier or from Texas or Arkansas. The country was long the natural haven of the lawless, as it has long been the designated home of a wild population. In this region the creed has been much the same even after the wild ethics of the cow men yielded to the scarcely more lawful methods of the land boomer.

Each man in the older days had his own notion of personal conduct, as each had his own opinions about the sacredness of property. It was natural that train robbing and bank looting should become recognised industries when the railroads and towns came into this fertile region, so long left sacred to the chase. The gangs of such men as the Cook boys, the Wickcliffe boys, or the Dalton boys, were natural and logical products of an environment. That this should be the more likely may be seen from the fact that for a decade or more preceding the great rushes of the land grabbers, the exploits of the James and Younger boys in train and bank robbing had filled all the country with the belief that the law could be defied successfully through a long term of years. The Cook boys acted upon this basis, until at length marshals shot them both, killed one and sent the remnants of the other to the penitentiary.

Since it would be impossible to go into any detailed mention of the scores and hundreds of desperadoes who have at different times been produced by the Nations, it may be sufficient to give a few of the salient features of the careers of the band which, as well as any, may be called typical of the Indian Nations brand of desperadoism—the once notorious Dalton boys.

The Dalton family lived in lower Kansas, near Coffeyville, which was situated almost directly upon the border of the Nations. They engaged in farming, and indeed two of the family were respectable farmers near Coffeyville within the last three or four years. The mother of the family still lives near Oklahoma City, where she secured a good claim at the time of the opening of the Oklahoma lands to white settlement. The father, Lewis Dalton, was a Kentucky man and served in the Mexican war.

He later moved to Jackson County, Missouri, near the home of the notorious James and Younger boys, and in 1851 married Adelaide Younger, they removing some years later from Missouri to Kansas. Thirteen children were born to them, nine sons and four daughters. Charles, Henry, Littleton and Coleman Dalton were respected and quiet citizens. All the boys had nerve, and many of them reached office as deputy marshals. Franklin Dalton was killed while serving as deputy United States marshal near Fort Smith, in 1887, his brother Bob being a member of the same posse at the time his fight was made with a band of horse thieves who resisted arrest. Grattan Dalton, after the death of his brother Franklin, was made a deputy United States marshal, after the curious but efficient Western fashion of setting dangerous men to work at catching dangerous men.

He and his posse in 1888 went after a bad Indian, who, in the melee, shot Grattan in the arm and escaped. Grattan later served as United States deputy marshal in Muskogee district, where the courts certainly needed men of stern courage as executives, for they had to deal with the most desperate and fearless class of criminals the world ever knew. Robert R. Dalton, better known as Bob Dalton, served on the posses of his brothers, and soon learned what it was to stand up and shoot while being shot at. He turned out to be about the boldest of the family, and was accepted as the clan leader later on in their exploits. He also was a deputy United States marshal at the dangerous stations of Fort Smith and Wichita, having much to do with the desperadoes of the Nations. He was chief of the Osage police for some time, and saw abundance of violent scenes.

Emmett Dalton was also possessed of cool nerve, and was soon known as a dangerous man to affront. All the boys were good shots, but they seemed to have cared more for the Winchester than the six-shooter in their exploits. In which they were perhaps wise, for the rifle is of course far the surer when it is possible of use; and men mostly rode in that country with rifle under leg. Uncle Sam is obliged to take such material for his frontier peace officers as proves itself efficient in serving processes. A coward may be highly moral, but he will not do as a border deputy. The personal character of some of the most famous Western deputies would scarcely bear careful scrutiny, but the government at Washington is often obliged to wink at that sort of thing. There came a time when it remained difficult longer to wink at the methods of the Daltons as deputies. In one case they ran off with a big bunch of horses and sold them in a Kansas town.

On account of this episode, Grattan, William, and Emmett Dalton made a hurried trip to California. Here they became restless, and went back at their old trade, thinking that no one even on the Pacific Slope had any right to cause them fear. They held up a train in Tulare county and killed a fireman, but were repulsed. Later arrested and tried, William was cleared, but Grattan was sentenced to twenty years in the penitentiary. He escaped from jail before he got to the penitentiary, and rejoined Emmett at the old haunts in the Nations, Emmett having evaded arrest in California. The Southern Pacific railway had a standing offer of $6,000 for the robbers at the time they were killed.

The Daltons were now more or less obliged to hide out, and to make a living as best they could, which meant by robbery. On May 9, 1891, the Santa Fé train was held up at Wharton, Oklahoma Territory, and the express car was robbed, the bandits supposedly being the Daltons. In June of the following year another Santa Fé train was robbed at Red Rock, in the Cherokee strip. The 'Frisco train was robbed at Vinita, Indian Territory. An epidemic of the old methods of the James and Younger bands seemed to have broken out in the new railway region of the Southwest. The next month the Missouri, Kansas and Texas train was held up at Adair, Indian Territory, and a general fight ensued between the robbers and the armed guard of the train, assisted by citizens of the town.

A local physician was killed and several officers and citizens wounded, but none of the bandits was hurt, and they got away with a heavy loot of the express and baggage cars. At Wharton they had been less fortunate, for though they killed the station agent, they were rounded up and one of their men, Dan Bryant, was captured, later killing and being killed by United States Deputy Ed. Short, as mentioned in an earlier chapter. Dick Broadwell joined the Dalton gang about now, and they nearly always had a few members besides those of their own family; their gang being made up and conducted on much the same lines of the James boys gang of Missouri, whose exploits they imitated and used as text for their bolder deeds. In fact, it was the boast of the leader, Bob Dalton, in the Coffeyville raid, that he was going to beat anything the James boys ever did: to rob two banks in one town at the same time.

Bank robbing was a side line of activity with the Daltons, but they did fairly well at it. They held up the bank at El Reno, at a time when no one was in the bank except the president's wife, and took $10,000, obliging the bank to suspend business. By this time the whole country was aroused against them, as it had been against the James and Younger boys. Pinkerton detectives had blanket commissions offered, and railway and express companies offered rewards running into the thousands. Each train across the Indian Nations was accompanied for months by a heavily armed guard concealed in the baggage and express cars.

Passengers dreaded the journey across that country, and the slightest halt of the train for any cause was sure to bring to the lips of all the word of fear, "the Daltons!" it seems almost incredible of belief that, in these modern days of fast railway service, of the telegraph and of rapidly increasing settlements, the work of these men could so long have been continued; but such, none the less, was the case. The law was powerless, and demonstrated its own unfitness to safeguard life and property, as so often it has in this country. And, as so often has been the case, outraged society at length took the law into its own hands and settled the matter.

The full tale of the Dalton robberies and murders will never be known, for the region in which they operated was reticent, having its own secrets to protect; but at last there came the climax in which the band was brought into the limelight of civilized publicity. They lived on the border of savagery and civilization. Now the press, the telegraph, the whole fabric of modern life, lay near at hand. Their last bold raid, therefore, in which they crossed from the country of reticence into that of garrulous news gathering, made them more famous than they had ever been before. The raid on Coffeyville, October 5, 1892, both established and ended their reputation as desperadoes of the border.

The rumour got out that the Daltons were down in the Nations, waiting for a chance to raid the town of Coffeyville, but the dreaded attack did not come off when it was expected. When it was delivered, therefore, it found the town quite unprepared. Bob Dalton was the leader in this enterprise. Emmett did not want to go. He declared that too many people knew them in Coffeyville, and that the job would prove too big for them to handle. He consented to join the party, however, when he found Bob determined to make the attempt in any case. There were in the band at that time Bob, Emmett, and Grattan Dalton, Bill Powers and Dick Broadwell. These lay in rendezvous near Tulsa, in the Osage country, two days before the raid, and spent the night before in the timber on Onion creek, not far below town. They rode into Coffeyville at half-past nine the following morning. The street being somewhat torn up, they turned aside into an alley about a hundred yards from the main street, and, dismounting, tied their horses, which were thus left some distance from the banks, the First National and the bank of C. M. Condon & Co., which were the objects of their design.

Grattan Dalton, Dick Broadwell and Bill Powers stepped over to the Condon bank, which was occupied at the time by C. T. Carpenter, C. M. Ball, the cashier, and T. C. Babb, a bookkeeper. Grattan Dalton threw down his rifle on Carpenter, with the customary command to put up his hands; the others being attended to by Powers and Broadwell. Producing a two-bushel sack, the leader ordered Carpenter to put all the cash into it, and the latter obeyed, placing three thousand dollars in silver and one thousand in currency in the sack. Grattan wanted the gold, and demanded that an inner safe inside the vault should be opened.

The cashier, Ball, with a shifty falsehood, told him that they could not open that safe, for it was set on a time lock, and no one could open it before half-past nine o'clock. He told the outlaw that it was now twenty minutes after nine (although it was really twenty minutes of ten); and the latter said they could wait ten minutes. He was, however, uneasy, and was much of the mind to kill Ball on the spot, for he suspected treachery, and knew how dangerous any delay must be.

It was a daring thing to do—to sit down in the heart of a civilized city, in broad daylight and on the most public street, and wait for a time lock to open a burglar-proof safe. Daring as it was, it was foolish and futile. As the robbers stood uneasily guarding their prisoners, the alarm was spread. A moment later firing began, and the windows of the bank were splintered with bullets. The robbers were trapped, Broadwell being now shot through the arm, probably by P. L. Williams from across the street. Yet they coolly went on with their work as they best could, Grattan Dalton ordering Ball to cut the string of the bag and pour out the heavy silver, which would have encumbered them too much in their flight. He asked If there was not a back way out, by which they could escape. He was shown a rear door, and the robbers stepped out, to find themselves in the middle of the hottest street fight any of them had ever known. The city marshal, Charles T. Connolly, had given the alarm, and citizens were hurrying to the street with such weapons as they could find at the hardware stores and in their own homes.

Meantime Bob and Emmett Dalton had held up the First National Bank, ordering cashier Ayres to hand out the money, and terrorizing two or three customers of the bank who happened to be present at the time. Bob knew Thos. G. Ayres, and called him by his first name, "Tom," said he, "go into the safe and get out that money—get the gold, too." He followed Ayres into the vault, and discovered two packages of $5,000 each in currency, which he tossed into his meal sack. The robbers here also poured out the silver, and having cleaned up the bank as they supposed, drove the occupants out of the door in front of them. As they got into the street they were fired upon by George Cubine and C. S. Cox; but neither shot took effect.

Emmett Dalton stood with his rifle under his arm, coolly tying up the neck of the sack which held the money. They then both stepped back into the bank, and went out through the back door, which was opened for them by W. H. Shepherd, the bank teller, who, with Tom Ayres and B. S. Ayres, the bookkeeper, made the bank force on hand. J. H. Brewster, C. H. Hollingsworth and A. W. Knotts were in the bank on business, and were joined by E. S. Boothby; all these being left unhurt.

The firing became general as soon as the robbers emerged from the two bank buildings. The first man to be shot by the robbers was

Charles T. Gump, who stood not far from the First National Bank armed with a shotgun. Before he could fire Bob Dalton shot him through the hand, the same bullet disabling his shotgun. A moment later, a young man named Lucius Baldwin started down the alley, armed with a revolver. He met Bob and Emmett, who ordered him to halt, but for some reason he kept on toward them. Bob Dalton said, "I'll have to kill you," and so shot him through the chest. He died three hours later.

Bob and Emmett Dalton now passed out of the alley back of the First National Bank, and came into Union street. Here they saw George B. Cubine standing with his Winchester in his hands, and an instant later Cubine fell dead, with three balls through his body. Near him was Charles Brown, an old man, who was also armed. He was the next victim, his body falling near that of Cubine, though he lived for a few hours after being shot. All four of these victims of the Daltons were shot at distances of about forty or fifty yards, and with rifles, the revolver being more or less uncertain at such ranges even in practiced hands. All the gang had revolvers, but none used them.

Thos. G. Ayres, late prisoner in the First National Bank, ran into a store nearby as soon as he was released, caught up a Winchester and took a station near the street door, waiting for the bandits to come out at that entrance of the bank. Here he was seen by Bob Dalton, who had gone through the alley. Bob took aim and at seventy-five yards shot Ayres through the head. Friends tried to draw his body back into the store, but these now met the fire of Grattan Dalton and Powers, who, with the crippled Broadwell, were now coming out of their alleyway.

T. A. Reynolds, a clerk in the same store, who went to the door armed, received a shot through the foot, and thus made the third wounded man then in that building. H. H. Isham, one of the owners of the store, aided by M. A. Anderson and Charles K. Smith, joined in the firing. Grattan Dalton and Bill Powers were shot mortally before they had gone more than a few steps from the door of the Condon bank. Powers tried to get into a door when he was shot, and kept his feet when he found the door locked, managing to get to his horse in the alley before he was killed by a second shot. Grattan Dalton also kept his feet, and reached cover back of a barn about seventy yards from Walnut Street, the main thoroughfare. He stood at bay here, and kept on firing.

City marshal Connolly, carrying a rifle, ran across to a spot near the corner of this barn. He had his eye on the horses of the bandits, which were still hitched in the alley. His back was turned toward Grattan Dalton. The latter must have been crippled somewhere in his right arm or shoulder, for he did not raise his rifle to his face, but fired from his hip, shooting Connolly down at a distance of about twenty feet or so.

There was a slight lull at this point of the street fight, and during this Dick Broadwell, who had been wounded again in the back, crawled into concealment in a lumber yard near by the alley where the horses were tied. He crept out to his horse and mounted, but just as he started away met the livery man, John J. Kloehr, who did some of the best shooting recorded by the citizens. Kloehr was hurrying thither with Carey Seaman, the latter armed with a shotgun. Kloehr fired his rifle and Seaman his shotgun, and both struck Broadwell, who rode away, but fell dead from his horse a short distance outside the town.

Bob and Emmett Dalton, after killing Cubine and Brown and shooting Ayres, hurried on to join their companions and to get to their horses. At an alleyway junction they spied F. D. Benson climbing out of a window, and fired at him, but missed. An instant later, as Bob stepped into full view of those who were firing from the Isham store, he was struck by a ball and badly wounded. He walked slowly across the alley and sat down on a pile of stones, but like his brother Grattan, he kept his rifle going, though mortally shot. He fired once at Kloehr, but was unsteady and missed him. Rising to his feet he walked a few paces and leaned against the corner of a barn, firing two more shots. He was then killed by Kloehr, who shot him through the chest.

By this time Grattan Dalton was feebly trying to get to his horse. He passed the body of Connolly, whom he had killed, faced toward his pursuers and tried to fire. He, too, fell before Kloehr's Winchester, shot through the throat, dropping close to the body of Connolly.

Emmett Dalton was now the only one of the band left alive. He was as yet unwounded, and he got to his horse. As he attempted to mount a number of shots were fired at him, and these killed the two horses belonging to Bob Dalton and Bill Powers, who by this time had no further use for horses. Two horses hitched to an oil wagon in the street were also killed by wild shots.

Emmett got into his saddle, but was shot through the right arm and through the left hip and groin. He still clung to the sack of money they had taken at the First National Bank, and he still kept his nerve and his wits even under such pressure of peril. He might have escaped, but instead he rode back to where Bob was lying, and reached down his hand to help him up behind himself on the horse. Bob was dying and told him it was no use to try to help him. As Emmett stooped down to reach Bob's arm, Carey Seaman fired both barrels of his shotgun into his back, Emmett dropping near Bob and falling upon the sack, containing over $20,000 in cash. Men hurried up and called to him to throw up his hands. He raised his one unhurt arm and begged for mercy. It was supposed he would die, and he was not lynched, but hurried away to a doctor's office nearby.

In the little alley where the last scene of this bloody fight took place there were found three dead men, one dying man and one badly wounded. Three dead horses lay near the same spot. In the whole fight, which was of course all over in a few moments, there were killed four citizens and four outlaws, three citizens and one outlaw being wounded. Less than a dozen citizens did most of the shooting, of which there was considerable, eighty bullet marks being found on the front of the Condon bank alone.

The news of this bloody encounter was instantly flashed over the country, and within a few hours the town was crowded with sightseers who came in by train loads. The dead bandits were photographed, and the story of the fight was told over and over again, not always with uniformity of detail. Emmett Dalton, before he was sent to the penitentiary, confessed to different crimes, not all of them hitherto known, which the gang had at different times committed.

So, ended in blood the career of as bloody a band as might well be discovered in the robber history of any land or time of the world. Indeed, it is doubtful if any country ever saw leagues of robbers so desperate as those which have existed in America, any with hands so red in blood. This fact is largely due to the peculiar history of this country, with its rapid development under swift modern methods of transportation. In America the advance to the westward of the fighting edge of civilization, where it meets and mingles with savagery, has been more rapid than has ever been known in the settlement of any country of the world.

Moreover, this has taken place at precisely that time when weapons of the most deadly nature have been invented and made at a price permitting all to own them and many to become extremely skilled with them. The temptation and the means of murder have gone hand in hand. And in time the people, not the organised law courts, have applied the remedy when the time has come for it. Today, (1905), the Indian Nations are no more than a name. Civilization has taken them over. Statehood has followed territorial organisation. Presently rich farms will make a continuous sea of grain across what was once a flood of crime, and the wheat will grow yellow, and the cotton white, where so long the grass was red.

Chapter 22

# Desperadoes of the Cities

It was stated early in these pages that the great cities and the great wildernesses are the two homes for bold crimes; but we have been most largely concerned with the latter in our studies of desperadoes and in our search for examples of disregard of the law. We have found a turbulence, a self-insistence, a vigour and self-reliance in the American character which at times has led on to lawlessness on our Western frontier.

Conditions have changed. We still revel in Wild West literature, but there is little of the wild left in the West of today, little of the old lawlessness. The most lawless time of America is today, (1905), but the most lawless parts of America are the most highly civilized parts. The most dangerous section of America is not the West, but the East.

The worst men are no longer those of the mountains or the plains, but of the great cities. The most absolute lawlessness exists under the shadow of the tallest temples of the law, and in the penetralia of that society which vaunts itself as the supreme civilization of the world. We have had no purpose in these pages to praise any sort of crime or to glorify any manner of bad deeds; but if we were forced to make choice among criminals, then by all means that choice should be, must be, not the brutal murderer of the cities, but the desperado of the old West. The one is an assassin, the other was a warrior; the one is a dastard, the other was something of a man.

A lawlessness which arises to magnitude is not called lawlessness; and killing more than murder is called war. The great industrial centres show us what ruthlessness may mean, more cruel and more dangerous than the worst deeds of our border fighting men. As for the criminal records of our great cities, they surpass by Infinity those of the rudest wilderness anarchy. Their nature at times would cause a hardened desperado of the West to blush for shame.

One distinguished feature of city badness is the great number of crimes against women, ranging from robbery to murder. Now, the desperado, the bandit, the robber of the wildest West never made war on any woman, rarely ever robbed a woman, even when women mingled with the victims of a "stand and deliver" general robbery of a stage or train. The man who would kill a woman in the West could never meet his fellow in fair fight again. The rope was ready for him, and that right quickly.

But how is it in the great cities, under the shadow of the law? Forget the crimes of industrialism, the sweat-shops and factories, which undermine the last hope of a nation—the constitution of its women—and take the open and admitted crimes. One city will suffice for this, and that may be the city of Chicago.

In Chicago, in the past twenty-four years, very nearly two thousand murders have been committed; and of these, two hundred remain mysteries today, (1905), their perpetrators having gone free and undetected. In the past year, seventeen women have been murdered in Chicago, some under circumstances too horrible to mention. In a list of fifty murders by unknown parties during the last few years, the whole gamut of dastardly crime has been run. The slaughter list is appalling. The story of this killing of women is so repellent that one turns to the bloodiest deeds of Western personal combats with a feeling of relief; and as one does so one adds, "Here at least were men."

The story of Chicago is little worse, according to her population, than that of New York, of Boston, of any large city. Foot up the total of the thousands of murders committed every year in America. Then, if you wish to become a criminal statistician, compare that record with those of England, France or Germany. We kill ten persons to England's one; and we kill them in the cities.

In the cities it is unlawful to wear arms, and to protect one's self against armed attack is therefore impossible. In the cities we have policemen. Against real fighting men, the average policeman would be helpless. Yet, such as he is, he must be the sole fence against the bloody-minded who do not scruple at robbery and murder. In the labour riots, the streets of a city are avenues of anarchy, and none of our weak-souled officials, held in the cursed thrall of politics, seems able to prevent it. A dozen town marshals of the old stripe would restore peace and fill a graveyard in one day of any strike; and their peace would be permanent. A real town marshal at the head of a city police force, with real fighting men under him, could restore peace and fill a graveyard in one month in any city; and that peace would be permanent. If we wished the law, we could have it.

The history of the bloodiest lawlessness of the American past shows continual repetitions. First, liberty is construed to mean license, and license unrebuked leads on to insolence. Still left unrebuked, license organises against the law, taking the form of gangs, factions, bandit clans. Then in time the spirit of law arises, and not the law, but the offended individuals wronged by too much license, take the matter into their own hands, not waiting for the courts, but executing a swifter justice. It is the terror of lynch law which has, in countless instances, been the foundation of the later courts, with their slow moving and absurdly inefficient methods.

In time the inefficiency of the courts once more begets impatience and contempt. The people again rebel at the fact that their government gives them no government, that their courts give them no justice, that their peace officers give them no protection. Then they take matters into their hands once more, and show both courts and criminals that the people still are strong and terrible.

The deprecation of lynch law, and the whining cry that the law should be supported, that the courts should pass on the punishment, is in the first place the plea of the weak, and in the second place, the plea of the ignorant. He has not read the history of this country, and has never understood the American character who says lynch law is wrong. It has been the salvation of America a thousand times. It may perhaps again be her salvation.

In one way or another the American people will assert the old vigilante principle that a man's life, given him by God, and a man's property, earned by his own labour, are things he is entitled to defend or have defended. He never wholly delegates this right to any government. He may rescind his qualified delegation when he finds his chosen servants unfaithful or inefficient; and so, have back again clean his own great and imperishable human rights. A wise law and one enforced is tolerable. An unjust and impure law is intolerable, and it is no wrong to cast off allegiance to it. If so, Magna Charta was wrong, and the American Revolution earth's greatest example of lynch law!

Conclusions parallel to these are expressed by no less a citizen than Andrew D. White, long United States Minister to Germany, who, in the course of an address at a prominent university of America, in the year 1906, made the following bold remarks:

"AFTERWARD"
(Fritz Graveyard, New Mexico. Many victims of the Lincoln County War buried here)

There is a well-defined criminal class in all of our cities; a class of men who make crime a profession. Deaths by violence are increasing rapidly. Our record is now larger than any other country of the world. The number of homicides that are punished by lynching exceeds the number punished by due process of law. There is nothing more nonsensical or ridiculous than the goody-goody talk about lynching. Much may be said in favour of Goldwin Smith's quotation, that 'there are communities in which lynch law is better than any other.'

The pendulum has swung from extreme severity in the last century to extreme laxity in this century. There has sprung up a certain sentimental sympathy. In the word of a distinguished jurist, 'the taking of life for the highest crime after due process of law is the only taking of life which the American people condemn.'

In the next year 9,000 people will be murdered. As I stand here today I tell you that 9,000 are doomed to death with all the cruelty of the criminal heart, and with no regard for home and families; and two-thirds will be due to the maudlin sentiment sometimes called mercy.

I have no sympathy for the criminal. My sympathy is for those who will be murdered; for their families and for their children. This sham humanitarianism has become a stench. The cry now is for righteousness. The past generation has abolished human slavery. It is for the present to deal with the problems of the future, and among them this problem of crime.

Against doctrine of this sort none will protest but the politicians in power, under whose lax administration of a great trust there has arisen one of the saddest spectacles of human history, the decay of the great American principles of liberty and fair play. The criminals of our city are bold, because they, if not ourselves, know of this decay. They, if not ourselves, know the weakness of that political system to which we have, in carelessness equalling that of the California miners of old—a carelessness based upon a madness of money equal to or surpassing that of the gold stampedes—delegated our sacred personal rights to live freely, to own property, and to protect each for himself his home.

# The Passing of the Frontier

# Contents

| | |
|---|---|
| The Frontier in History | 235 |
| The Range | 240 |
| The Cattle Trails | 248 |
| The Cowboy | 254 |
| The Mines | 262 |
| The Pathways of the West | 276 |
| The Indian Wars | 291 |
| The Cattle Kings | 304 |
| The Homesteader | 311 |

CHAPTER 1

# The Frontier in History

The frontier! There is no word in the English language more stirring, more intimate, or more beloved. It has in it all the *élan* of the old French phrase, *En avant!* It carries all of the old Saxon command, *Forward!* It means all that America ever meant. It means the old hope of a real personal liberty, and yet a real human advance in character and achievement. To a genuine American it is the dearest word in all the world.

What is, or was, the frontier? Where was it? Under what stars did it lie? Because, as the vague Iliads of ancient heroes or the nebulous records of the savage gentlemen of the Middle Ages make small specific impingement on our consciousness today, so also even now begin the tales of our own old frontier to assume a haziness, an unreality, which makes them seem less history than folklore. Now the truth is that the American frontier of history has many a local habitation and many a name. And this is why it lies somewhat indefinite under the blue haze of the years, all the more alluring for its lack of definition, like some old mountain range, the softer and more beautiful for its own shadows.

The fascination of the frontier is and has ever been an undying thing. Adventure is the meat of the strong men who have built the world for those more timid. Adventure and the frontier are one and inseparable. They suggest strength, courage, hardihood—qualities beloved in men since the world began—qualities which are the very soul of the United States, itself an experiment, an adventure, a risk accepted. Take away all our history of political regimes, the story of the rise and fall of this or that partisan aggregation in our government; take away our somewhat inglorious military past; but leave us forever the tradition of the American frontier! There lies our comfort and our pride. There we never have failed. There, indeed, we always realised our ambitions. There, indeed, we were efficient, before that hateful phrase was known. There we were a melting-pot for character, before we came to know that odious appellation which classifies us as the melting-pot of the nations.

The frontier was the place and the time of the strong man, of the self-sufficient but restless individual. It was the home of the rebel, the protestant, the unreconciled, the intolerant, the ardent—and the resolute. It was not the conservative and tender man who made our history; it was the man sometimes illiterate, oftentimes uncultured, the man of coarse garb and rude weapons. But the frontiersmen were the true dreamers of the nation. They really were the possessors of a national vision. Not statesmen but riflemen and riders made America. The noblest conclusions of American history still rest upon premises which they laid.

But, in its broadest significance, the frontier knows no country. It lies also in other lands and in other times than our own. When and what was the Great Frontier? We need go back only to the time of Drake and the sea-dogs, the Elizabethan Age, when all North America was a frontier, almost wholly unknown, compellingly alluring to all bold men. That was the day of new stirrings in the human heart. Some strange impulse seemed to act upon the soul of the braver and bolder Europeans; and they moved westward, nor could have helped that had they tried. They lived largely and blithely, and died handsomely, those old Elizabethan adventurers, and they lie today in thousands of unrecorded graves upon two continents, each having found out that any place is good enough for a man to die upon, provided that he be a man.

The American frontier was Elizabethan in its quality—childlike, simple, and savage. It has not entirely passed; for both Elizabethan folk and Elizabethan customs are yet to be found in the United States. While the half-savage civilization of the farther West was roaring on its way across the continent—while the day of the keel-boatman and the plainsman, of the Indian-fighter and the miner, even the day of the cowboy, was dawning and setting there still was a frontier left far behind in the East, near the top of the mountain range which made the first great barrier across our pathway to the West. That frontier, the frontier of Boone and Kenton, of Robertson and Sevier, still exists and may be seen in the Cumberlands—the only remaining part of America which is all American. There we may find trace of the Elizabethan

Age—idioms lost from English literature and American speech long ago. There we may see the American home life as it went on more than a hundred years ago. We may see hanging on the wall the long muzzle-loading rifle of an earlier day. We may see the spinning-wheel and the loom. The women still make in part the clothing for their families, and the men still make their own household furniture, their own farming implements, their own boots.

This overhanging frontier of America is a true survival of the days of Drake as well as of the days of Boone. The people are at once godly and savage. They breed freely; they love their homes; they are ever ready for adventure; they are frugal, abstemious, but violent and strong. They carry on still the half-religious blood feuds of the old Scotch Highlands or the North of Ireland, whence they came. They reverence good women. They care little for material accumulations. They believe in personal ease and personal independence. With them life goes on not in the slow monotony of reiterated performance, but in ragged profile, with large exertions followed by large repose. Now that has been the fashion of the frontier in every age and every land of all the world. And so, by studying these people, we may even yet arrive at a just and comprehensive notion of what we might call the "feel" of the old frontier.

There exists, too, yet another Saxon frontier in a far-off portion of the world. In that strange country, Australia, tremendous unknown regions still remain, and the wild pastoral life of such regions bids fair to exist yet for many years. A cattle king of Queensland held at one time sixty thousand square miles of land. It is said that the average size of pastoral holdings in the northern territory of Australia is two hundred and seventy-five thousand acres. Does this not recall the old times of free range in the American West?

This strange antipodal civilization also retains a curious flavour of Elizabethan ideas. It does not plan for inordinate fortunes, the continual amassing of money, but it does deliberately plan for the use by the individual of his individual life. Australian business hours are shorter than American. Routine is less general. The individual takes upon himself a smaller load of effort. He is restive under monotony. He sets aside a great part of his life for sport. He lives in a large and young day of the world. Here we may see a remote picture of our own American West—better, as it seems to me, than that reflected in the rapid and wholly commercialised development of Western Canada, which is not flavoured by any age but this.

But much of the frontier of Australia is occupied by men of means who had behind them government aid and a semi-paternal encouragement in their adventures. The same is true in part of the government-fostered settlement of Western Canada. It was not so with the American West. Here was not the place of the rich man but of the poor man, and he had no one to aid him or encourage him. Perhaps no man ever understood the American West who did not himself go there and make his living in that country, as did the men who found it and held it first. Each life on our old frontier was a personal adventure. The individual had no government behind him and he lacked even the protection of any law.

Our frontier crawled west from the first seaport settlements, afoot, on horseback, in barges, or with slow wagon-trains. It crawled across the Alleghanies, down the great river valleys and up them yet again; and at last, in days of new transportation, it leaped across divides, from one river valley to another. Its history, at first so halting, came to be very swift—so swift that it worked great elisions in its own story.

In our own day, however, the Old West generally means the old cow country of the West the high plains and the lower foothills running from the Rio Grande to the northern boundary. The still more ancient cattle-range of the lower Pacific Slope will never come into acceptance as the Old West. Always, when we use these words, we think of buffalo plains and of Indians, and of their passing before the footmen and riders who carried the phantom flag of Drake and the Virgin Queen from the Appalachians to the Rockies—before the men who eventually made good that glorious and vaunting vision of the Virginia cavaliers, whose party turned back from the Rockfish Gap after laying claim in the name of King George on all the country lying west of them, as far as the South Sea!

The American cow country may with very good logic arrogate to itself the title of the real and typical frontier of all the world. We call the spirit of the frontier Elizabethan, and so it was; but even as the Elizabethan Age was marked by its contact with the Spanish civilization in Europe, on the high seas, and in both the Americas, so the last frontier of the American West also was affected, and largely, deeply, by Spanish influence and Spanish customs. The very phraseology of range work bears proof of this. Scores of Spanish words are written indelibly in the language of the Plains. The frontier of the cow-range never was Saxon alone.

It is a curious fact also, seldom if ever noted, that this Old West of the Plains was very largely Southern and not Northern on its Saxon side. No States so much as Kentucky and Tennessee and, later, Missouri—daughters of Old Virginia in her glory—contributed to the forces of the frontiersmen. Texas, farther to the south, put her stamp indelibly upon the entire cattle industry of the West. Visionary, impractical, restless, adventurous, these later Elizabethan heroes—bowing to no yoke, insisting on their own rights and scorning often the laws of others, yet careful to retain the best and most advantageous customs of any conquered country naturally—came from those nearest Elizabethan countries which lay abandoned behind them.

If the atmosphere of the Elizabethan Age still, (1918), may be found in the forgotten Cumberlands, let us lay claim to kinship with yonder roystering heroes of a gallant day; for this was ever the atmosphere of our own frontier. To feel again the following breezes of the *Golden Hind,* or see again, floating high in the cloudless skies, the sails of the Great Armada, was the privilege of Americans for a double decade within the memory of men yet living, (1918), in that country, so unfailingly beloved, which we call the Old West of America.

CHAPTER 2

# The Range

When, in 1803, those two immortal youths, Meriwether Lewis and William Clark, were about to go forth on their great journey across the continent, they were admonished by Thomas Jefferson that they would in all likelihood encounter in their travels, living and stalking about, the mammoth or the mastodon, whose bones had been found in the great salt-licks of Kentucky. We smile now at such a supposition; yet it was not unreasonable then. No man knew that tremendous country that lay beyond the mouth of the Missouri.

The explorers crossed one portion of a vast land which was like to nothing they had ever seen—the region later to become the great cattle-range of America. It reached, although they could know nothing of that, from the Spanish possessions on the south across a thousand miles of short grass lands to the present Canadian boundary line—which certain obdurate American souls still say ought to have been at 54° 40', and not where it is! From the Rio Grande to "Fifty-four forty," indeed, would have made nice measurements for the Saxon cattle-range.

Little, however, was the value of this land understood by the explorers; and, for more than half a century afterwards, it commonly was supposed to be useless for the occupation of white men and suitable only as a hunting-ground for savage tribes. Most of us can remember the school maps of our own youth, showing a vast region marked, vaguely, "The Great American Desert," which was considered hopeless for any human industry, but much of which has since proved as rich as any land anywhere on the globe.

Perhaps it was the treeless nature of the vast Plains which carried the first idea of their infertility, When the first settlers of Illinois and Indiana came up from south of the Ohio River they had their choice

240

of timber and prairie lands. Thinking the prairies worthless—since land which could not raise a tree certainly could not raise crops—these first occupants of the Middle West spent a generation or more, axe in hand, along the heavily timbered river-bottoms. The prairies were long in settling. No one then could have predicted that farm lands in that region would be worth three hundred dollars an acre or better, and that these prairies of the Mississippi Valley would, in a few generations, be studded with great towns and would form a part of the granary of the world.

But, if our early explorers, passing beyond the valley of the Missouri, found valueless the region of the Plains and the foothills, not so the wild creatures or the savage men who had lived there longer than science records. The buffalo then ranged from the Rio Grande to the Athabaska, from the Missouri to the Rockies, and beyond. No one seems to have concluded in those days that there was after all slight difference between the buffalo and the domestic ox. The native cattle, however, in untold thousands and millions, had even then proved beyond peradventure the sustaining and strengthening nature of the grasses of the Plains.

Now, each creature, even of human species, must adjust itself to its environment. Having done so, commonly it is disposed to love that environment. The Eskimo and the Zulu each thinks that he has the best land in the world. So with the American Indian, who, supported by the vast herds of buffalo, ranged all over that tremendous country which was later to be given over to the white man with his domestic cattle. No freer life ever was lived by any savages than by the Horse Indians of the Plains in the buffalo days; and never has the world known a physically higher type of savage.

On the buffalo-range—that is to say, on the cattle-range which was to be—Lewis and Clark met several bands of the Sioux the Mandans and the Assiniboines, the Blackfeet, the Shoshones. Farther south were the Pawnees, the Kaws, the Otoes, the Osages, most of whom depended in part upon the buffalo for their living, though the Otoes, the Pawnees, the Mandans, and certain others now and then raised a little corn or a few squashes to help out their bill of fare. Still farther south dwelt the Kiowas, the Comanches, and others. The Arapahoes, the Cheyennes, the Crows, and the Utes, all hunters, were soon to come into the ken of the white man. Of such of these tribes as they met, the youthful captains made accounting, gravely and with extraordinary accuracy, but without discovering in this region much future for Americans. They were explorers and not industrial investigators.

It was nearly half a century after the journey of Lewis and Clark that the Forty-Niners were crossing the Plains, whither, meanwhile, the Mormons had trekked in search of a country where they might live as they liked. Still the wealth of the Plains remained untouched. California was in the eyes of the world. The great cow-range was overleaped. But, in the early fifties, when the placer fields of California began to be less numerous and less rich, the half-savage population of the mines roared on northward, even across our northern line. Soon it was to roll back. Next it worked east and southeast and northeast over the great dry plains of Washington and Oregon, so that, as readily may be seen, the cow-range proper was not settled as most of the West was, by a directly westbound thrust of an eastern population; but, on the contrary, it was approached from several different angles—from the north, from the east, from the west and northwest, and finally from the south.

The early, turbulent population of miners and adventurers was crude, lawless, and aggressive. It cared nothing whatever for the Indian tribes. War, instant and merciless, where it meant murder for the most part, was set on foot as soon as white touched red in that far western region.

All these new white men who had crowded into the unknown country of the Plains, the Rockies, the Sierras, and the Cascades, had to be fed. They could not employ and remain content with the means by which the red man there had always fed himself. Hence a new industry sprang up in the United States, which of itself made certain history in that land. The business of freighting supplies to the West, whether by bull-train or by pack-train, was an industry *sui generis*, very highly specialised, and pursued by men of great business ability as well as by men of great hardihood and daring.

Each of these freight trains which went West carried hanging on its flank more and more of the white men. As the trains returned, more and more was learned in the States of the new country which lay between the Missouri and the Rockies, which ran no man knew how far north, and no man could guess how far south. Now appears in history Fort Benton, on the Missouri, the great northern supply post—just as at an earlier date there had appeared Fort Hall, one of the old fur-trading posts beyond the Rockies, Bent's Fort on the Arkansas, and many other outposts of the new Saxon civilization in the West.

Later came the pony express and the stage coach which made history and romance for a generation. Feverishly, boisterously, a strong, rugged, womanless population crowded westward and formed the wavering, now advancing, now receding line of the great frontier of American story.

But for long there was no sign of permanent settlement on the Plains, and no one thought of this region as the frontier. The men there who were prospecting and exploiting were classified as no more than adventurers. No one seems to have taken a lesson from the Indian and the buffalo. The reports of Frémont long since had called attention to the nourishing quality of those grasses of the high country, but the day of the cowboy had not yet dawned. There is a somewhat feeble story which runs to the effect that in 1866 one of the great wagon-trains, caught by the early snows of winter, was obliged to abandon its oxen on the range. It was supposed that, of course, the oxen must perish during the winter.

But next spring the owners were surprised to find that the oxen, so far from perishing, had flourished very much—indeed, were fat and in good condition. So, runs the story which is often repeated. It may be true, but to accredit to this incident the beginnings of the cattle industry in the Indian country would surely be going too far. The truth is that the cow industry was not a Saxon discovery. It was a Latin enterprise, flourishing in Mexico long before the first of these miners and adventurers came on the range.

Something was known of the Spanish lands to the south through the explorations of Pike, but more through the commerce of the prairies—the old wagon trade from the Missouri River to the Spanish cities of Sante Fé and Chihuahua. Now the cow business, south of the Rio Grande, was already well differentiated and developed at the time the first adventurers from the United States went into Texas and began to crowd their Latin neighbours for more room. There it was that our Saxon frontiersmen first discovered the cattle industry. But these southern and northern riflemen—ruthless and savage, yet strangely statesmanlike—though they might betimes drive away the owners of the herds, troubled little about the herds themselves.

There was a certain fascination to these rude strangers in the slow and easeful civilization of Old Spain which they encountered in the land below them. Little by little, and then largely and yet more largely, the warriors of San Jacinto reached out and began to claim lands for themselves—leagues and uncounted leagues of land, which had, however, no market value. Well within the memory of the present generation large tracts of good land were bought in Texas for six cents an acre; some was bought for half that price in a time not much earlier. Today, (1918), much of that land is producing wealth; but land then was worthless—and so were cows.

This civilization of the Southwest, of the new Republic of Texas, may be regarded as the first enduring American result of contact with the Spanish industry. The men who won Texas came mostly from Kentucky and Tennessee or southern Ohio, and the first coloniser of Texas was a Virginian, Stephen Fuller Austin. They came along the old Natchez Trace from Nashville to the Mississippi River-that highway which has so much history of its own. Down this old winding trail into the greatest valley of all the world, and beyond that valley out into the Spanish country, moved steadily the adventurers whose fathers had but recently crossed the Appalachians. One of the strongest thrusts of the American civilization thus entered the cattle-range at its lower end, between the Rio Grande and the Red River.

In all the several activities, mining, freighting, scouting, soldiering, riding pony express, or even sheer adventuring for what might come, there was ever a trading back and forth between home-staying men and adventuring men. Thus, there was an interchange of knowledge and of customs between East and West, between our old country and our new. There was an interchange, too, at the south, where our Saxon civilization came in touch with that of Mexico.

We have now to note some fundamental facts and principles of the cattle industry which our American cattlemen took over ready-made from the hands of Mexico.

The Mexicans in Texas had an abundance of small, hardy horses of African and Spanish breed, which Spain had brought into the New World—the same horses that the Moors had brought into Spain—a breed naturally hardy and able to subsist upon dry food. Without such horses there could have been no cattle industry. These horses, running wild in herds, had crossed to the upper Plains. La Vérendrye, and later Lewis and Clark, had found the Indians using horses in the north. The Indians, as we have seen, had learned to manage the horse. Formerly they had used dogs to drag the *travois*, but now they used the "elk-dog," as they first called the horse.

In the original cow country, that is, in Mexico and Texas, countless herds of cattle were held in a loose sort of ownership over wide and unknown plains. Like all wild animals in that warm country, they bred in extraordinary numbers. The southern range, indeed, has always been called the breeding range. The cattle had little value. He who wanted beef killed beef. He who wanted leather killed cattle for their hides. But beyond these scant and infrequent uses cattle had no definite value.

The Mexican, however, knew how to handle cows. He could ride a horse, and he could rope cattle and brand them. Most of the cattle of a wide range would go to certain water-holes more or less regularly, where they might be roughly collected or estimated. This coming of the cattle to the watering-places made it unnecessary for owners of cattle to acquire ranch land. It was enough to secure the water-front where the cows must go to drink. That gave the owner all the title he needed. His right to the increase he could prove by another phenomenon of nature, just as inevitable and invariable as that of thirst. The maternal instinct of a cow and the dependence of the calf upon its mother gave the old rancher of immemorial times sufficient proof of ownership in the increase of his herd. The calf would run with its own mother and with no other cow through its first season. So that if an old Mexican *ranchero* saw a certain number of cows at his watering-places, and with them calves, he knew that all before him were his property—or, at least, he claimed them as such and used them.

Still, this was loose-footed property. It might stray away after all, or it might be driven away. Hence, in some forgotten time, our shrewd Spaniard invented a system of proof of ownership which has always lain at the very bottom of the organised cow industry; he invented the method of branding. This meant his sign, his name, his trade-mark, his proof of ownership. The animal could not shake it off. It would not burn off in the sun or wash off in the rain. It went with the animal and could not be eradicated from the animal's hide. Wherever the bearer was seen, the brand upon its hide provided certain identification of the owner.

Now, all these basic ideas of the cow industry were old on the lower range in Texas when our white men first drifted thither. The cattle industry, although in its infancy, and although supposed to have no great future, was developed long before Texas became a republic. It never, indeed, changed very much from that time until the end of its own career.

One great principle was accepted religiously even in those early and crude days. A man's cow was *his* cow. A man's brand was *his* brand. There must be no interference with his ownership. Hence certain other phases of the industry followed inevitably. These cattle, these calves, each branded by the iron of the owner, in spite of all precautions, began to mingle as settlers became more numerous; hence came the idea of the round-up. The country was warm and lazy. If a hundred or a thousand cows were not collected, very well. If a calf were separated from its mother, very well.

The old ranchers never quarrelled among themselves. They never would have made in the South anything like a cattle association; it was left for the Yankees to do that at a time when cows had come to have far greater values. There were few arguments in the first *rodeos* of the lower range. One rancher would vie with his neighbour in generosity in the matter of unbranded calves. Haggling would have been held contemptible. On the lower range in the old times no one cared much about a cow. Why should one do so? There was no market for cows—no one who wished to buy them. If one tendered a Mexican *cinquo pesos* for a yearling or a two-year-old, the owner might perhaps offer the animal as a gift, or he might smile and say "*Con mucha gusto*" as he was handed a few pieces of silver. There were plenty of cows everywhere in the world!

Let us, therefore, give the old Spaniard full credit alike in picturesque romance and in the organised industry of the cow. The westbound thrust which came upon the upper part of the range in the days of more shrewd and exacting business methods was simply the best-known and most published phase of frontier life in the cow country; hence we have usually accepted it as typical. It would not be accurate to say that the cattle industry was basically much influenced or governed by northern or eastern men. In practically all of its great phenomena the frontier of the old cow-range was southern by birth and growth.

There lay, then, so long unused, that vast and splendid land so soon to write romantic history of its own, so soon to come into the admiration or the wonder of a great portion of the earth—a land of fascinating interest to the youth of every country, and a region whose story holds a charm for young and old alike even today. It was a region royal in its dimensions. Far on the west it was hedged by the grey-sided and white-topped mountains, the Rockies. Where the buffalo once lived, the cattle were to live, high up in the foothills of this great mountain range which ran from the Rio Grande to Canada. On the east, where lay the Prairies rather than the Plains, it was a country waving with high native grasses, with many brilliant flowers hiding among them, the sweet-william, the wild rose, and often great masses of the yellow sunflower.

From the Rio Grande to the Athabaska, for the greater part, the frontier sky was blue and cloudless during most of the year. The rainfall was not great. The atmosphere was dry. It was a cheerful country, one of optimism and not of gloom. In the extreme south, along the Rio Grande, the climate was moister, warmer, more enervating; but on the high steppes of the middle range in Colorado, Wyoming, Montana, western Nebraska, there lay the finest out-of-doors country, man's country the finest of the earth.

But for the time, busy with more accustomed things, mining and freighting and fighting and hunting and trading and trapping, we Americans who had arrived upon the range cared little for cows. The upper thrust of the great herds from the south into the north had not begun. It was after the Civil War that the first great drives of cattle from the south toward the north began, and after men had learned in the State of Texas that cattle moved from the Rio Grande to the upper portions of the State and fed on the mesquite grass would attain greater stature than in the hot coast country. Then swiftly, somewhat luridly, there leaped into our comprehension and our interest that strange country long loosely held under our flag, the region of the Plains, the region which we now call the Old West.

In great bands, in long lines, slowly, low-headed, sore-footed, the vast gatherings of the prolific lower range moved north, each cow with its title indelibly marked upon its hide. These cattle were now going to take the place of those on which the Indians had depended for their living these many years. A new day in American history had dawned.

CHAPTER 3

# The Cattle Trails

The customary method of studying history by means of a series of events and dates is not the method which we have chosen to employ in this study of the Old West. Speaking generally, our minds are unable to assimilate a condensed mass of events and dates; and that is precisely what would be required of us if we should attempt here to follow the ways of conventional history. Dates are at best no more than milestones on the pathway of time; and in the present instance it is not the milestones but the road itself with which we are concerned. Where does the road begin? Why comes it hither? Whither does it lead? These are the real questions.

Under all the exuberance of the life of the range there lay a steady business of tremendous size and enormous values. The "uproarious iniquity" of the West, its picturesqueness, its vividness—these were but froth on the stream. The stream itself was a steady and sombre flood. Beyond this picturesqueness of environment very few have cared to go, and therefore sometimes have had little realisation of the vastness of the cowboy's kingdom, the "magnitude of the interests in his care, or the fortitude, resolution, and instant readiness essential to his daily life." The American cowboy is the most modern representative of a human industry that is second to very few in antiquity.

Virgil strikes the note of real history: *Quorum pars magna fui*, says Æneas—"Of which I was a great part." If we seek the actual truth, we ought most to value contemporary records, representations made by men who were themselves a part of the scenes which they describe. In that way we shall arrive not merely upon lurid events, not alone upon the stereotyped characters of the "Wild West," but upon causes which are much more interesting and immensely more valuable than any merely titillating stories from the weirdly illustrated Apocrypha of the

West. We must go below such things if we would gain a just and lasting estimate of the times. We ought to look on the old range neither as a playground of idle men nor as a scene of hysterical and contorted human activities. We ought to look upon it from the point of view of its uses to mankind. The explorers found it a wilderness, the home of the red man and the buffalo. What were the underlying causes of its settlement and development?

There is in history no agency so wondrous in events, no working instrumentality so great as transportation. The great seeking of all human life is to find its level. Perhaps the first men travelled by hollowed logs downstream. Then possibly the idea of a sail was conceived. Early in the story of the United States men made commercial journeys from the head of the Ohio to the mouth of the Mississippi by flatboats, and came back by keelboats. The pole, the cordelle, the paddle, and the sail, in turn helped them to navigate the great streams which led out into the West. And presently there was to come that tremendous upheaval wrought by the advent of the iron trails which, scorning alike waterways and mountain ranges, flung themselves almost directly westward across the continent.

The iron trails, crossing the northern range soon after the Civil War, brought a market to the cattle country. Inevitably the men of the lower range would seek to reach the railroads with what they had to sell—their greatest natural product, cattle on the hoof. This was the primary cause of the great northbound drives already mentioned, the greatest pastoral phenomena in the story of the world.

The southern herds at that time had no market at their doors. They had to go to the market, and they had to go on foot. That meant that they must be driven northward by cattle handlers who had passed their days in the wild life of the lower range. These cowmen of course took their character and their customs northward with them, and so they were discovered by those enthusiastic observers, newly arrived by rail, whom the cowen were wont to call "pilgrims."

Now the trail of the great cattle drives—the Long Trail—was a thing of tremendous importance of itself and it is still full of interest. As it may not easily be possible for the author to better a description of it that was written some twenty years ago, that description is here again set down. (*The Story of the Cowboy*; 1897.)

The braiding of a hundred minor pathways, the Long Trail lay like a vast rope connecting the cattle country of the South with that of the North. Lying loose or coiling, it ran for more than two thousand miles along the eastern edge of the Rocky Mountains, sometimes close in at their feet, again hundreds of miles away across the hard tablelands or the well-flowered prairies. It traversed in a fair line the vast land of Texas, curled over the Indian Nations, over Kansas, Colorado, Nebraska, Wyoming, and Montana, and bent in wide overlapping circles as far west as Utah and Nevada; as far east as Missouri, Iowa, even Illinois; and as far north as the British possessions.

Even today, (1918), you may trace plainly its former course, from its faint beginnings in the lazy land of Mexico, the Ararat of the cattle-range. It is distinct across Texas, and multifold still in the Indian lands. Its many intermingling paths still scar the iron surface of the Neutral Strip, and the ploughs have not buried all the old furrows in the plains of Kansas. Parts of the path still remain visible in the mountain lands of the far North. You may see the ribbons banding the hillsides today along the valley of the Stillwater, and along the Yellowstone and toward the source of the Missouri. The hoof marks are beyond the Musselshell, over the Bad Lands and the coulees and the flat prairies; and far up into the land of the long cold you may see, even today if you like, the shadow of that unparalleled pathway, the Long Trail of the cattle-range. History has no other like it.

The Long Trail was surveyed and constructed in a century and a day. Over the Red River of the South, a stream even today perhaps known but vaguely in the minds of many inhabitants of the country, there appeared, almost without warning, vast processions of strange horned kine—processions of enormous wealth, owned by kings who paid no tribute, and guarded by men who never knew a master. Whither these were bound, what had conjured them forth, whence they came, were questions in the minds of the majority of the population of the North and East to whom the phenomenon appeared as the product of a day.

The answer to these questions lay deep in the laws of civilization, and extended far back into that civilization's history. The Long Trail was finished in a day. It was begun more than a century before that day, and came forward along the very appointed ways of time . . . . Thus, far down in the vague Southwest, at some distant time, in some distant portion of old, mysterious Mexico, there fell into line the hoof prints which made the first faint beginnings of the Long Trail, merely the path of a half nomadic movement along the line of the least resistance.

The Long Trail began to deepen and extend. It received then, as it did later, a baptism of human blood such as no other pathway of the continent has known. The nomadic and the warlike days passed, and there ensued a more quiet and pastoral time. It was the beginning of a feudalism of the range, a barony rude enough, but a glorious one, albeit it began, like all feudalism, in large-handed theft and generous murdering. The flocks of these strong men, carelessly interlapping, increased and multiplied amazingly. They were hardly looked upon as wealth. The people could not eat a tithe of the beef; they could not use a hundredth of the leather. Over hundreds and hundreds of miles of ownerless grass lands, by the rapid waters of the mountains, by the slow streams of the plains or the long and dark lagoons of the low coast country, the herds of tens grew into droves of hundreds and thousands and hundreds of thousands. This was really the dawning of the American cattle industry.

Chips and flakes of the great Southwestern herd began to be seen in the Northern States. As early as 1857 Texas cattle were driven to Illinois. In 1861 Louisiana was, without success, tried as an outlet. In 1867 a venturous drover took a herd across the Indian Nations, bound for California, and only abandoned the project because the Plains Indians were then very bad in the country to the north. In 1869 several herds were driven from Texas to Nevada. These were side trails of the main cattle road. It seemed clear that a great population in the North needed the cheap beef of Texas, and the main question appeared to be one of transportation. No proper means for this offered. The Civil War stopped almost all plans to market the range cattle, and the close of that war found the vast grazing lands of Texas covered fairly with millions of cattle which had no actual or determinate value. They were sorted and branded and herded after a fashion, but neither they nor their increase could be converted into anything but more cattle. The cry for a market became imperative.

Meantime the Anglo-Saxon civilization was rolling swiftly toward the upper West. The Indians were being driven from the Plains. A solid army was pressing behind the vanguard of soldier, scout, and plainsman. The railroads were pushing out into a new and untracked empire. They carried the market with them. The market halted, much nearer, though still some hundred of miles to the north of the great herd. The Long Trail tapped no more at the door of Illinois, Missouri, Arkansas, but leaped north again definitely, this time springing across the Red River and up to the railroads, along sharp and well-defined channels deepened in the year of 1866 alone by the hoofs of more than a quarter of a million cattle.

In 1871, only five years later, over six hundred thousand cattle crossed the Red River for the Northern markets. Abilene, Newton, Wichita, Ellsworth, Great Bend, Dodge, flared out into a swift and sometime evil blossoming. Thus, the men of the North first came to hear of the Long Trail and the men who made it, although really it had begun long ago and had been foreordained to grow.

By this time, 1867 and 1868, the northern portions of the region immediately to the east of the Rocky Mountains had been sufficiently cleared of their wild inhabitants to admit a gradual though precarious settlement. It had been learned yet again that the buffalo grass and the sweet waters of the far North would fatten a range broadhorn to a stature far beyond any it could attain on the southern range. The Long Trail pushed rapidly even farther to the north where there still remained "free grass" and a new market. The territorial ranges needed many thousands of cattle for their stocking, and this demand took a large part of the Texas drive which came to Abilene, Great Bend, and Fort Dodge. Moreover, the government was now feeding thousands of its new red wards, and these Indians needed thousands of beeves for rations, which were driven from the southern range to the upper army posts and reservations. Between this government demand and that of the territorial stock ranges there was occupation for the men who made the saddle their home.

The Long Trail, which had previously found the black corn lands of Illinois and Missouri, now crowded to the West, until it had reached Utah and Nevada, and penetrated every open park and mesa and valley of Colorado, and found all the high plains of Wyoming. Cheyenne and Laramie became common words now, and drovers spoke as wisely of the dangers of the Platte as a year before they had mentioned those of the Red River or the Arkansas. Nor did the Trail pause in its irresistible push to the north until it had found the last of the five great transcontinental lines, far in the British provinces. Here in spite of a long season of ice and snow the uttermost edges of the great herd might survive, in a certain percentage at least, each year in an almost unassisted struggle for existence, under conditions different enough, it would seem, from those obtaining at the opposite extreme of the wild roadway over which they came.

The Long Trail of the cattle-range was done! By magic the cattle industry had spread over the entire West. Today many men think of that industry as belonging only to the Southwest, and many would consider that it was transferred to the North. Really it was not transferred but extended, and the trail of the old drive marks the line of that extension.

Today, (1918), the Long Trail is replaced by other trails, product of the swift development of the West, and it remains as the connection, now for the most part historical only, between two phases of an industry which, in spite of differences of climate and condition, retain a similarity in all essential features. When the last steer of the first herd was driven into the corral at the Ultima Thule of the range, it was the pony of the American cowboy which squatted and wheeled under the spur and burst down the straggling street of the little frontier town. Before that time, and since that time, it was and has been the same pony and the same man who have travelled the range, guarding and guiding the wild herds, from the romantic to the commonplace days of the West.

## Chapter 4

# The Cowboy

The Great West, vast and rude, brought forth men also vast and rude. We pass today over parts of that matchless region, and we see the red hills and ragged mountain-fronts cut and crushed into huge indefinite shapes, to which even a small imagination may give a human or more than human form. It would almost seem that the same great hand which chiselled out these monumental forms had also laid its fingers upon the people of this region and fashioned them rude and ironlike, in harmony with the stern faces set about them.

Of all the babes of that primeval mother, the West, the cowboy was perhaps her dearest because he was her last. Some of her children lived for centuries; this one for not a triple decade before he began to be old. What was really the life of this child of the wild region of America, and what were the conditions of the experience that bore him, can never be fully known by those who have not seen the West with wide eyes—for the cowboy was simply a part of the West. He who does not understand the one can never understand the other.

If we care truly to see the cowboy as he was and seek to give our wish the dignity of a real purpose, we should study him in connection with his surroundings and in relation to his work. Then we shall see him not as a curiosity but as a product—not as an eccentric driver of horned cattle but as a man suited to his times.

Large tracts of that domain where once the cowboy reigned supreme have been turned into farms by the irrigator's ditch or by the dry-farmer's plan. The farmer in overalls is in many instances his own stockman today. On the ranges of Arizona, Wyoming, and Texas and parts of Nevada we may find the cowboy, it is true, even today: but he is no longer the Homeric figure that once dominated the plains. In what we say as to his trade, therefore, or his fashion in the practice of it, we speak in terms of thirty or forty years ago, when wire was unknown, when the round-up still was necessary, and the cowboy's life was indeed that of the open.

By the costume we may often know the man. The cowboy's costume was harmonious with its surroundings. It was planned upon lines of such stern utility as to leave no possible thing which we may call dispensable. The typical cowboy costume could hardly be said to contain a coat and waistcoat. The heavy woollen shirt, loose and open at the neck, was the common wear at all seasons of the year excepting winter, and one has often seen cowboys in the winter-time engaged in work about the yard or corral of the ranch wearing no other cover for the upper part of the body but one or more of these heavy shirts.

If the cowboy wore a coat he would wear it open and loose as much as possible. If he wore a "vest" he would wear it slouchily, hanging open or partly unbuttoned most of the time. There was a reason for this slouchy habit. The cowboy would say that the vest closely buttoned about the body would cause perspiration, so that the wearer would quickly chill upon ceasing exercise. If the wind were blowing keenly when the cowboy dismounted to sit upon the ground for dinner, he would button up his waistcoat and be warm. If it were very cold he would button up his coat also.

The cowboy's boots were of fine leather and fitted tightly, with light narrow soles, extremely small and high heels. Surely a more irrational foot-covering never was invented; yet these tight, peaked cowboy boots had a great significance and may indeed be called the insignia of a calling. There was no prouder soul on earth than the cowboy. He was proud of being a horseman and had a contempt for all human beings who walked. On foot in his tight-toed boots he was lost; but he wished it to be understood that he never was on foot.

If we rode beside him and watched his seat in the big cow saddle we found that his high and narrow heels prevented the slipping forward of the foot in the stirrup, into which he jammed his feet nearly full length. If there was a fall, the cowboy's foot never hung in the stirrup. In the corral roping, afoot, his heels anchored him. So, he found his little boots not so unserviceable and retained them as a matter of pride. Boots made for the cowboy trade sometimes had fancy tops of bright-coloured leather. The Lone Star of Texas was not infrequent in their ornamentation.

The curious pride of the horseman extended also to his gloves. The cowboy was very careful in the selection of his gloves. They were made of the finest buckskin, which could not be injured by wetting. Generally, they were tanned white and cut with a deep cuff or gauntlet from which hung a little fringe to flutter in the wind when he rode at full speed on horseback.

The cowboy's hat was one of the typical and striking features of his costumes. It was a heavy, wide, white felt hat with a heavy leather band buckled about it. There has been no other head covering devised so suitable as the Stetson for the uses of the Plains, although high and heavy black hats have in part supplanted it today among stockmen. The boardlike felt was practically indestructible. The brim flapped a little and, in time, was turned up and perhaps held fast to the crown by a thong. The wearer might sometimes stiffen the brim by passing a thong through a series of holes pierced through the outer edge. He could depend upon his hat in all weathers. In the rain it was an umbrella; in the sun a shield; in the winter he could tie it down about his ears with his handkerchief.

Loosely thrown about the cowboy's shirt collar was a silk kerchief. It was tied in a hard knot in front, and though it could scarcely be said to be devoted to the uses of a neck scarf, yet it was a great comfort to the back of the neck when one was riding in a hot wind. It was sure to be of some bright colour, usually red. Modern would-be cowpunchers do not willingly let this old kerchief die, and right often they over-play it. For the cowboy of the "movies," however, let us register an unqualified contempt. The real range would never have been safe for him.

A peculiar and distinctive feature of the cowboy's costume was his "chaps" (*chaparéjos*). The chaps were two very wide and full-length trouser-legs made of heavy calfskin and connected by a narrow belt or strap. They were cut away entirely at front and back so that they covered only the thigh and lower legs and did not heat the body as a complete leather garment would. They were intended solely as a protection against branches, thorns, briers, and the like, but they were prized in cold or wet weather. Sometimes there was seen, more often on the southern range, a cowboy wearing chaps made of skins tanned with the hair on; for the cowboy of the Southwest early learned that goatskin left with the hair on would turn the cactus thorns better than any other material. Later, the chaps became a sort of affectation on the part of new men on the range; but the old-time cowboy wore them for use, not as a uniform. In hot weather he laid them off.

In the times when some men needed guns and all men carried

them, no pistol of less than 44-caliber was tolerated on the range, the solid framed 45caliber being the one almost universally used. The barrel was eight inches long, and it shot a rifle cartridge of forty grains of powder and a blunt-ended bullet that made a terrible missile. This weapon depended from a belt worn loose resting upon the left hip and hanging low down on the right hip so that none of the weight came upon the abdomen. This was typical, for the cowboy was neither fancy gunman nor army officer. The latter carries the revolver on the left, the butt pointing forward.

An essential part of the cow-puncher's outfit was his "rope." This was carried in a close coil at the side of the saddle-horn, fastened by one of the many thongs scattered over the saddle. In the Spanish country it was called *reata* and even today is sometimes seen in the Southwest made of rawhide. In the South it was called a *lariat*. The modern rope is a well-made three-quarter-inch hemp rope about thirty feet in length, with a leather or rawhide eye. The cowboy's quirt was a short heavy whip, the stock being of wood or iron covered with braided leather and carrying a lash made of two or three heavy loose thongs. The spur in the old days had a very large rowel with blunt teeth an inch long. It was often ornamented with little bells or oblongs of metal, the tinkling of which appealed to the childlike nature of the Plains rider. Their use was to lock the rowel.

His bridle—for, since the cowboy and his mount are inseparable, we may as well speak of his horse's dress also—was noticeable for its tremendously heavy and cruel curbed bit, known as the "Spanish bit." But in the ordinary riding and even in the exciting work of the old round-up and in "cutting out," the cowboy used the bit very little, nor exerted any pressure on the reins. He laid the reins against the neck of the pony opposite to the direction in which he wished it to go, merely turning his hand in the direction and inclining his body in the same way. He rode with the pressure of the knee and the inclination of the body and the light side-shifting of both reins. The saddle was the most important part of the outfit.

It was a curious thing, this saddle developed by the cattle trade, and the world has no other like it. Its great weight—from thirty to forty pounds—was readily excusable when one remembers that it was not only seat but workbench for the cowman. A light saddle would be torn to pieces at the first rush of a maddened steer, but the sturdy frame of a cow-saddle would throw the heaviest bull on the range. The high cantle would give a firmness to the cowboy's seat when he snubbed a steer with a sternness sufficient to send it rolling heels overhead. The high pommel, or "horn," steel-forged and covered with cross braids of leather, served as anchor post for this same steer, a turn of the rope about it accomplishing that purpose at once. The saddle-tree forked low down over the pony's back so that the saddle sat firmly and could not readily be pulled off. The great broad cinches bound the saddle fast till horse and saddle were practically one fabric. The strong wooden house of the old heavy stirrup protected the foot from being crushed by the impact of the herd. The form of the cow-saddle has changed but little, although today one sees a shorter seat and smaller horn, a "swell front" or roll, and a stirrup of open "ox-bow" pattern.

The round-up was the harvest of the range. The time of the calf round-up was in the spring after the grass had become good and after the calves had grown large enough for the branding, The State Cattle Association divided the entire State range into a number of round-up districts. Under an elected round-up captain were all the bosses in charge of the different ranch outfits sent by men having cattle in the round-up. Let us briefly draw a picture of this scene as it was.

Each cowboy would have eight or ten horses for his own use, for he had now before him the hardest riding of the year. When the cow-puncher went into the herd to cut out calves he mounted a fresh horse, and every few hours he again changed horses, for there was no horse which could long endure the fatigue of the rapid and intense work of cutting. Before the rider stretched a sea of interwoven horns, waving and whirling as the densely packed ranks of cattle closed in or swayed apart.

It was no prospect for a weakling, but into it went the cow-puncher on his determined little horse, heeding not the plunging, crushing, and thrusting of the excited cattle. Down under the bulks of the herd, half hid in the whirl of dust, he would spy a little curly calf running, dodging, and twisting, always at the heels of its mother; and he would dart after, following the two through the thick of surging and plunging beasts. The sharp-eyed pony would see almost as soon as his rider which cow was wanted and he needed small guidance from that time on. He would follow hard at her heels, edging her constantly toward the flank of the herd, at times nipping her hide as a reminder of his own superiority. In spite of herself the cow would gradually turn out toward the edge, and at last would be swept clear of the crush, the calf following close behind her. There was a whirl of the rope and the calf was laid by the heels and dragged to the fire where the branding irons were heated and ready.

Meanwhile other cow-punchers are rushing calves to the branding. The hubbub and turmoil increase. Taut ropes cross the ground in many directions. The cutting ponies pant and sweat, rear and plunge. The garb of the cowboy is now one of white alkali which hangs grey in his eyebrows and moustache. Steers bellow as they surge to and fro. Cows charge on their persecutors. Fleet yearlings break and run for the open, pursued by men who care not how or where they ride.

We have spoken in terms of the past. There is no calf round-up of the open range today. The last of the round-ups was held in Routt County, Colorado, several years ago, so far as the writer knows, and it had only to do with shifting cattle from the summer to the winter range.

After the calf round-up came the beef round-up, the cowman's final harvest. This began in July or August. Only the mature or fatted animals were cut out from the herd. This "beef cut" was held apart and driven on ahead from place to place as the round-up progressed. It was then driven in by easy stages to the shipping point on the railroad, whence the long trainloads of cattle went to the great markets.

In the heyday of the cowboy it was natural that his chief amusements should be those of the outdoor air and those more or less in line with his employment. He was accustomed to the sight of big game, and so had the edge of his appetite for its pursuit worn off. Yet he was a hunter, just as every Western man was a hunter in the times of the Western game. His weapons were the rifle, revolver, and rope; the latter two were always with him. With the rope at times he captured the coyote, and under special conditions he has taken deer and even antelope in this way, though this was of course most unusual and only possible under chance conditions of ground and cover.

Elk have been roped by cowboys many times, and it is known that even the mountain sheep has been so taken, almost incredible as that may seem. The young buffalo were easy prey for the cowboy and these he often roped and made captive. In fact the beginnings of all the herds of buffalo now in captivity in this country were the calves roped and secured by cowboys: and these few scattered individuals of a grand race of animals remain as melancholy reminders alike of a national shiftlessness and an individual skill and daring.

The grizzly was at times seen by the cowboys on the range, and if it chanced that several cowboys were together it was not unusual to give him chase. They did not always rope him, for it was rarely that the nature of the country made this possible. Sometimes they roped him and wished they could let him go, for a grizzly bear is uncommonly active and straightforward in his habits at close quarters. The extreme difficulty of such a combat, however, gave it its chief fascination for the cowboy. Of course, no one horse could hold the bear after it was roped, but, as one after another came up, the bear was caught by neck and foot and body, until at last he was tangled and tripped and haled about till he was helpless, strangled, and nearly dead. It is said that cowboys have so brought into camp a grizzly bear, forcing him to half walk and half slide at the end of the ropes. No feat better than this could show the courage of the plainsman and of the horse which he so perfectly controlled.

Of such wild and dangerous exploits were the cowboy's amusements on the range. It may be imagined what were his amusements when he visited the "settlements." The cow-punchers, reared in the free life of the open air, under circumstances of the utmost freedom of individual action, perhaps came off the drive or round-up after weeks or months of unusual restraint or hardship, and felt that the time had arrived for them to "celebrate." Merely great rude children, as wild and untamed and untaught as the herds they led, they regarded their first look at the "settlements" of the railroads as a glimpse of a wider world. They pursued to the uttermost such avenues of new experience as lay before them, almost without exception avenues of vice. It is strange that the records of those days should be chosen by the public to be held as the measure of the American cowboy. Those days were brief, and they are long since gone. The American cowboy atoned for them by a quarter of a century of faithful labour.

The amusements of the cowboy were like the features of his daily surroundings and occupation—they were intense, large, Homeric. Yet, judged at his work, no higher type of employee ever existed, nor one more dependable. He was the soul of honour in all the ways of his calling. The very blue of the sky, bending evenly over all men alike, seemed to symbolize his instinct for justice. Faithfulness and manliness were his chief traits; his standard—to be a "square man."

Not all the open range will ever be farmed, but very much that was long thought to be irreclaimable has gone under irrigation or is being more or less successfully "dry-farmed." The man who brought water upon the arid lands of the West changed the entire complexion of a vast country and with it the industries of that country. Acres redeemed from the desert and added to the realm of the American farmer were taken from the realm of the American cowboy.

The West has changed. The curtain has dropped between us and its wild and stirring scenes. The old days are gone. The house dog sits on the hill where yesterday the coyote sang. There are fenced fields and in them stand sleek round beasts, deep in crops such as their ancestors never saw. In a little town nearby is the hurry and bustle of modern life. This town is far out upon what was called the frontier, long after the frontier has really gone. Guarding its ghost here stood a little army post, once one of the pillars, now one of the monuments of the West.

Out from the tiny settlement in the dusk of evening, always facing toward where the sun is sinking, might be seen riding, not so long ago, a figure we should know. He would thread the little lane among the fences, following the guidance of hands other than his own, a thing he would once have scorned to do. He would ride as lightly and as easily as ever, sitting erect and jaunty in the saddle, his reins held high and loose in the hand whose fingers turn up gracefully, his whole body free yet firm in the saddle with the seat of the perfect horseman. At the boom of the cannon, when the flag dropped fluttering down to sleep, he would rise in his stirrups and wave his hat to the flag. Then, toward the edge, out into the evening, he would ride on. The dust of his riding would mingle with the dusk of night. We could not see which was the one or the other. We could only hear the hoofbeats passing, boldly and steadily still, but growing fainter, fainter, and more faint. (*The Story of the Cowboy*.)

CHAPTER 5

# The Mines

If the influence of the cattle industry was paramount in the development of the frontier region found by the first railways, it should not be concluded that this upthrust of the southern cattle constituted the only contribution to the West of that day. There were indeed earlier influences, the chief of which was the advent of the wild population of the placer mines. The riches of the gold-fields hastened the building of the first transcontinental railroads and the men of the mines set their mark also indelibly upon the range.

It is no part of our business here to follow the great discoveries of 1849 in California. (See Stewart Edward White: *The Forty-Niners, Chronicles of America*). Neither shall we chronicle the once-famous rushes from California north into the Fraser River Valley of British Columbia; neither is it necessary to mention in much detail the great camps of Nevada; nor yet the short-lived stampede of 1859 to the Pike's Peak country in Colorado. The rich placer fields of Idaho and Montana, from which enormous amounts were taken, offer typical examples of the mining communities of the Rockies.

We may never know how much history remains forever unwritten. Of the beginnings of the Idaho camps there have trickled back into record only brief, inconsequent, and partial stories. The miners who surged this way and that all through the Sierras, the upper Cascades, north into the Selkirks, and thence back again into the Rockies were a turbulent mob. Having overrun all our mountain ranges, following the earlier trails of the traders and trappers, they now recoiled upon themselves and rolled back eastward to meet the advancing civilization of the westbound rails, caring nothing for history and less for the civilized society in which they formerly had lived. This story of bedlam broken loose, of men gone crazed by the sudden subversion of all known values and all standards of life, was at first something which had no historian and can be recorded only by way of hearsay stories which did not always tally as to the truth.

The mad treasure-hunter of the California mines, restless, insubordinate, incapable of restraint, possessed of the belief that there might be gold elsewhere than in California, and having heard reports of strikes to the north, went hurrying out into the mountains of Oregon and Washington, in a wild stampede, all eager again to engage in the glorious gamble where by one lucky stroke of the pick a man might be set free of the old limitations of human existence.

So, the flood of gold-seekers—passing north into the Fraser River country, south again into Oregon and Washington, and across the great desert plains into Nevada and Idaho—made new centres of lurid activity, such as Oro Fino, Florence, and Carson. Then it was that Walla Walla and Lewiston, outfitting points on the western side of the range, found place upon the maps of the land, such as they were.

Before these adventurers, now eastbound and no longer facing west, there arose the vast and formidable mountain ranges which in their time had daunted even the calm minds of Meriwether Lewis and William Clark. But the prospectors and the pack-trains alike penetrated the Salmon River Range. Oro Fino, in Idaho, was old in 1861. The next great strikes were to be made around Florence. Here the indomitable packer from the West, conquering unheard-of difficulties, brought in whiskey, women, pianos, food, mining-tools. Naturally all these commanded fabulous prices. The price for each and all lay underfoot. Man, grown superman, could overleap time itself by a stroke of the pick! What wonder delirium reigned!

These events became known in the Mississippi Valley and farther eastward. And now there came hurrying out from the older regions many more hundreds and thousands eager to reach a land not so far as California, but reputed to be quite as rich. It was then, as the bull-trains came in from the East, from the head of navigation on the Missouri River, that the western outfitting points of Walla Walla and Lewiston lost their importance.

Southward of the Idaho camps the same sort of story was repeating itself. Nevada had drawn to herself a portion of the wild men of the stampedes. Carson for its day (1859-60) was a capital not unlike the others. Some of its men had come down from the upper fields, some had arrived from the East over the old Santa Fé Trail, and yet others had drifted in from California.

All the camps were very much alike. A straggling row of log cabins or huts of motley construction; a few stores so-called, sometimes of logs, or, if a saw-mill was at hand, of rude sawn boards; a number of saloons, each of which customarily also supported a dance-hall; a series of cabins or huts where dwelt individual men, each doing his own cooking and washing; and outside these huts the uptorn earth—such were the camps which dotted the trails of the stampedes across inhospitable deserts and mountain ranges Church and school were unknown. Law there was none, for of organised society there was none. The women who lived there were unworthy of the name of woman. The men strode about in the loose dress of the camp, sometimes without waistcoat, sometimes coatless, shod with heavy boots, always armed.

If we look for causes contributory to the history of the mining-camp, we shall find one which ordinarily is overlooked—the invention of Colt's revolving pistol. At the time of the Civil War, though this weapon was not old, yet it had attained very general use throughout the frontier. That was before the day of modern ammunition. The six-shooter of the placer days was of the old cap-and-ball type, heavy, long-barrelled, and usually wooden-handled. It was the general ownership of these deadly weapons which caused so much bloodshed in the camps. The revolver in the hands of a tyro is not especially serviceable, but it attained great deadliness in the hands of an expert user. Such a man, naturally of quick nerve reflexes, skilful and accurate in the use of the weapon through long practice, became a dangerous, and for a time an unconquerable, antagonist.

It is a curious fact that the great Montana fields were doubly discovered, in part by men coming east from California, and in part by men passing west in search of new gold-fields. The first discovery of gold in Montana was made on Gold Creek by a half-breed trapper named François, better known as Be-net-see. This was in 1852, but the news seems to have lain dormant for a time—naturally enough, for there was small ingress or egress for that wild and unknown country. In 1857, however, a party of miners who had wandered down the Big Hole River on their way back east from California decided to look into the Gold Creek discovery, of which they had heard.

This party was led by James and Granville Stuart, and among others in the party were Jake Meeks, Robert Hereford, Robert Dempsey, John W. Powell, John M. Jacobs, Thomas Adams, and some others. These men did some work on Gold Creek in 1858, but seem not to have struck it very rich, and to have withdrawn to Fort Bridger in Utah until the autumn of 1860. Then a prospector by the name of Tom Golddigger turned up at Bridger with additional stories of creeks to the north, so that there was a gradual straggling back toward Gold Creek and other gulches. This prospector had been all over the Alder Gulch, which was ere long to prove fabulously rich.

It was not, however, until 1863 that the Montana camps sprang into fame. It was not Gold Creek or Alder Gulch, but Florence and other Idaho camps, that, in the summer and autumn of 1862, brought into the mountains no less than five parties of gold-seekers, who remained in Montana because they could not penetrate the mountain barrier which lay between them and the Salmon River camps in Idaho.

The first of these parties arrived at Gold Creek by wagon-train from Fort Benton and the second hailed from Salt Lake. An election was held for the purpose of forming a sort of community organisation, the first election ever known in Montana. The men from the East had brought with them some idea of law and organisation. There were now in the Montana fields many good men such as the Stuart Brothers, Samuel T. Hauser, Walter Dance, and others later well known in the State. These men were prominent in the organisation of the first miners' court, which had occasion to try—and promptly to hang—Stillman and Jernigan, two ruffians who had been in from the Salmon River mines only about four days when they thus met retribution for their early crimes. An associate of theirs, Arnett, had been killed while resisting arrest. The reputation of Florence for lawlessness and bloodshed was well known; and, as the outrages of the well-organised band of desperadoes operating in Idaho might be expected to begin at any time in Montana, a certain uneasiness existed among the newcomers from the States.

Two more parties, likewise bound for Idaho and likewise baffled by the Salmon River range, arrived at the Montana camps in the same summer. Both these were from the Pike's Peak country in Colorado. And in the autumn came a fifth—this one under military protection, Captain James L. Fisk commanding, and having in the party a number of settlers bound for Oregon as well as miners for Idaho. This expedition arrived in the Prickly Pear Valley in Montana on September 21, 1862, having left St. Paul on the 16th of June, traveling by steamboat and wagon-train. While Captain Fisk and his expedition pushed on to Walla Walla, nearly half of the immigrants stayed to try their luck at placer-mining.

But the yield was not great and the distant Salmon River mines, their original destination, still awaited them. Winter was approaching. It was now too late in the season to reach the Salmon River mines, five hundred miles across the mountains, and it was four hundred miles to Salt Lake, the nearest supply post; therefore, most of the men joined this little army of prospectors in Montana. Some of them drifted to the Grasshopper diggings, soon to be known under the name of Bannack—one of the wildest mining-camps of its day.

These different origins of the population of the first Montana camps are interesting because of the fact that they indicate a difference in the two currents of population which now met here in the new placer fields. In general, the wildest and most desperate of the old-time adventurers, those coming from the West, had located in the Idaho camps, and might be expected in Montana at any time. In contrast to these, the men lately out from the States were of a different type, many of them sober, most of them law-abiding, men who had come out to better their fortunes and not merely to drop into the wild and licentious life of a placer-camp. Law and order always did prevail eventually in any mining community. In the case of Montana, law and order arrived almost synchronously with lawlessness and desperadoism.

Law and order had not long to wait before the arrival of the notorious Henry Plummer and his band from Florence. Plummer was already known as a bad man, but was not yet recognised as the leader of that secret association of robbers and murderers which had terrorised the Idaho camps. He celebrated his arrival in Bannack by killing a man named Cleveland. He was acquitted in the miners' court that tried him, on the usual plea of self-defence. He was a man of considerable personal address.

The same tribunal soon assembled once more to try three other murderers, Moore, Reeves, and Mitchell, with the agreement that the men should have a jury and should be provided with counsel. They were all practically freed; and after that the roughs grew bolder than ever. The Plummer band swore to kill every man who had served in that court, whether as juryman or officer. So well did they make good their threat that out of the twenty-seven men thus engaged all but seven were either killed or driven out of the country, nine being murdered outright.

The man who had acted as sheriff of this miners' court, Hank Crawford, was unceasingly hounded by Plummer, who sought time and again to fix a quarrel on him. Plummer was the best shot in the mountains at that time, and he thought it would be easy for him to kill his man and enter the usual plea of self-defence. By good fortune, however, Crawford caught Plummer off his guard and fired upon him with a rifle, breaking his right arm. Plummer's friends called in Dr. Glick, the best physician in Bannack, to treat the wounded man, warning him that if he told anything about the visit he would be shot down. Glick held his peace, and later was obliged to attend many of the wounded outlaws, who were always engaged in affairs with firearms.

Of all these wild affrays, of the savage life which they denoted, and of the stern ways in which retribution overtook the desperadoes of the mines, there is no better historian than Nathaniel P. Langford, a prominent citizen of the West, who accompanied the overland expedition of 1862 and took part in the earliest life of Montana. His work, *Vigilante Days and Ways*, is an invaluable contemporary record.

It is mentally difficult for us now fully to restore these scenes, although the events occurred no earlier than the Civil War. Langford says:

> Life in Bannack at this time, was perfect isolation from the rest of the world. Napoleon was not more of an exile on St. Helena than a newly arrived immigrant from the States in this region of lakes and mountains. All the great battles of the season of 1862—Antietam, Fredericksburg, Second Bull Run—all the exciting debates of Congress, and the more exciting combats at sea, first became known to us on the arrival of newspapers and letters in the spring of 1863.

The Territory of Idaho, which included Montana and nearly all Wyoming, was organised March 3, 1863. Previous to that time western Montana and Idaho formed a part of Washington Territory, of which Olympia was the capital, and Montana, east of the mountains, belonged to the Territory of Dakota, of which the capital was Yankton, on the Missouri. Langford makes clear the political uncertainties of the time, the difficulty of enforcing the laws, and narrates the circumstances which led to the erection in 1864 of the new Territory of Montana, comprising the limits of the present State.

★★★★★★

The Acts of Congress organising Territories and admitting States are milestones in the occupation of this last West. On the eve of the Civil War, Kansas was admitted into the Union; during the war, the Territories of Colorado, Nevada, Dakota, Arizona, Idaho, and Montana were organised, and Nevada was admitted as a State. Immediately after the war, Nebraska was admitted and Wyoming was organised as a Territory. In the Centennial Year (1876) Colorado became a State. In 1889 and 1890 North and South Dakota, Montana, Washington, Idaho, and Wyoming were admitted as States. In the latter year Oklahoma was carved out of the Indian Territory. Utah with its Mormon population was kept waiting at the doors of the Union until 1896. Oklahoma became a State in 1907; Arizona and New Mexico were admitted in 1912.

★★★★★★

In Montana as elsewhere in these days of great sectional bitterness, there was much political strife; and this no doubt accounts for an astonishing political event that now took place. Henry Plummer, the most active outlaw of his day, was elected sheriff and entrusted with the enforcement of the laws! He made indeed a great show of enforcing the laws. He married, settled down, and for a time was thought by some of the ill-advised to have reformed his ways, although in truth he could not have reformed.

By June, 1863, the extraordinarily rich strike in Alder Gulch had been made. The news of this spread like wildfire to Bannack and to the Salmon River mines in Idaho as well, and the result was one of the fiercest of all the stampedes, and the rise, almost overnight, of Virginia City. Meanwhile some Indian fighting had taken place and in a pitched battle on the Bear River General Connor had beaten decisively the Bannack Indians, who for years had preyed on the emigrant trains. This made travel on the mountain trails safer than it had been; and the rich Last Chance Gulch on which the city of Helena now stands attracted a tremendous population almost at once. The historian above cited lived there. Let him tell of the life:

> One long stream of active life filled the little creek on its auriferous course from Bald Mountain, through a canyon of wild and picturesque character, until it emerged into the large and fertile valley of the Pas-sama-ri ... the mountain stream called by Lewis and Clark in their journal "Philanthropy River." Lateral streams of great beauty pour down the sides of the mountain chain bounding the valley. . . . Gold placers were found

upon these streams and occupied soon after the settlement at Virginia City was commenced. . . . This human hive, numbering at least ten thousand people, was the product of ninety days. Into it were crowded all the elements of a rough and active civilization. Thousands of cabins and tents and brush *wakiups* . . . were seen on every hand. Every foot of the gulch . . . was undergoing displacement, and it was already disfigured by huge heaps of gravel which had been passed through the sluices and rifled of their glittering contents. . . . Gold was abundant, and every possible device was employed by the gamblers, the traders, the vile men and women that had come in with the miners into the locality, to obtain it.

Nearly every third cabin was a saloon where vile whiskey was peddled out for fifty cents a drink in gold dust. Many of these places were filled with gambling tables and gamblers. . . . Hurdy-gurdy dance-houses were numerous. . . . Not a day or night passed which did not yield its full fruition of vice, quarrels, wounds, or murders. The crack of the revolver was often heard above the merry notes of the violin. Street fights were frequent, and as no one knew when or where they would occur, everyone was on his guard against a random shot.

Sunday was always a gala day. . . . The stores were all open. . . . Thousands of people crowded the thoroughfares ready to rush in the direction of any promised excitement. Horse-racing was among the most favoured amusements. Prize rings were formed, and brawny men engaged in fisticuffs until their sight was lost and their bodies pommelled to a jelly, while hundreds of onlookers cheered the victor. . . . Pistols flashed, bowie knives flourished, and braggart oaths filled the air, as often as men's passions triumphed over their reason. This was indeed the reign of unbridled license, and men who at first regarded it with disgust and terror, by constant exposure soon learned to become a part of it and forget that they had ever been aught else. All classes of society were represented at this general exhibition. Judges, lawyers, doctors, even clergymen, could not claim exemption. Culture and religion afforded feeble protection, where allurement and indulgence ruled the hour.

Imagine, therefore, a fabulously rich mountain valley, twelve miles in extent, occupied by more than ten thousand men and producing more than ten millions of dollars before the close of the first year! It is a stupendous demand on any imagination. How might all this gold be sent out in safe-keeping? We are told that the only stage route extended from Virginia City no farther than Bannack. Between Virginia City and Salt Lake City there was an absolute wilderness, wholly unsettled, four hundred and seventy-five miles in width.

> There was no post office in the Territory. Letters were brought from Salt Lake first at a cost of two dollars and a half each, and later in the season at one dollar each. All money at infinite risk was sent to the nearest ex press office at Salt Lake City by private hands.

Practically every man in the new gold-fields was aware of the existence of a secret band of well-organised ruffians and robbers. The general feeling was one of extreme uneasiness. There were plenty of men who had taken out of the ground considerable quantities of gold, and who would have been glad to get back to the East with their little fortunes, but they dared not start. Time after time the express coach, the solitary rider, the unguarded wagon-train, were held up and robbed, usually with the concomitant of murder. When the miners did start out from one camp to another they took all manner of precautions to conceal their gold dust. We are told that on one occasion one party bored a hole in the end of the wagon tongue with an auger and filled it full of gold dust, thus escaping observation!

The robbers learned to know the express agents, and always had advice of every large shipment of gold. It was almost useless to undertake to conceal anything from them; and resistance was met with death. Such a reign of terror, such an organised system of highway robbery, such a light valuing of human life, has been seldom found in any other time or place.

There were, as we have seen, good men in these camps—although the best of them probably let down the standards of living somewhat after their arrival there; but the trouble was that the good men did not know one another, had no organisation, and scarcely dared at first to attempt one. On the other hand, the robbers' organisation was complete and kept its secrets as the grave; indeed, many and many a lonesome grave held secrets none ever was to know. How many men went out from Eastern States and disappeared, their fate always to remain a mystery, is a part of the untold story of the mining frontier.

There are known to have been a hundred and two men killed by

Plummer and his gang; how many were murdered without their fate ever being discovered cannot be told. Plummer was the leader of the band, but, arch-hypocrite that he was, he managed to keep his own connection with it a secret. His position as sheriff gave him many advantages. He posed as being a silver-mine expert, among other things, and often would be called out to "expert" some new mine. That usually meant that he left town in order to commit some desperate robbery. The boldest outrages always required Plummer as the leader. Sometimes he would go away on the pretence of following some fugitive from justice. His horse, the fleetest in the country, often was found, labouring and sweating, at the rear of his house. That meant that Plummer had been away on some secret errand of his own. He was suspected many times, but nothing could be fastened upon him; or there lacked sufficient boldness and sufficient organisation on the part of the law-and-order men to undertake his punishment.

We are not concerned with repeating thrilling tales, bloody almost beyond belief, and indicative of an incomprehensible depravity in human nature, so much as we are with the causes and effects of this wild civilization which raged here quite alone in the midst of one of the wildest of the western mountain regions. It will best serve our purpose to retain in mind the twofold character of this population, and to remember that the frontier caught to itself not only ruffians and desperadoes, men undaunted by any risk, but also men possessed of a yet steadier personal courage and hardihood. There were men rough, coarse, brutal, murderous; but against them were other men self-reliant, stern, just, and resolved upon fair play.

That was indeed the touchstone of the entire civilization which followed upon the heels of these scenes of violence. It was fair play which really animated the great Montana Vigilante movement and which eventually cleaned up the merciless gang of Henry Plummer and his associates. The centres of civilization were far removed. The courts were powerless. In some cases, even the machinery of the law was in the hands of these ruffians. But so violent were their deeds, so brutal, so murderous, so unfair, that slowly the indignation of the good men arose to the white-hot point of open resentment and of swift retribution. What the good men of the frontier loved most of all was justice. They now enforced justice in the only way left open to them. They did this as California earlier had done; and they did it so well that there was small need to repeat the lesson.

The actual extermination of the Henry Plummer band occurred

rather promptly when the Vigilantes once got under way. One of the band by the name of Red Yager, in company with yet another by the name of Brown, had been concerned in the murder of Lloyd Magruder, a merchant of the Territory. The capture of these two followed closely upon the hanging of George Ives, also accused of more than one murder. Ives was an example of the degrading influence of the mines. He was a decent young man until he left his home in Wisconsin. He was in California from 1857 to 1858. When he appeared in Idaho he seemed to have thrown off all restraint and to have become a common rowdy and desperado. It is said of him that "few men of his age ever had been guilty of so many fiendish crimes."

Yager and Brown, knowing the fate which Ives had met, gave up hope when they fell into the hands of the newly organised Vigilantes. Brown was hanged; so was Yager; but Yager, before his death, made a full confession which put the Vigilantes in possession of information they had never yet been able to secure.

******

Langford gives these names disclosed by Yager as follows: "Henry Plummer was chief of the band; Bill Bunton, stool pigeon and second in command; George Brown, secretary; Sam Bunton, roadster; Cyrus Skinner, fence, spy, and roadster; George Shears, horse thief and roadster; Frank Parish, horst thief and roadster; Hayes Lyons, telegraph man and roadster; Bill Hunter, telegraph man and roadster; Ned Ray, council-room keeper at Bannack City; George Ives, Stephen Marshland, Dutch John (Wagner), Alex Carter, Whiskey Bill (Graves), Johnny Cooper, Buck Stinson, Mexican Frank, Bob Zachary, Boone Helm, Clubfoot George (Lane), Billy Terwiliger, Gad Moore, were roadsters."

Practically all these were executed by the Vigilantes, with many others, and eventually the band of outlaws was entirely broken up.

******

Much has been written and much romanced about the conduct of these desperadoes when they met their fate. Some of them were brave and some proved cowards at the last. For a time, Plummer begged abjectly, his eyes streaming with tears. Suddenly he was smitten with remorse as the whole picture of his past life appeared before him. He promised everything, begged everything, if only life might be spared him—asked his captors to cut off his ears, to cut out his tongue, then strip him naked and banish him. At the very last, however, he seems to have become composed. Stinson and Ray went to their fate alternately swearing and whining. Some of the ruffians faced death boldly. More than one himself jumped from the ladder or kicked from under him the box which was the only foothold between him and eternity.

Boone Helm was as hardened as any of them. This man was a cannibal and murderer. He seems to have had no better nature whatever. His last words as he sprang off were "Hurrah for Jeff Davis! Let her rip!" Another man remarked calmly that he cared no more for hanging than for drinking a glass of water. But each after his own fashion met the end foreordained for him by his own lack of compassion; and of compassion he received none at the hands of the men who had resolved that the law should be established and should remain forever.

There was an instant improvement in the social life of Virginia City, Bannack, and the adjoining camps as soon as it was understood that the Vigilantes were afoot. Langford, who undoubtedly knew intimately of the activities of this organisation, makes no apology for the acts of the Vigilantes, although they did not have back of them the colour of the actual law. He says:

> The retribution dispensed to these daring freebooters in no respect exceeded the demands of absolute justice.... There was no other remedy. Practically the citizens had no law, but if law had existed it could not have afforded adequate redress. This was proven by the feeling of security consequent upon the destruction of the band. When the robbers were dead the people felt safe, not for themselves alone but for their pursuits and their property. They could travel without fear. They had reasonable assurance of safety in the transmission of money to the States and in the arrival of property over the unguarded route from Salt Lake.
> The crack of pistols had ceased, and they could walk the streets without constant exposure to danger. There was an omnipresent spirit of protection, akin to that omnipresent spirit of law which pervaded older and more civilized communities....
> Young men who had learned to believe that the roughs were destined to rule and who, under the influence of that faith, were fast drifting into crime shrunk appalled before the thorough work of the Vigilantes. Fear, more potent than conscience, forced even the worst of men to observe the requirements of

society, and a feeling of comparative security among all classes was the result.

Naturally it was not the case that all the bad men were thus exterminated. From time to time there appeared vividly in the midst of these surroundings additional figures of solitary desperadoes, each to have his list of victims, and each himself to fall before the weapons of his enemies or to meet the justice of the law or the sterner meed of the Vigilantes. It would not be wholly pleasant to read even the names of a long list of these; perhaps it will be sufficient to select one, the notorious Joseph Slade, one of the "picturesque" characters of whom a great deal of inaccurate and puerile history has been written. The truth about Slade is that he was a good man at first, faithful in the discharge of his duties as an agent of the stage company. Needing at times to use violence lawfully, he then began to use it unlawfully. He drank and soon went from bad to worse. At length his outrages became so numerous that the men of the community took him out and hanged him. His fate taught many others the risk of going too far in defiance of law and decency.

What has been true regarding the camps of Florence, Bannack, and Virginia City, had been true in part in earlier camps and was to be repeated perhaps a trifle less vividly in other camps yet to come. The Black Hills gold rush, for instance, which came after the railroad but before the Indians were entirely cleared away, made a certain wild history of its own. We had our Deadwood stage line then, and our Deadwood City with all its wild life of drinking, gambling, and shooting—the place where more than one notorious bad man lost his life, and some capable officers of the peace shared their fate. To describe in detail the life of this stampede and the wild scenes ensuing upon it is perhaps not needful here. The main thing is that the great quartz lodes of the Black Hills support in the end a steady, thrifty, and law-abiding population.

All over that West, once so unspeakably wild and reckless, there now rise great cities where recently were scattered only mining-camps scarce fit to be called units of any social compact. It was but yesterday that these men fought and drank and dug their own graves in their own sluices. At the city of Helena, on the site of Last Chance Gulch, one recalls that not so long ago, (as at 1918), citizens could show with a certain contemporary pride the old dead tree once known as "Hangman's Tree."

It marked a spot which might be called a focus of the old frontier. Around it, and in the country immediately adjoining, was fought out the great battle whose issue could not be doubted—that between the new and the old days; between law and order and individual lawlessness; between the school and the saloon; between the home and the dance-hall; between society united and resolved and the individual reverted to worse than savagery.

CHAPTER 6

# The Pathways of the West

Since we have declared ourselves to be less interested in bald chronology than in the naturally connected causes of events which make chronology worthwhile, we may now, perhaps, double back upon the path of chronology, and take up the great early highways of the West—what we might call the points of attack against the frontier.

The story of the Santa Fé Trail, now passing into oblivion, once was on the tongue of every man. This old highroad in its heyday presented the most romantic and appealing features of the earlier frontier life. The Santa Fé Trail was the great path of commerce between our frontier and the Spanish towns trading through Santa Fé. This commerce began in 1822, when about threescore men shipped certain goods across the lower Plains by pack-animals.

By 1826 it was employing a hundred men and was using wagons and mules. In 1830, when oxen first were used on the trail, the trade amounted to $120,000 annually; and by 1843, when the Spanish ports were closed, it had reached the value of $450,000, involving the use of 230 wagons and 350 men. It was this great wagon trail which first brought us into touch with the Spanish civilization of the South west. Its commercial totals do not bulk large today, but the old trail itself was a thing titanic in its historic value.

This was the day not of water but of land transport; yet the wheeled vehicles which passed out into the West as common carriers of civilization clung to the river valleys—natural highways and natural resting places of home-building man. This has been the story of the advance of civilization from the first movements of the world's peoples. The valleys are the cleats of civilization's golden sluices.

There lay the great valley of the Arkansas, offering food and water, an easy grade and a direct course reaching out into the West, even to the edge of the lands of Spain; and here stood wheeled vehicles able to traverse it and to carry dry-goods and hardware, and especially domestic cotton fabrics, which formed the great staple of a "Santa Fé assortment." The people of the Middle West were now, in short, able to feed and clothe themselves and to offer a little of their surplus merchandise to someone else in sale. They had begun to export! Out yonder, in a strange and unknown land, lay one of the original markets of America!

On the heels of Lewis and Clark, who had just explored the Missouri River route to the Northwest, Captain Zebulon Pike of the Army, long before the first wheeled traffic started West, had employed this valley of the Arkansas in his search for the southwestern delimitations of the United States. Pike thought he had found the head of the Red River when after a toilsome and dangerous march he reached the headwaters of the Rio Grande. But it was not our river. It belonged to Spain, as he learned to his sorrow, when he marched all the way to Chihuahua in old Mexico and lay there during certain weary months.

It was Pike's story of the far Southwest that first started the idea of the commerce of the Santa Fé Trail. In that day geography was a human thing, a thing of vital importance to all men. Men did not read the stock markets; they read stories of adventure, tales of men returned from lands out yonder in the West. Heretofore the swarthy Mexicans, folk of the dry plains and hills around the head of the Rio Grande and the Red, had carried their cotton goods and many other small and needful things all the way from Vera Cruz on the seacoast, over trails that were long, tedious, uncertain, and expensive. A far shorter and more natural trade route went west along the Arkansas, which would bring the American goods to the doors of the Spanish settlements. After Pike and one or two others had returned with reports of the country, the possibilities of this trade were clear to any one with the merchant's imagination.

There is rivalry for the title of "Father of the Santa Fé Trail." As early as 1812, when the United States was at war with England, a party of men on horseback trading into the West, commonly called the McKnight, Baird, and Chambers party, made their way west to Santa Fé. There, however, they met with disaster. All their goods were confiscated and they themselves lay in Mexican jails for nine years. Eventually the returning survivors of this party told their stories, and those stories, far from chilling, only inflamed the ardour of other adventurous traders. In 1821 more than one American trader reached Santa Fé;

and, now that the Spanish yoke had been thrown off by the Mexicans, the goods, instead of being confiscated, were purchased eagerly.

It is to be remembered, of course, that trading of this sort to Mexico was not altogether a new thing. Sutlers of the old fur traders and trappers already had found the way to New Spain from the valley of the Platte, south along the eastern edge of the Rockies, through Wyoming and Colorado. By some such route as that at least one trader, a French Creole, agent of the firm of Bryant & Morrison at Kaskaskia, had penetrated to the Spanish lands as early as 1804, while Lewis and Clark were still absent in the upper wilderness. Each year the great mountain rendezvous of the trappers—now at Bent's Fort on the Arkansas, now at Horse Creek in Wyoming, now on Green River in Utah, or even farther beyond the mountains—demanded supplies of food and traps and ammunition to enable the hunters to continue their work for another year. Perhaps many of the pack-trains which regularly supplied this shifting mountain market already had traded in the Spanish country.

It is not necessary to go into further details regarding this primitive commerce of the prairies. It yielded a certain profit; it shaped the character of the men who carried it on. But what is yet more important, it greatly influenced the country which lay back of the border on the Missouri River. It called yet more men from the eastern settlements to those portions which lay upon the edge of the Great Plains. There crowded yet more thickly, up to the line between the certain and the uncertain, the restless westbound population of all the country.

If on the south the valley of the Arkansas led outward to New Spain, yet other pathways made out from the Mississippi River into the unknown lands. The Missouri was the first and last of our great natural frontier roads. Its lower course swept along the eastern edge of the Plains, far to the south, down to the very doors of the most adventurous settlements in the Mississippi Valley. Those who dared its stained and turbulent current had to push up, onward, northward, past the mouth of the Platte, far to the north across degrees of latitude, steadily forward through a vast virgin land. Then the river bent boldly and strongly off to the west, across another empire. Its great falls indicated that it headed high; beyond the great falls its steady sweep westward and at last southward, led into yet other kingdoms.

When we travel by horse or by modern motor car in that now accessible region and look about us, we should not fail to reflect on the long trail of the upbound boats which Manuel Lisa and other traders sent out almost immediately upon the return of the Lewis and Clark expedition. We should see them struggling up against that tremendous current before steam was known, driven by their lust for new lands. We may then understand fully what we have read of the enterprises of the old American Fur Company, and bring to mind the forgotten names of Campbell and Sublette, of General Ashley and of Wyeth— names to be followed by others really of less importance, as those of Bonneville and Frémont. That there could be farms, that there ever might be homes, in this strange wild country, was, to these early adventurers, unthinkable.

Then we should picture the millions of buffalo which once covered these plains and think of the waste and folly of their slaughtering. We should see the long streams of the Mackinaw boats swimming down the Missouri, bound for St. Louis, laden with bales of buffalo and beaver peltry, every pound of which would be worth ten dollars at the capital of the fur trade; and we should restore to our minds the old pictures of savage tribesmen, decked in fur-trimmed war-shirts and plumed bonnets, armed with lance and sinewed bow and bull-neck shield, not forgetting whence they got their horses and how they got their food.

The great early mid-continental highway, known as the Oregon Trail or the Overland Trail, was by way of the Missouri up the Platte Valley, thence across the mountains. We know more of this route because it was not discontinued, but came steadily more and more into use, for one reason after another. The fur traders used it, the Forty-Niners used it, the cattlemen used it in part, the railroads used it; and, lastly, the settlers and farmers used it most of all.

In physical features the Platte River route was similar to that of the Arkansas Valley. Each at its eastern extremity, for a few days' travel, passed over the rolling grass-covered and flower-besprinkled prairies ere it broke into the high and dry lands of the Plains, with their green or grey or brown covering of practically flowerless short grasses. But between the two trails of the Arkansas and the Platte there existed certain wide differences. At the middle of the nineteenth century the two trails were quite distinct in personnel, if that word may be used. The Santa Fé Trail showed Spanish influences; that of the Platte Valley remained far more nearly American.

Thus far the frontier had always been altering the man who came to it; and, indirectly, always altering those who dwelt back of the frontier, nearer to the Appalachians or the Atlantic. A new people now was in process of formation—a people born of a new environment. America and the American were conceiving. There was soon to be born, soon swiftly to grow, a new and lasting type of man. Man changes an environment only by bringing into it new or better transportation. Environment changes man. Here in the mid-continent, at the mid-century, the frontier and the ways of the frontier were writing their imprint on the human product of our land.

The first great caravans of the Platte Valley, when the wagon-trains went out hundreds strong, were not the same as the scattering cavalcade of the fur hunters, not the same as the ox-trains and mule-trains of the Santa Fé traffic. The men who wore deepest the wheel marks of the Oregon Trail were neither trading nor trapping men, but home-building men—the first real emigrants to go West with the intent of making homes beyond the Rockies.

The Oregon Trail had been laid out by the explorers of the fur trade. Zealous missionaries had made their way over the trail in the thirties. The Argonauts of '49 passed over it and left it only after crossing the Rockies. But, before gold in California was dreamed of, there had come back to the States reports of lands rich in resources other than gold, lying in the far Northwest, beyond the great mountain ranges; and, before the Forty-Niners were heard of, farmers, home-builders, emigrants, men with their families, men with their household goods, were steadily passing out for the far-off and unknown country of Oregon.

The Oregon Trail was the pathway for Frémont in 1842, perhaps the most overvalued explorer of all the West; albeit this comment may to some seem harsh. Kit Carson and Bill Williams led Frémont across the Rockies almost by the hand. Carson and Williams themselves had been taken across by the Indian tribes. But Frémont could write; and the story which he set down of his first expedition inflamed the zeal of all. Men began to head out for that far-away country beyond the Rockies. Not a few scattered bands, but very many, passed up the valley of the Platte. There began a tremendous trek of thousands of men who wanted homes somewhere out beyond the frontier. And that was more than ten years before the Civil War. The cow trade was not dreamed of; the coming cow country was overleaped and ignored.

Our national horizon extended immeasurably along that dusty way. In the use of the Oregon Trail we first began to be great. The chief figure of the American West, the figure of the ages, is not the long-haired, fringed-legging man riding a raw-boned pony, but the gaunt and sad-faced woman sitting on the front seat of the wagon, following her lord where he might lead, her face hidden in the same ragged sunbonnet which had crossed the Appalachians and the Missouri long before. That was America, my brethren! There was the seed of America's wealth. There was the great romance of all America—the woman in the sunbonnet; and not, after all, the hero with the rifle across his saddle horn. Who has written her story? Who has painted her picture?

They were large days, those of the great Oregon Trail, not always pleasingly dramatic, but oftentimes tragic and terrible. We speak of the Oregon Trail, but it means little to us today; nor will any mere generalities ever make it mean much to us. But what did it mean to the men and women of that day? What and who were those men and women? What did it mean to take the Overland Trail in the great adventure of abandoning forever the known and the safe and setting out for Oregon or California at a time when everything in the far West was new and unknown? How did those good folk travel? Why and whither did they travel?

There is a book done by C. F. McGlashan, a resident of Truckee, California, known as The *History of the Donner Party*, (also republished by Leonaur), holding a great deal of actual history. McGlashan, living close to Donner Lake, wrote in 1879, describing scenes with which he was perfectly familiar, and recounting facts which he had from direct association with participants in the ill-fated Donner Party. He chronicles events which happened in 1846—a date before the discovery of gold in California. The Donner Party was one of the typical American caravans of homeseekers who started for the Pacific Slope with no other purpose than that of founding homes there, and with no expectation of sudden wealth to be gained in the mines. I desire therefore to quote largely from the pages of this book, believing that, in this fashion, we shall come upon history of a fundamental sort, which shall make us acquainted with the men and women of that day, with the purposes and the ambitions which animated them, and with the hardships which they encountered.

> The States along the Mississippi were but sparsely settled in 1846, yet the fame of the fruitfulness, the healthfulness, and the almost tropical beauty of the land bordering the Pacific, tempted the members of the Donner Party to leave their homes. These homes were situated in Illinois, Iowa, Tennessee, Mis-

souri, and Ohio. Families from each of these States joined the train and participated in its terrible fate; yet the party proper was organised in Sangamon County, Illinois, by George and Jacob Donner and James F. Reed. Early in April, 1846, the party set out from Springfield, Illinois, and by the first week in May reached Independence, Missouri. Here the party was increased by additional members, and the train comprised about one hundred persons. . . .

In the party were aged fathers with their trusting families about them, mothers whose very lives were wrapped up in their children, men in the prime and vigour of manhood, maidens in all the sweetness and freshness of budding womanhood, children full of glee and mirthfulness, and babes nestling on maternal breasts. Lovers there were, to whom the journey was tinged with rainbow hues of joy and happiness, and strong, manly hearts whose constant support and encouragement was the memory of dear ones left behind in homeland.

The wonderment which all experience in viewing the scenery along the line of the old emigrant road was peculiarly vivid to these people. Few descriptions had been given of the route, and all was novel and unexpected. In later years the road was broadly and deeply marked, and good camping grounds were distinctly indicated. The bleaching bones of cattle that had perished, or the broken fragments of wagons or castaway articles, were thickly strewn on either side of the highway.

But in 1846 the way was through almost trackless valleys waving with grass, along rivers where few paths were visible, save those made by the feet of buffalo and antelope, and over mountains and plains where little more than the westward course of the sun guided the travellers. Trading-posts were stationed at only a few widely distant points, and rarely did the party meet with any human beings, save wandering bands of Indians. Yet these first days are spoken of by all of the survivors as being crowned with peaceful enjoyment and pleasant anticipations. There were beautiful flowers by the roadside, an abundance of game in the meadows and mountains, and at night there were singing, dancing, and innocent plays. Several musical instruments, and many excellent voices, were in the party, and the kindliest feeling and goodfellowship prevailed among the members.

The formation of the company known as the Donner Party

was purely accidental. The union of so many emigrants into one train was not occasioned by any preconcerted arrangement. Many composing the Donner Party were not aware, at the outset, that such a tide of emigration was sweeping to California. In many instances small parties would hear of the mammoth train just ahead of them or just behind them, and by hastening their pace, or halting for a few days, joined themselves to the party.

Many were with the train during a portion of the journey, but from some cause or other became parted from the Donner company before reaching Donner Lake. Soon after the train left Independence it contained between two and three hundred wagons, and when in motion was two miles in length. The members of the party proper numbered ninety.

This caravan, like many others of the great assemblage westbound at that time, had great extremes in personnel. Some were out for mere adventure; some were single men looking for a location. Most of them were fathers of families, among them several persons of considerable means and of good standing in the community which they were leaving. While we may suppose that most of them were folk of no extraordinary sort, certainly some were persons of education and intelligence. Among these was the wife of George Donner—Tamsen Donner, a woman of education, a musician, a linguist, a botanist, and of the most sublime heroism.

Tamsen Donner sent back now and then along the route some story of the daily doings of the caravan; and such letters as these are of the utmost interest to any who desire precise information of that time. It would seem that the emigrants themselves for a great part of their route met with no great adventures, nor indeed, appeared to be undertaking any unusual affair. They followed a route up the Platte Valley already long known to those of the eastern settlements.

Near the Junction of the North<br>and South Platte, June 16, 1846.

My Old Friend: We are now on the Platte, two hundred miles from Fort Laramie. Our journey so far has been pleasant, the roads have been good, and food plentiful. The water for part of the way has been indifferent, but at no time have our cattle suffered for it. Wood is now very scarce, but "buffalo chips" are excellent; they kindle quickly and retain heat surprisingly. We had this morning buffalo steaks broiled upon them that had the same flavour they would have had upon hickory coals.

We feel no fear of Indians; our cattle graze quietly around our encampment unmolested. Two or three men will go hunting twenty miles from camp; and last night two of our men lay out in the wilderness rather than ride their horses after a hard chase. Indeed, if I do not experience something far worse than I have yet done, I shall say the trouble is all in getting started. Our wagons have not needed much repair, and I cannot yet tell in what respects they could be improved. Certain it is, they cannot be too strong. Our preparations for the journey might have been in some respects bettered.

Bread has been the principal article of food in our camp. We laid in one hundred and fifty pounds of flour and seventy-five pounds of meat for each individual, and I fear bread will be scarce. Meat is abundant. Rice and beans are good articles on the road; cornmeal too, is acceptable. Linsey dresses are the most suitable for children. Indeed, if I had one, it would be acceptable. There is so cool a breeze at all times on the Plains that the sun does not feel so hot as one would suppose.

We are now four hundred and fifty miles from Independence. Our route at first was rough, and through a timbered country, which appeared to be fertile. After striking the prairie, we found a first-rate road, and the only difficulty we have had, has been in crossing the creeks. In that, however, there has been no danger.

I never could have believed we could have travelled so far with so little difficulty. The prairie between the Blue and the Platte Rivers is beautiful beyond description. Never have I seen so varied a country, so suitable for cultivation. Everything is new and pleasing, the Indians frequently come to see us, and the chiefs of a tribe breakfasted at our tent this morning. All are so friendly that I cannot help feeling sympathy and friendship for them. But on one sheet what can I say?

Since we have been on the Platte, we have had the river on one side and the ever varying mounds on the other, and have travelled through the bottom lands from one to two miles wide, with little or no timber. The soil is sandy, and last year, on account of the dry season, the emigrants found grass here scarce. Our cattle are in good order, and when proper care has been taken, none have been lost. Our milch cows have been of great service, indeed. They have been of more advantage than our meat. We have plenty of butter and milk.

We are commanded by Captain Russell, an amiable man. George Donner is himself yet. He crows in the morning and shouts out, "Chain up, boys chain up,"—with as much authority as though he was "something in particular." John Denton is still with us. We find him useful in the camp. Hiram Miller and Noah James are in good health and doing well. We have of the best people in our company, and some, too, that are not so good. Buffalo show themselves frequently. We have found the wild tulip, the primrose, the lupine, the eardrop, the larkspur, and creeping hollyhock, and a beautiful flower resembling the bloom of the beech tree, but in bunches as large as a small sugarloaf, and of every variety of shade, to red and green.

I botanise, and read some, but cook "heaps" more. There are four hundred and twenty wagons, as far as we have heard, on the road between here and Oregon and California.

Give our love to all inquiring friends. God bless them.

    Yours truly,

                    Mrs. George Donner.

By the Fourth of July the Dormer Party had reached Fort Laramie. They pushed on west over the old trail up the Sweetwater River and across the South Pass, the easiest of all the mountain passes known to the early travellers. Without much adventure they reached Fort Bridger, then only a trading-post. Here occurred the fatal mistake of the Donner Party.

Someone at the fort strongly advised them to take a new route, a cut-off said to shorten the distance by about three hundred miles. This cut-off passed along the south shore of Great Salt Lake and caught up the old California Trail from Fort Hall—then well established and well known—along the Humboldt River. The great Donner caravan delayed for some days at Fort Bridger, hesitating over the decision of which route to follow. The party divided. All those who took the old road north of Salt Lake by of Fort Hall reached California in complete safety. Of the original Dormer Party there remained eighty-seven persons. All of these took the cut-off, being eager to save time in their travel. They reached Salt Lake after unspeakable difficulties. Farther west, in the deserts of Nevada, they lost many of their cattle.

Now began among the party dissensions and grumblings. The story is a long one. It reached its tragic *dénouement* just below the summit of the Sierras, on the shores of Donner Lake. The words of McGlashan may now best serve our purpose.

> Generally, the ascent of the Sierra brought joy and gladness to weary overland emigrants. To the Donner Party it brought terror and dismay. The company had hardly obtained a glimpse of the mountains, ere the winter storm clouds began to assemble their hosts around the loftier crests. Every day the weather appeared more ominous and threatening. The delay at the Truckee Meadows had been brief, but every day ultimately cost a dozen lives. On the twenty-third of October, they became thoroughly alarmed at the angry heralds of the gathering storm, and with all haste resumed the journey. It was too late! At Prosser Creek, three miles below Truckee, they found themselves encompassed with six inches of snow. On the summits, the snow was from two to five feet in depth. This was October 28, 1846. Almost a month earlier than usual, the Sieira had donned its mantle of ice and snow. The party were prisoners!
> All was consternation. The wildest confusion prevailed. In their eagerness, many went far in advance of the main train. There was little concert of action or harmony of plan. All did not arrive at Donner Lake the same day. Some wagons and families did not reach the lake until the thirty-first day of October, some never went farther than Prosser Creek, while others, on the evening of the twenty-ninth, struggled through the snow, and reached the foot of the precipitous cliffs between the summit and the upper end of the lake. Here, baffled, wearied, disheartened, they turned back to the foot of the lake.

These emigrants did not lack in health, strength, or resolution, but here they were in surroundings absolutely new to them. A sort of panic seized them now. They scattered; their organisation disintegrated. All thought of conjoint action, of a social compact, a community of interests, seems to have left them. It was a history of every man for himself, or at least every family for itself. All track of the road was now lost under the snow. At the last pitch up to the summit of the Sierras precipitous cliffs abounded. No one knew the way. And now the snows came once again.

The emigrants suffered a thousand deaths. The pitiless snow

came down in large, steady masses. All understood that the storm meant death. One of the Indians silently wrapped his blanket about him and in deepest dejection seated himself beside a tall pine. In this position he passed the entire night, only moving occasionally to keep from being covered with snow. Mrs. Reed spread down a shawl, placed her four children—Virginia, Patty, James, and Thomas—thereon, and putting another shawl over them, sat by the side of her babies during all the long hours of darkness. Every little while she was compelled to lift the upper shawl and shake off the rapidly accumulating snow. With slight interruptions, the storm continued several days. The mules and oxen that had always hovered about camp were blinded and bewildered by the storm, and straying away were literally buried alive in the drifts. What pen can describe the horror of the position in which the emigrants found themselves? It was impossible to move through the deep, soft snow without the greatest effort. The mules were gone, and were never found. Most of the cattle had perished, and were wholly hidden from sight. The few oxen which were found were slaughtered for beef.

The travellers knew that the supplies they had could not last long. On the 12th of November a relief party essayed to go forward, but after struggling a short distance toward the summit, came back wearied and broken-hearted, unable to make way through the deep, soft snow. Then someone—said to have been F. W. Graves of Vermont—bethought himself of making snowshoes out of the oxbows and the hides of the slaughtered oxen. With these they did better.

Volunteers were called for yet another party to cross the mountains into California. Fifteen persons volunteered. Not all of them were men—some were mothers, and one was a young woman. Their mental condition was little short of desperation. Only, in the midst of their intense hardships it seemed to all, somewhere to the westward was California, and that there alone lay any hope. The party travelled four miles the first day; and their camp fires were visible below the summit. The next day they travelled six miles and crossed the divide.

They were starving, cold, worn out, their feet frozen to bursting, their blood chilled. At times they were caught in some of the furious storms of the Sierras. They did not know their way. On the 27th of December certain of the party resolved themselves to that last recourse which alone might mean life. Surrounded by horrors as they were, it seemed they could endure the thought of yet an additional horror.... There were the dead, the victims who already had perished! ...

Seven of the fifteen got through to the Sacramento Valley, among these the young girl, Mary Graves, described as "a very beautiful girl, of tall and slender build, and exceptionally graceful character." The story brought out by these survivors of the first party to cross the Sierras from the starving camp set all California aflame. There were no less than three relief expeditions formed, which at varying dates crossed the mountains to the east. Some men crossed the snow belt five times in all. The rescuers were often in as much danger as the victims they sought to save.

And they could not save them. Back there in their tents and hovels around Donner Lake starvation was doing its work steadily. There is contemporary history also covering the details of this. Tamsen Donner, heroine that she was, kept a diary which would have been valuable for us, but this was lost along with her paintings and her botanical collections. The best preserved diary is that of Patrick Breen, done in simple and matter-of-fact fashion throughout most of the starving winter. Thus:

> *Dec. 17.* Pleasant; William Murphy returned from the mountain party last evening; Baylis Williams died night before last; Milton and Noah started for Donner's eight days ago; not returned yet; think they are lost in the snow.
>
> *Dec. 21.* Milton got back last night from Donners camp. Sad news; Jacob Donner, Samuel Shoemaker, Rhineheart, and Smith are dead; the rest of them in a low situation; snowed all night, with a strong southwest wind.
>
> *Dec. 23.* Clear today; Milton took some of his meat away; all well at their camp. Began this day to read the *Thirty Days' Prayers*; Almighty God, grant the requests of unworthy sinners!
>
> *Jan. 13.* Snowing fast; snow higher than the shanty; it must be thirteen feet deep. Cannot get wood this morning; it is a dreadful sight for us to look upon.
>
> *Jan. 27.* Commenced snowing yesterday; still continues today. Lewis Keseberg, Jr., died three days ago; food growing scarce; don't have fire enough to cook our hides.

*Jan. 31.* The sun does not shine out brilliant this morning; froze hard last night; wind northwest. Landrum Murphy died last night about ten o'clock; Mrs. Reed went to Graves's this morning to look after goods.

*Feb. 4.* Snowed hard until twelve o'clock last night; many uneasy for fear we shall all perish with hunger; we have but little meat left, and only three hides; Mrs. Reed has nothing but one hide, and that is on Graves's house; Milton lives there, and likely will keep that. Eddy's child died last night.

*Feb. 7.* Ceased to snow at last; today it is quite pleasant. McCutchen's child died on the second of this month.

(This child died and was buried in the Graves's cabin. Mr. W. C. Graves helped dig the grave near one side of the cabin, and laid the little one to rest One of the most heart-rending features of this Donner tragedy is the number of infants that perished. Mrs. Breen, Mrs. Pike, Mrs. Foster, Mrs. McCutchen, Mrs. Eddy, and Mrs. Graves each had nursing babes when the fatal camp was pitched at Donner Lake.)

*Feb. 8.* Fine, clear morning. Spitzer died last night, and we will bury him in the snow; Mrs. Eddy died on the night of the seventh.

*Feb. 9.* Mrs. Pike's child all but dead; Milton is at Murphy's, not able to get out of bed; Mrs. Eddy and child buried today; wind southeast.

*Feb. 10.* Beautiful morning; thawing in the sun; Milton Elliott died last night at Murphy's cabin, and Mrs. Reed went there this morning to see about his effects. John Denton trying to borrow meat for Graves; had none to give; they had nothing but hides; all are entirely out of meat, but a little we have; our hides are nearly all eat up, but with God's help spring will soon smile upon us."

There was one survivor of the camp at Donner Lake, a man named Lewis Keseberg, of German descent. That he was guilty of repeated cannibalism cannot be doubted. It was in his cabin that, after losing all her loved ones, the heroic Tamsen Donner met her end. Many thought he killed her for the one horrid purpose. (Many years later, 1879, Keseberg declared under oath to C. F, McGlashan that he did not take her life. See *History of the Donner Party*.)

Such then is the story of one of the great emigrant parties who started West on a hazard of new fortunes in the early days of the Oregon Trail. Happily, there has been no parallel to the misadventures of this ill-fated caravan. It is difficult—without reading these bald and awful details—to realise the vast difference between that day and this. Today, (1918), we may by the gentle stages of a pleasant railway journey arrive at Donner Lake. Little trace remains, nor does any kindly soul wish for more definite traces, of those awful scenes. Only a cross here and there with a legend, faint and becoming fainter every year, may be seen, marking the more prominent spots of the historic starving camp.

Up on the high mountain side, for the most part hid in the forest, lie the snow-sheds and tunnels of the railway, now encountering its stiffest climb up the steep slopes to the summit of the Sierras. The author visited this spot of melancholy history in company with the vice-president of the great railway line which here swings up so steadily and easily over the Sierras. Bit by bit we checked out as best we might the fateful spots mentioned in the story of the Donner Party. A splendid motor highway runs by the lakeside now, (1918). While we halted our own car there, a motor car drove up from the westward—following that practical automobile highway which now exists from the plains of California across the Sierras and east over precisely that trail where once the weary feet of the oxen dragged the wagons of the early emigrants. It was a small car of no expensive type. It was loaded down with camping equipment until the wheels scarcely could be seen. It carried five human occupants—an Iowa farmer and his family. They had been out to California for a season. Casually they had left Los Angeles, had travelled north up the valleys of California, east across the summit of the Sierras, and were here now bound for Iowa over the old emigrant trail!

We hailed this new traveller on the old trail. I do not know whether or not he had any idea of the early days of that great highway; I suspect that he could tell only of its present motoring possibilities. But his wheels were passing over the marks left more than half a century ago by the cracked felloes of the emigrant wagons going west in search of homes. If we seek history, let us ponder that chance pause of the eastbound family, traveling by motor for pleasure, here by the side of the graves of the travellers of another day, itself so briefly gone. What an epoch was spanned in the passing of that frontier!

CHAPTER 7

# The Indian Wars

It might well be urged against the method employed in these pages that, although we undertook to speak of the last American frontier, all that we really thus far have done has been to describe a series of frontiers from the Missouri westward. In part this is true. But it was precisely in this large, loose, and irregular fashion that we actually arrived at our last frontier. Certainly, our westbound civilization never advanced by any steady or regular process. It would be a singularly illuminating map—and one which I wish we might show—which would depict in different colours the great occupied areas of the West, with the earliest dates of their final and permanent occupation. Such a map as this would show us that the last frontier of America was overleaped and left behind not once but a score of times.

The land between the Missouri and the Rockies, along the Great Plains and the high foothills, was crossed over and forgotten by the men who were forging on into farther countries in search of lands where fortune was swift and easy. California, Oregon, all the early farming and timbering lands of the distant Northwest—these lay far beyond the Plains; and as we have noted, they were sought for, even before gold was dreamed of upon the Pacific Slope.

So here, somewhere between the Missouri and the Rockies, lay our last frontier, wavering, receding, advancing, gaining and losing, changing a little more every decade—and at last so rapidly changed as to be outworn and abolished in one swift decade all its own.

This unsettled land so long held in small repute by the early Americans, was, as we have pointed out, the buffalo-range and the country of the Horse Indians—the Plains tribes who lived upon the buffalo. For a long time, it was this Indian population which held back the white settlements of Kansas, Nebraska, the Dakotas, Montana, Wyoming, Colorado. But as men began to work farther and farther westward in search of homes in Oregon, or in quest of gold in California or Idaho or Montana, the Indian question came to be a serious one.

To the army, soon after the Civil War, fell the task of exterminating, or at least evicting, the savage tribes over all this unvalued and unknown Middle West. This was a process not altogether simple. For a considerable time, the Indians themselves were able to offer very effective resistance to the enterprise. They were accustomed to living upon that country, and did not need to bring in their own supplies; hence the army fought them at a certain disadvantage. In sooth, the army had to learn to become half Indian before it could fight the Indians on anything like even terms. We seem not so much to have coveted the lands in the first Indian-fighting days; we fought rather for the trails than for the soil. The Indians themselves had lived there all their lives, had conquered their environment, and were happy in it. They made a bitter fight; nor are they to be blamed for doing so.

The greatest of our Indian wars have taken place since our own Civil War; and perhaps the most notable of all the battles are those which were fought on the old cow range—in the land of our last frontier. We do not lack abundant records of this time of our history. Soon after the Civil War the railroads began edging out into the Plains. They brought, besides many new settlers, an abundance of chroniclers and historians and writers of hectic fiction or supposed fact. A multitude of books came out at this time of our history, most of which were accepted as truth. That was the time when we set up as Wild West heroes rough skin-clad hunters and so-called scouts, each of whom was allowed to tell his own story and to have it accepted at par.

As a matter of fact, at about the time the army had succeeded in subduing the last of the Indian tribes on the buffalo-range, the most of our Wild West history, at least so far as concerned the boldest adventure, was a thing of the past. It was easy to write of a past which everyone now was too new, too ignorant, or too busy critically to remember.

Even as early as 1866, Colonel Marcy, an experienced army officer and Indian-fighter, took the attitude of writing about a vanishing phase of American life. In his *Army Life on the Border*, he says:

> I have been persuaded by many friends that the contents of the book which is herewith presented to the public are not

without value as records of a fast-vanishing age, and as truthful sketches of men of various races whose memory will shortly depend only on romance, unless someone who knew them shall undertake to leave outlines of their peculiar characteristics.... I am persuaded that excuse may be found in the simple fact that all these peoples of my description—men, conditions of life, races of aboriginal inhabitants and adventurous hunters and pioneers—are passing away.

A few years more and the prairie will be transformed into farms. The mountain ravines will be the abodes of busy manufacturers, and the gigantic power of American civilization will have taken possession of the land from the great river of the West to the very shores of the Pacific.... The world is fast filling up. I trust I am not in error when I venture to place some value, however small, on everything which goes to form the truthful history of a condition of men incident to the advances of civilization over the continent—a condition which forms peculiar types of character, breeds remarkable developments of human nature—a condition also which can hardly again exist on this or any other continent, and which has, therefore, a special value in the sum of human history.

Such words as the foregoing bespeak a large and dignified point of view. No one who follows Marcy's pages can close them with anything but respect and admiration. It is in books such as this, then, that we may find something about the last stages of the clearing of the frontier.

Even in Marcy's times the question of our Government's Indian policy was a mooted one. He himself as an army officer looked at the matter philosophically, but his estimate of conditions was exact. Long ago as he wrote, his conclusions were such as might have been given forty years later.

> The limits of their accustomed range are rapidly contracting, and their means of subsistence undergoing a corresponding diminution. The white man is advancing with rapid strides upon all sides of them, and they are forced to give way to his encroachments. The time is not far distant when the buffalo will become extinct, and they will then be compelled to adopt some other mode of life than the chase for a subsistence.... No man will quietly submit to starvation when food is within

his reach, and if he cannot obtain it honestly he will steal it or take it by force. If, therefore, we do not induce them to engage in agricultural avocations we shall in a few years have before us the alternative of exterminating them or fighting them perpetually. That they are destined ultimately to extinction does not in my mind admit of a doubt. For the reasons above mentioned it may at first be necessary for our government to assert its authority over them by a prompt and vigorous exercise of the military arm. . . . The tendency of the policy I have indicated will be to assemble these people in communities where they will be more readily controlled; and I predict from it the most gratifying results.

Another well-informed army officer, Colonel Richard Dodge, himself a hunter, a trailer, and a rider able to compete with the savages in their own fields, penetrated to the heart of the Indian problem when he wrote:

The conception of Indian character is almost impossible to a man who has passed the greater portion of his life surrounded by the influences of a cultivated, refined, and moral society. . . . The truth is simply too shocking, and the revolted mind takes refuge in disbelief as the less painful horn of the dilemma. As a first step toward an understanding of his character we must get at his standpoint of morality. As a child he is not brought up. . . . From the dawn of intelligence his own will is his law. There is no right and no wrong to him. . . . No dread of punishment restrains him from any act that boyish fun or fury may prompt. No lessons inculcating the beauty and sure reward of goodness or the hideousness and certain punishment of vice are ever wasted on him. The men by whom he is surrounded, and to whom he looks as models for his future life, are great and renowned just in proportion to their ferocity, to the scalps they have taken, or the thefts they have committed.

His earliest boyish memory is probably a dance of rejoicing over the scalps of strangers, all of whom he is taught to regard as enemies. The lessons of his mother awaken only a desire to take his place as soon as possible in fight and foray. The instruction of his father is only such as is calculated to fit him best to act a prominent part in the chase, in theft, and in murder. . . . Virtue, morality, generosity, honour, are words not only absolutely without significance to him, but are not accurately translatable into any Indian language on the Plains.

These are sterner, less kindly, less philosophic words than Marcy's, but they keenly outline the duty of the army on the frontier. We made treaties with the Indians and broke them. In turn men such as these ignorant savages might well be expected to break their treaties also; and they did. Unhappily our Indian policy at that time was one of mingled ferocity and wheedling. The Indians did not understand us any more than we did them. When we withdrew some of the old frontier posts from the old hunting-range, the action was construed by the tribesmen as an admission that we feared them, and they acted upon that idea. In one point of view they had right with them, for now we were moving out into the last of the great buffalo country. Their war was one of desperation, whereas ours was one of conquest, no better and no worse than all the wars of conquest by which the strong have taken the possessions of the weak.

Our Army at the close of the Civil War and at the beginning of the wars with the Plains tribes was in better condition than it has ever been since that day. It was made up of the soundest and best-seasoned soldiers that ever fought under our flag; and at that time, it represented a greater proportion of our fighting strength than it ever has before or since. In 1860 the Regular Army, not counting the volunteer forces, was 16,000. In 1870 it was 37,000—one soldier to each one thousand of our population.

Against this force, pioneers of the vaster advancing army of peaceful settlers now surging West, there was arrayed practically all the population of fighting tribes such as the Sioux, the two bands of the Cheyennes, the Piegans, the Assiniboines, the Arapahoes, the Kiowas, the Comanches, and the Apaches. These were the leaders of many other tribes in savage campaigns which set the land aflame from the Rio Grande to our northern line. The Sioux and Cheyennes were more especially the leaders, and they always did what they could to enlist the aid of the less warlike tribes such as the Crows, the Snakes, the Bannacks, the Utes—indeed all of the savage or semi-civilized tribes which had hung on the flanks of the traffic of the westbound trail.

The Sioux, then at the height of their power, were distinguished by many warlike qualities. They fought hard and were quick to seize upon any signs of weakness in their enemies. When we, in the course of our Civil War, had withdrawn some of the upper posts, the Sioux edged in at once and pressed back the whites quite to the eastern confines of the Plains. When we were locked in the death grip of internecine war in 1862, they rose in one savage wave of rebellion of their own and massacred with the most horrible ferocity not less than six hundred and forty-four whites in Minnesota and South Dakota. When General Sibley went out among them on his later punitive campaign he had his hands full for many a long and weary day.

Events following the close of the Civil War did not mend matters in the Indian situation. The railroads had large land grants given to them along their lines, and they began to offer these lands for sale to settlers. Soldier scrip entitling the holder to locate on public lands now began to float about. Some of the engineers, even some of the laborers, upon the railroads, seeing how really feasible was the settlement of these Plains, began to edge out and to set up their homes, usually not far from the railway lines. All this increase in the numbers of the white population not only infuriated the Indians the more, but gave them the better chance to inflict damage upon our people. Our Army therefore became very little more than a vast body of police, and it was always afoot with the purpose of punishing these offending tribesmen, who knew nothing of the higher laws of war and who committed atrocities that have never been equalled in history; unless it be by one of the belligerents of the Great War in Europe, with whom we are at this writing engaged—once more in the interest of a sane and human civilization. The last great struggle for the occupation of the frontier was on. It involved the ownership of the last of our open lands; and hence may be called the war of our last frontier.

The settler who pushed West continued to be the man who shared his time between his rifle and his plough. The numerous buffalo were butchered with an endless avidity by the men who now appeared upon the range. As the great herds regularly migrated southward with each winter's snows, they were met by the settlers along the lower railway lines and in a brutal commerce were killed in thousands and in millions. The Indians saw this sudden and appalling shrinkage of their means of livelihood. It meant death to them. To their minds, especially when they thought we feared them, there was but one answer to all this—the whites must all be killed.

Red Cloud, Crazy Horse, Roman Nose, American Horse, Black Kettle—these were names of great Indian generals who proved their ability to fight. At times they brought into the open country, which as yet remained unoccupied by the great pastoral movement from the south, as many as five thousand mounted warriors in one body, and they were well armed and well supplied with ammunition. Those were the days when the Indian agents were carrying on their lists twice as many Indians as actually existed—and receiving twice as many supplies as really were issued to the tribes. The curse of politics was ours even at that time, and it cost us then, as now, unestimated millions of our nation's dearest treasures. As to the reservations which the Indians were urged to occupy, they left them when they liked. In the end, when they were beaten, all they were asked to do was to return to these reservations and be fed.

There were fought in the West from 1869 to 1875 more than two hundred pitched actions between the army and the Indians. In most cases the white men were heavily outnumbered. The account which the army gave of itself on scores of unremembered minor fields—which meant life or death to all engaged—would make one of the best pages of our history, could it be written today. The enlisted men of the frontier army were riding and shooting men, able to live as the Indians did and able to beat them at their own game. They were led by army officers whose type has never been improved upon in any later stage of our army itself, or of any army in the world.

There are certain great battles which may at least receive notice, although it would be impossible to mention more than a few of the encounters of the great Indian wars on the buffalo-range at about the time of the buffalo's disappearance. The Fetterman Massacre in 1866, near Fort Phil Kearney, a post located at the edge of the Big Horn Mountains, was a blow which the army never has forgotten.

> In a place of fifty feet square lay the bodies of Colonel Fetterman, Captain Brown, and sixty-five enlisted men. Each man was stripped naked and hacked and scalped, the skulls beaten in with war clubs and the bodies gashed with knives almost beyond recognition, with other ghastly mutilations that the civilized pen hesitates to record. (*Ab-sa-ra-ka or Wyoming Opened* by Margaret Irvin Carrington, *My Army Life and the Fort Phil. Kearney Massacre* by Frances C. Carrington both republished by Leonaur contain details about the massacre.)

This tragedy brought the Indian problem before the country as never before. The hand of the Western rancher and trader was implacably against the tribesmen of the plains; the city-dweller of the East, with hazy notions of the Indian character, was disposed to urge lenient methods upon those responsible for governmental policy. While the Sioux and Cheyenne wars dragged on, Congress created, by act of July 20, 1867, a peace commission of four civilians and three army officers to deal with the hostile tribes. For more than a year, with scant sympathy from the military members, this commission endeavoured to remove the causes of friction by amicable conference with the Indian chiefs. The attitude of the army is reflected in a letter of General Sherman to his brother:

> We have now selected and provided reservations for all, off the great roads. All who cling to their old hunting-grounds are hostile and will remain so till killed off. We will have a sort of predatory war for years—every now and then be shocked by the indiscriminate murder of travelers and settlers, but the country is so large, and the advantage of the Indians so great, that we cannot make a single war and end it. From the nature of things, we must take chances and clean out Indians as we encounter them.

Segregation of the Indian tribes upon reservations seemed to the commission the only solution of the vexing problem. Various treaties were made and others were projected looking toward the removal of the tribesmen from the highways of continental travel. The result was misgiving and increased unrest among the Indians.

In midsummer of 1868 forays occurred at many points along the border of the Indian Territory. General Sheridan, who now commanded the Department of the Missouri, believed that a general war was imminent. He determined to teach the southern tribesmen a lesson they would not forget. In the dead of winter our troops marched against the Cheyennes, then in their encampments below the Kansas line. The Indians did not believe that white men could march in weather forty below zero, during which they themselves sat in their *tepees* around their fires; but our cavalrymen did march in such weather, and under conditions such as our cavalry perhaps could not endure today. Among these troops was the Seventh Cavalry, Custer's Regiment, formed after the Civil War, and it was led by Lieutenant-Colonel George A. Custer himself, that gallant officer whose name was to go into further and more melancholy history of the Plains.

Custer marched until he got in touch with the trails of the Cheyennes, whom he knew to belong to Black Kettle's band, He did not at the time know that below them, in the same valley of the Washita, were also the winter encampments of the Kiowas, the Comanches, the Arapahoes, and even a few Apaches. He attacked at dawn of a bleak winter morning, November 27, 1868, after taking the precaution of surrounding the camp, and killed Black Kettle, and another chief, Little Rock, and over a hundred of their warriors. Many women and children also were killed in this attack. The result was one which sank deep into the Indian mind. They began to respect the men who could outmarch them and outlive them on the range. Surely, they thought, these were not the same men who had abandoned Forts Phil Kearney, C. F. Smith, and Reno. There had been some mistake about this matter. The Indians began to think it over. The result was a pacifying of all the country south of the Platte. The lower Indians began to come in and give themselves up to the reservation life.

One of the hardest of pitched battles ever fought with an Indian tribe occurred in September, 1868, on the Arickaree or South Fork of the Republican River, where General "Sandy" Forsyth, and his scouts, for nine days fought over six hundred Cheyennes and Arapahoes. These savages had been committing atrocities upon the settlers of the Saline, the Solomon, and the Republican valleys, and were known to have killed some sixty-four men and women at the time General Sheridan resolved to punish them. Forsyth had no chance to get a command of troops, but he was allowed to enlist fifty scouts, all "first-class, hardened frontiersmen," and with this body of fighting men he carried out the most dramatic battle perhaps ever waged on the Plains.

Forsyth ran into the trail of two or three large Indian villages, but none the less he followed on until he came to the valley of the South Fork. Here the Cheyennes under the redoubtable Roman Nose surrounded him on the 17th of September. The small band of scouts took refuge on a brushy island some sixty yards from shore, and hastily dug themselves in under fire.

They stood at bay outnumbered ten to one, with small prospect of escape, for the little island offered no protection of itself, and was in point-blank range from the banks of the river. All their horses soon were shot down, and the men lay in the rifle pits with no hope of escape. Roman Nose, enraged at the resistance put up by Forsyth's men, led a band of some four hundred of his warriors in the most desperate charge that has been recorded in all our Indian fighting annals. It was rarely that the Indian would charge at all; but these tribesmen, stripped naked for the encounter, and led at first by that giant warrior, who came on shouting his defiance, charged in full view not only once but three times in one day, and got within a hundred feet of the foot of the island where the scouts were lying.

According to Forsyth's report, the Indians came on in regular ranks like the cavalry of the white men, more than four hundred strong. They were met by the fire of repeating carbines and revolvers, and they stood for the first, second, third, fourth, and fifth fire of repeating weapons, and still charged in! Roman Nose was killed at last within touch of the rifle pits against which he was leading his men. The second charge was less desperate, for the savages lost heart after the loss of their leader. The third one, delivered towards the evening of that same day, was desultory. By that time the bed of the shallow stream was well filled with fallen horses and dead warriors.

Forsyth ordered meat cut from the bodies of his dead horses and buried in the wet sand so that it might keep as long as possible. Lieutenant Beecher, his chief of scouts, was killed, as also were Surgeon Mooers, and Scouts Smith, Chalmers, Wilson, Farley, and Day. Seventeen others of the party were wounded, some severely. Forsyth himself was shot three times, once in the head. His left leg was broken below the knee, and his right thigh was ripped up by a rifle ball, which caused him extreme pain. Later he cut the bullet out of his own leg, and was relieved from some part of the pain. After his rescue, when his broken leg was set it did not suit him, and he had the leg broken twice in the hospital and reset until it knitted properly.

Forsyth's men lay under fire under a blazing sun in their holes on the sandbar for nine days. But the savages never dislodged them, and at last they made off, their women and children beating the death drums, and the entire village mourning the unreturning brave. On the second day of the fighting Forsyth had got out messengers at extreme risk, and at length the party was rescued by a detachment of the Tenth Cavalry. The Indians later said that they had in all over six hundred warriors in this fight. Their losses, though variously estimated, were undoubtedly heavy.

It was encounters such as this which gradually were teaching the Indians that they could not beat the white men, so that after a time they began to yield to the inevitable.

What is known as the Baker Massacre was the turning-point in the half-century of warfare with the Blackfeet, the savage tribe which had preyed upon the men of the fur trade in a long-continued series of robberies and murders. On January 22, 1870, Major E. M. Baker, led by half-breeds who knew the country, surprised the Piegans in their winter camp on the Marias River, just below the border. He, like Custer, attacked at. dawn, opening the encounter with a general fire into the tepees. He killed a hundred and seventy-three of the Piegans, including very many women and children, as was unhappily the case so often in these surprise attacks. It was deplorable warfare. But it ended the resistance of the savage Blackfeet. They have been disposed for peace from that day to this, (1918).

The terrible revenge which the Sioux and Cheyennes took in the battle which annihilated Custer and his men on the Little Big Horn in the summer of 1876; the Homeric running fight made by Chief Joseph of the Nez Percés—a flight which baffled our best generals and their men for a hundred and ten days over more than fourteen hundred miles of wilderness—these are events so well known that it seems needless to do more than to refer to them. The Nez Percés in turn went down forever when Joseph came out and surrendered, saying:

> From where the sun now stands I fight against the white man no more forever.

His surrender to fate did not lack its dignity. Indeed, a mournful interest attached to the inevitable destiny of all these savage leaders, who, no doubt, according to their standards, were doing what men should do and all that men could do. (*The Nez Percé Campaign*, 1877, by G. O. Shields & Edmond Stephen Meany, also published by Leonaur).

The main difficulty in administering full punishment to such bands was that after a defeat they scattered, so that they could not be overtaken in any detailed fashion. After the Custer fight many of the tribe went north of the Canadian line and remained there for some time. The writer himself has seen along the Qu'Appelle River in Saskatchewan some of the wheels taken out of the watches of Glister's men. The savages broke them up and used the wheels for jewellery. They even offered the Canadians for trade boots, hats, and clothing taken from the bodies of Custer's men.

The Modoc war against the warriors of Captain Jack in 1873 was waged in the lava beds of Oregon, and it had the distinction of being one of the first Indian wars to be well reported in the newspapers. (In *Wigwam and War-Path* by A. B. Meacham published by Leonaur, this war is described by an eyewitness.) We heard a great deal of the long and trying campaigns waged by the army in revenge for the murder of

General Canby in his council tent. We got small glory out of that war, perhaps, but at last we hanged the ringleader of the murderers; and the extreme Northwest remained free from that time on.

Far in the dry Southwest, where home-building man did not as yet essay a general occupation of the soil, the blood-thirsty Apache long waged a warfare which tried the mettle of our army as perhaps no other tribes ever have done. The Spaniards had fought these Apaches for nearly three hundred years, and had not beaten them. They offered three hundred dollars each for Apache scalps, and took a certain number of them. But they left all the remaining braves sworn to an eternal enmity. The Apaches became mountain outlaws, whose blood-mad thirst for revenge never died. No tribe ever fought more bitterly. Hemmed in and surrounded, with no hope of escape, in some instances they perished literally to the last man.

General George Crook finished the work of cleaning up the Apache outlaws only by use of the trailers of their own people who sided with the whites for pay. Without the Pima scouts he never could have run down the Apaches as he did. Perhaps these were the hardest of all the Plains Indians to find and to fight. But in 1872 Crook subdued them and concentrated them in reservations in Arizona. Ten years later, under Geronimo, a tribe of the Apaches broke loose and yielded to General Crook only after a prolonged war. Once again, they raided New Mexico and Arizona in 1885-6. This was the last raid of Geronimo. He was forced by General Miles to surrender and, together with his chief warriors, was deported to For Pickens in Florida. (See *Geronimo* by Geronimo and *On the Border With Crook* by his officer, John G. Bourke, by Leonaur, which give eyewitness accounts of these times.)

In all these savage pitched battles and bloody skirmishes, the surprises and murderous assaults all over the old range, there were hundreds of settlers killed, hundreds also of our army men, including some splendid officers. In the Custer fight alone, on the Little Big Horn, the army lost Custer himself, thirteen commissioned officers, and two hundred and fifty-six enlisted men killed, with two officers and fifty-one men wounded: a total of three hundred and twenty-three killed and wounded in one battle. Custer had in his full column about seven hundred men. The number of the Indians has been variously estimated. They had perhaps five thousand men in their villages when they met Custer in this, the most historic and most ghastly battle of the Plains. It would be bootless to revive any of the old discussions regarding Custer and his rash courage. Whether in error or in wisdom, he died, and gallantly. He and his men helped clear the frontier for those who were to follow, and the task took its toll.

Thus, slowly but steadily, even though handicapped by a vacillating governmental policy regarding the Indians, we muddled through these great Indian wars of the frontier, our soldiers doing their work splendidly and uncomplainingly, such work as no other body of civilized troops has ever been asked to do or could have done if asked. At the close of the Civil War we ourselves were a nation of fighting men. We were fit and we were prepared. The average of our warlike qualities never has been so high as then. The frontier produced its own pathfinders, its own saviours, its own fighting men.

So now the frontier lay ready, waiting for the man with the plough. The dawn of that last day at hand.

CHAPTER 8

# The Cattle Kings

It is proper now to look back yet again over the scenes with which we hitherto have had to do. It is after the railways have come to the Plains. The Indians now are vanishing. The buffalo have not yet gone, but are soon to pass.

Until the closing days of the Civil War the northern range was a wide, open domain, the greatest ever offered for the use of a people. None claimed it then in fee; none wanted it in fee. The grasses and the sweet waters offered accessible and profitable chemistry for all men who had cows to range. The land laws still were vague and inexact in application, and each man could construe them much as he liked. The excellent homestead law of 1862, one of the few really good land laws that have been put on our national statute books, worked well enough so long as we had good farming lands for homesteading—lands of which a quarter section would support a home and a family.

This same homestead law was the only one available for use on the cattle-range. In practice it was violated thousands of times—in fact, of necessity violated by any cattle man who wished to acquire sufficient range to run a considerable herd. Our great timber kings, our great cattle kings, made their fortunes out of their open contempt for the homestead law, which was designed to give all the people an even chance for a home and a farm. It made, and lost, America.

Swiftly enough, here and there along all the great waterways of the northern range, ranchers and their men filed claims on the water fronts. The dry land thus lay tributary to them. For the most part the open lands were held practically under squatter right; the first cow-man in any valley usually had his rights respected, at least for a time. These were the days of the open range. Fences had not come, nor had farms been staked out.

From the South now appeared that tremendous and elemental force—most revolutionary of all the great changes we have noted in the swiftly changing West—the bringing in of thousands of horned kine along the northbound trails. The trails were hurrying from the Rio Grande to the upper plains of Texas and northward, along the north and south line of the Frontier—that land which now we have been seeking less to define and to mark precisely than fundamentally to understand.

The Indian wars had much to do with the cow trade. The Indians were crowded upon the reservations, and they had to be fed, and fed on beef. Corrupt Indian agents made fortunes, and the Beef Ring at Washington, one of the most despicable lobbies which ever fattened there, now wrote its brief and unworthy history. In a strange way corrupt politics and corrupt business affected the phases of the cattle industry as they had affected our relations with the Indians. More than once a herd of some thousand beeves driven up from Texas on contract, and arriving late in autumn, was not accepted on its arrival at the army post—some pet of Washington perhaps had his own herd to sell! All that could be done then would be to seek out a "holding range." In this way, more and more, the capacity of the northern Plains to nourish and improve cattle became established.

Naturally, the price of cows began to rise; and naturally, also, the demand for open range steadily increased. There now began the whole complex story of leased lands and fenced lands. The frontier still was offering opportunity for the bold man to reap where he had not sown. Lands leased to the Indians of the civilized tribes began to cut large figure in the cow trade—as well as some figure in politics—until at length the thorny situation was handled by a firm hand at Washington. The methods of the East were swiftly overrunning those of the West. Politics and graft and pull, things hitherto unknown, soon wrote their hurrying story also over all this newly won region from which the rifle-smoke had scarcely yet cleared away.

But every herd which passed north for delivery of one sort or the other advanced the education of the cowman, whether of the northern or the southern ranges. Some of the southern men began to start feeding ranges in the North, retaining their breeding ranges in the South. The demand of the great upper range for cattle seemed for the time insatiable.

To the vision of the railroad builders a tremendous potential freightage now appeared. The railroad builders began to calculate that one day they would parallel the northbound cow trail with iron trails of their own and compete with nature for the carrying of this beef. The whole swift story of all that development, while the westbound rails were crossing and criss-crossing the newly won frontier, scarce lasted twenty years. Presently we began to hear in the East of the Chisholm Trail and of the Western Trail which lay beyond it, and of many smaller and intermingling branches. We heard of Ogallalla, in Nebraska, the "Gomorrah of the Range," the first great upper market-place for distribution of cattle to the swiftly forming northern ranches. The names of new rivers came upon our maps; and beyond the first railroads we began to hear of the Yellowstone, the Powder, the Musselshell, the Tongue, the Big Horn, the Little Missouri.

The wild life, bold and carefree, coming up from the South now in a mighty surging wave, spread all over that new West which offered to the people of older lands a strange and fascinating interest. Everyone on the range had money; everyone was independent. Once more it seemed that man had been able to overleap the confining limitations of his life, and to attain independence, self-indulgence, ease and liberty. A chorus of Homeric, riotous mirth, as of a land in laughter, rose up all over the great range. After all, it seemed that we had a new world left, a land not yet used. We still were young! The cry arose that there was land enough for all out West. And at first the trains of white-topped wagons rivalled the crowded coaches westbound on the rails.

In consequence there came an entire readjustment of values. This country, but yesterday barren and worthless, now was covered with gold, deeper than the gold of California or any of the old placers. New securities and new values appeared. Banks did not care much for the land as security—it was practically worthless without the cattle—but they would lend money on cattle at rates which did not then seem usurious. A new system of finance came into use. Side by side with the expansion of credits went the expansion of the cattle business. Literally in hundreds of thousands the cows came north from the exhaustless ranges of the lower country.

It was a wild, strange day. But withal it was the kindliest and most generous time, alike the most contented and the boldest time, in all the history of our frontiers. There never was a better life than that of the cowman who had a good range on the Plains and cattle enough to stock his range. There never will be found a better man's country in all the world than that which ran from the Missouri up to the low foothills of the Rockies.

The lower cities took their tribute of the northbound cattle for quite a time. Wichita, Coffeyville, and other towns of lower Kansas in turn made bids for prominence as cattle marts. Agents of the Chicago stockyards would come down along the trails into the Indian Nations to meet the northbound herds and to try to divert them to this or that market as a shipping-point. The Kiowas and Comanches, not yet wholly confined to their reservations, sometimes took tribute, whether in theft or in open extortion, of the herds labouring upward through the long slow season.

Trail-cutters and herd-combers, licensed or unlicensed hangers-on to the northbound throngs of cattle, appeared along the lower trails—with some reason, occasionally; for in a great northbound herd there might be many cows included under brands other than those of the road brands registered for the drovers of that particular herd. Cattle thieving became an industry of certain value, rivalling in some localities the operations of the bandits of the placer camps. There was great wealth suddenly to be seen. The weak and the lawless, as well as the strong and the unscrupulous, set out to reap after their own fashion where they had not sown.

If a grave here or there appeared along the trail or at the edge of the straggling town, it mattered little. If the gamblers and the desperadoes of the cow towns such as Newton, Ellsworth, Abilene, Dodge, furnished a man for breakfast day after day, it mattered little, for plenty of men remained, as good or better. The life was large and careless, and bloodshed was but an incident. During the early and unregulated days of the cattle industry, the frontier insisted on its own creed, its own standards. But all the time, coming out from the East, were scores and hundreds of men of exacter notions of trade and business. The enormous waste of the cattle range could not long endure. The toll taken by the thievery of the men who came to be called range-rustlers made an element of loss which could not long be sustained by thinking men.

As the Vigilantes regulated things in the mining camps so now in slightly different fashion the new property owners on the upper range established their own ideas, their own sense of proportion as to law and order. The cattle associations, the banding together of many owners of vast herds, for mutual protection and mutual gain were a natural and logical development. Outside of these there was for a time a highly efficient corps of cattle-range Vigilantes, who shot and hanged some scores of rustlers.

It was a frenzied life while it lasted—this lurid outburst, the last flare of the frontier. Such towns as Dodge and Ogallalla offered extraordinary phenomena of unrestraint. But fortunately, into the worst of these capitals of license came the best men of the new regime, and the new officers of the law, the agents of the Vigilantes, the advance-guard of civilization now crowding on the heels of the wild men of the West. In time the lights of the dance-halls and the saloons and the gambling parlours went out one by one all along the frontier. By 1885 Dodge City, a famed capital of the cow trade, which will live as long as the history of that industry is known, resigned its eminence and declared that from where the sun then stood it would be a cow camp no more! The men of Dodge knew that another day had dawned. But this was after the homesteaders had arrived and put up their wire fences, cutting off from the town the holding grounds of the north-bound herds.

This innovation of barb-wire fences in the seventies had caused a tremendous alteration of conditions over all the country. It had enabled men to fence in their own water-fronts, their own homesteads. Casually, and at first without any objection filed by any one, they had included in their fences many hundreds of thousands of acres of range land to which they had no title whatever. These men—like the large-handed cow barons of the Indian Nations, who had things much as they willed in a little unnoted realm all their own—had money and political influence. And there seemed still range enough for all. If a man wished to throw a drift fence here or there, what mattered it?

Up to this time not much attention had been paid to the Little Fellow, the man of small capital who registered a brand of his own, and who—with a Maverick here and there and the natural increase, and perhaps a trifle of unnatural increase here and there—had proved able to accumulate with more or less rapidity a herd of his own.

******

In the early days a rancher by the name of Maverick, a Texas man, had made himself rich simply by riding out on the open range and branding loose and unmarked occupants of the free lands. Hence the term "Maverick" was applied to any unbranded animal running loose on the range. No one cared to interfere with these early activities in collecting unclaimed cattle. Many a foundation for a great fortune was laid in precisely that way. It was not until the more canny days in the North that Mavericks were regarded with jealous eyes.

✶✶✶✶✶✶

Now the cattle associations passed rules that no foreman should be allowed to have or register a brand of his own. Not that any foreman could be suspected—not at all!—but the foreman who insisted on his old right to own a running iron and a registered brand was politely asked to find his employment somewhere else.

The large-handed and once generous methods of the old range now began to narrow themselves. Even if the Little Fellow were able to throw a fence around his own land, very often he did not have land enough to support his herd with profit. A certain antipathy now began to arise between the great cattle owners and the small ones, especially on the upper range, where some rather bitter wars were fought—the cow kings accusing their smaller rivals of rustling cows; the small men accusing the larger operators of having for year? clone the same thing, and of having grown rich at it.

The cattle associations, thrifty and shifty, sending their brand inspectors as far east as the stockyards of Kansas City and Chicago, naturally had the whip hand of the smaller men. They employed detectives who regularly combed out the country in search of men who had loose ideas of mine and thine. All the time the cow game was becoming stricter and harder. Easterners brought on the East's idea of property, of low interest, sure returns, and good security. In short, there was set on once more—as there had been in every great movement across the entire West—the old contest between property rights and human independence in action. It was now once more the Frontier against the States, and the States were foredoomed to win.

The barb-wire fence, which was at first used extensively by the great operators, came at last to be the greatest friend of the Little Fellow on the range. The Little Fellow, who under the provisions of the homestead act began to push West and to depart farther and farther from the protecting lines of the railways, could locate land and water for himself and fence in both. "I've got the law back of me," was what he said; and what he said was true. Around the old cow camps of the trails, and around the young settlements which did not aspire to be called cow camps, the homesteaders fenced in land—so much land that there came to be no place near any of the shipping-points where a big herd from the South could be held. Along the southern range artificial barriers to the long drive began to be raised. It would be hard to say whether fear of Texas competition or of Texas cattle fever was the more powerful motive in the minds of ranchers in Colorado and

Kansas. But the cattle quarantine laws of 1885 nearly broke up the long drive of that year. Men began to talk of fencing off the trails, and keeping the northbound herds within the fences—a thing obviously impossible.

The railroads soon rendered this discussion needless. Their agents went down to Texas and convinced the shippers that it would be cheaper and safer to put their cows on cattle trains and ship them directly to the ranges where they were to be delivered. And in time the rails running north and south across the Staked Plains into the heart of the lower range began to carry most of the cattle. So, ended the old cattle trails.

What date shall we fix for the setting of the sun of that last frontier? Perhaps the year 1885 is as accurate as any the time when the cattle trails practically ceased to bring north their vast tribute. But, in fact, there is no exact date for the passing of the frontier. Its decline set in on what day the first lank "nester" from the States outspanned his sun-burned team as he pulled up beside some sweet water on the rolling lands, somewhere in the West, and looked about him. and looked again at the land map held in his hand.

"I reckon this is our land, Mother," said he.

When he said that, he pronounced the doom of the old frontier.

CHAPTER 9

# The Homesteader

His name was usually Nester or Little Fellow It was the old story of the tortoise and the hare. The Little Fellow was from the first destined to win. His steady advance, now on this flank, now on that, just back of the vanguard pushing westward, had marked the end of all our earlier frontiers. The same story now was being written on the frontier of the Plains.

But in the passing of this last frontier the type of the land-seeking man, the type of the American, began to alter distinctly. The million dead of our cruel Civil War left a great gap in the American population which otherwise would have occupied the West and Northwest after the clearing away of the Indians. For three decades we had been receiving a strong and valuable immigration from the north of Europe. It was in great part this continuous immigration which occupied the farming lands of upper Iowa, Minnesota, and the Dakotas. Thus, the population of the Northwest became largely foreign. Each German or Scandinavian who found himself prospering in this rich new country was himself an immigration agency. He sent back word to his friends and relatives in the Old World and these came to swell the steadily thickening population of the New.

We have seen that the enterprising cattlemen had not been slow to reach out for such resources as they might. Perhaps at one time between 1885 and 1890 there were over ten million acres of land illegally fenced in on the upper range by large cattle companies. This had been done without any colour of law whatever; a man simply threw out his fences as far as he liked, and took in range enough to pasture all the cattle that he owned. His only pretext was "I saw it first." For the Nester who wanted a way through these fences out into the open public lands, he cherished a bitter resentment. And yet the Nester must in time win through, must eventually find the little piece of land which he was seeking.

The government at Washington was finally obliged to take action. In the summer of 1885, acting under authorisation of Congress, President Cleveland ordered the removal of all illegal enclosures and forbade any person or association to prevent the peaceful occupation of the public land by homesteaders. The President had already cancelled the leases by which a great cattle company had occupied grazing lands in the Indian Territory. Yet, with even-handed justice he kept the land boomers also out of these coveted lands, until the Dawes Act of 1887 allotted the tribal lands to the Indians in severalty and threw open the remainder to the impatient homeseekers. Waiting thousands were ready at the Kansas line, eager for the starting gun which was to let loose a mad stampede of crazed human beings.

It always was contended by the cowman that these settlers coming in on the semi-arid range could not make a living there, that all they could do was legally to starve to death some good woman. True, many of them could not last out in the bitter combined fight with nature and the grasping conditions of commerce and transportation of that time. The western Canadian farmer of today is a cherished, almost a petted being. But no one ever showed any mercy to the American farmer who moved out West.

As always has been the case, a certain number of wagons might be seen passing back East, as well as the somewhat larger number steadily moving westward. There were lean years and dry years, hot years, yellow years here and there upon the range. The phrase written on one disheartened farmer's wagon top, "Going back to my wife's folks," became historic.

The railways were finding profit in carrying human beings out to the cow-range just as once they had in transporting cattle. Indeed, it did not take the wiser railroad men long to see that they could afford to set down a farmer, at almost no cost for transportation, in any part of the new West. He would after that be dependent upon the railroad in every way. The railroads deliberately devised the great land boom of 1886, which was more especially virulent in the State of Kansas. Many of the roads had lands of their own for sale, but what they wanted most was the traffic of the settlers. They knew the profit to be derived from the industry of a dense population raising products which must be shipped, and requiring imports which also must be shipped. One railroad even offered choice breeding-stock free on request. The same road, and others also, preached steadily the doctrine of diversified farming. In short, the railroads, m their own interests, did all they could to make prosperous the farms or ranches of the West. The usual Western homestead now was part ranch and part farm, although the term "ranch" continued for many years to cover all the meanings of the farm of whatever sort.

There appeared now in the new country yet another figure of the Western civilization, the land-boomer, with his irresponsible and unregulated statements in regard to the values of these Western lands. These men were not always desirable citizens, although of course no industry was more solid or more valuable than that of legitimate handling of the desirable lands. "Public spirit" became a phrase now well known in any one of scores of new towns springing up on the old cow-range, each of which laid claims to be the future metropolis of the world. In any one of these towns the main industry was that of selling lands or "real estate." During the Kansas boom of 1886 the land-boomers had their desks in the lobbies of banks, the windows of hardware stores—any place and every place offering room for a desk and chair.

Now also flourished apace the industry of mortgage loans. Eastern money began to flood the western Plains, attracted by the high rates of interest. In 1886 the customary banking interest in western Kansas was two *per cent* a month. It is easy to see that very soon such a state of affairs as this must collapse. The industry of selling town lots far out in the cornfields, and of buying unimproved subdivision property with borrowed money at usurious rates of interest, was one riding for its own fall.

None the less the Little Fellow kept on going out into the West. We did not change our land laws for his sake, and for a time he needed no sympathy. The homestead law in combination with the pre-emption act and the tree claim act would enable a family to get hold of a very sizable tract of land. The foundations of many comfortable fortunes were laid in precisely this way by thrifty men who were willing to work and willing to wait.

It was not until 1917 that the old homestead law limiting the settler to a hundred and sixty acres of land was modified for the benefit of the stock-raiser. The stock-raising homestead law, as it is called, permits a man to make entry for not more than six hundred and forty acres of unappropriated land which shall have been designated by the Secretary of the Interior as "stock-raising land." Cultivation of the land is not required, but the holder is required to make "permanent improvements" to the value of a dollar and twenty-five cents an acre, and at least one-half of these improvements must be made within three years after the date of entry. In the old times the question of proof in 'proving up' was very leniently considered. A man would stroll down to the land office and swear solemnly that he had lived the legal length of time on his homestead, whereas perhaps he had never seen it or had no more than ridden across it. Today, (1918), matters perhaps will be administered somewhat more strictly; for of all those millions of acres of open land once in the West there is almost none left worth the holding for farm purposes.

Such dishonest practices were, however, indignantly denied by those who fostered the irrigation and dry-farming booms which made the last phase of exploitation of the old range. A vast amount of disaster was worked by the failure of numberless irrigation companies, each of them offering lands to the settlers through the medium of most alluring advertising. In almost every case the engineers underestimated the cost of getting water on the land. Very often the amount of water available was not sufficient to irrigate the land which had been sold to settlers. In countless cases the district irrigation bonds—which were offered broadcast by Eastern banks to their small investors—were hardly worth the paper on which they were written. One after another these wildcat irrigation schemes, purporting to assure sudden wealth in apples, pears, celery, garden truck, cherries, small fruits, alfalfa, pecans, eucalyptus or catalpa trees—anything you liked—went to the wall. Sometimes whole communities became straitened by the collapse of these overblown enterprises. The recovery was slow, though usually the result of that recovery was a far healthier and more stable condition of society.

This whole question of irrigation and dry farming, this or that phase of the last scrambling, feverish settling on the last lands, was sorely wasteful of human enterprise and human happiness. It was much like the spawning rush of the salmon from the sea. Many perish. A few survive. Certainly, there never was more cruel injustice done than that to the sober-minded Eastern farmers, some of them young men in search of cheaper homes, who sold out all they had in the East and went out to the dry country to farm under the ditch, or to take up that still more hazardous occupation—successful sometimes, though always hard and always risky—dry farming on the benches which cannot be reached with irrigating waters.

Strangely changed was all the face of the cattle range by these successive and startling innovations. The smoke of many little homes rose now, scattered over all that tremendous country from the Rockies to the edge of the short grass country, from Texas to the Canadian line. The cattle were not banished from the range, for each little farmer would probably have a few cows of his own; and in some fashion the great cowmen were managing to get in fee tracts of land sufficient for their purposes. There were land leases of all sorts which enabled the thrifty Westerner who knew the inside and out of local politics to pick up permanently considerable tracts of land. Some of these ranches held together as late as 1916; indeed, there are some such old-time holdings still existent in the West, although far more rare than formerly was the case.

Under all these conditions the price of land went up steadily. Land was taken eagerly which would have been refused with contempt a decade earlier. The parings and scraps and crumbs of the Old West now were fought for avidly.

The need of capital became more and more important in many of the great land operations. Even the government reclamation enterprises could not open lands to the settler on anything like the old homestead basis. The water right cost money—sometimes twenty-five or thirty dollars an acre; in some of the private reclamation enterprises, fifty dollars an acre, or even more. Very frequently when the Eastern farmer came out to settle on such a tract and to meet the hard, new, and expensive conditions of life in the semi-arid regions he found that he could not pay out on the land. Perhaps he brought two or three thousand dollars with him. It usually was the industrial mistake of the land-boomer to take from this intending settler practically all of his capital at the start. Naturally, when the new farmers were starved out and in one way or another had made other plans, the country itself went to pieces. That part of it was wisest which did not kill the goose of the golden egg. But be these things as they may be and as they were, the whole readjustment in agricultural values over the once measureless and valueless cow country was a stupendous and staggering thing.

Now appeared yet another agency of change. The high dry lands of many of the Rocky Mountain States had long been regarded covetously by an industry even more cordially disliked by the cattleman than the industry of farming. The sheepman began to raise his head and to plan certain things for himself in turn. Once the herder of sheep was a meek and lowly man, content to slink away when ordered. The writer himself in the dry Southwest once knew a flock of six thousand sheep to be rounded up and killed by the cattlemen of a range into which they had intruded. The herders went with the sheep. All over the range the feud between the sheepmen and the cowmen was bitter and implacable. The issues in those quarrels rarely got into the courts but were fought out on the ground. The old Wyoming dead-line of the cowmen against intruding bands of Green River sheep made a considerable amount of history which was never recorded.

The sheepmen at length began to succeed in their plans. Themselves not paying many taxes, not supporting the civilization of the country, not building the schools or roads or bridges, they none the less claimed the earth and the fullness thereof.

After the establishment of the great forest reserves, the sheepmen coveted the range thus included. It has been the governmental policy to sell range privileges in the forest reserves for sheep, on a per capita basis. Like privileges have been extended to cattlemen in certain of the reserves. Always the contact and the contest between the two industries of sheep and cows have remained. Of course, the issue even in this ancient contest is foregone—as the cowman has had to raise his cows under fence, so ultimately must the sheepman also buy his range in fee and raise his product under fence.

The wandering bands of sheep belong nowhere. They ruin a country. It is a pathetic spectacle to see parts of the Old West in which sheep steadily have been ranged. They utterly destroy all the game; they even drive the fish out of the streams and cut the grasses and weeds down to the surface of the earth. The denuded soil crumbles under their countless hoofs, becomes dust, and blows away. They leave a waste, a desert, an abomination.

There were yet other phases of change which followed hard upon the heels of our soldiers after they had completed their task of subjugating the tribes of the buffalo Indians. After the homesteads had been proved up in some of the North-western States, such as Montana and the Dakotas, large bodies of land were acquired by certain capitalistic farmers. All this new land had been proved to be exceedingly prolific of wheat, the great new-land crop. The farmers of the Northwest had not yet learned that no country long can thrive which depends upon a single crop. But the once familiar figures of the bonanza farms of the Northwest—the pictures of their long lines of reapers or self-binders, twenty, thirty, forty, or fifty machines, one after the other, advancing through the golden grain—the pictures of their innumerable stacks of wheat—the figures of the vast mileage of their fencing—the yet more stupendous figures of the outlay required to operate these farms, and the splendid totals of the receipts from such operations—these at one time were familiar and proudly presented features of boom advertising in the upper portions of our black land belt, which lay just at the eastern edge of the old Plains.

There was to be repeated in this country something of the history of California. In the great valleys, such as the San Joaquin, the first interests were pastoral, and the cowmen found a vast realm which seemed to be theirs forever. There came to them, however, the bonanza wheat farmers, who flourished there about 1875 and through the next decade. Their highly specialized industry boasted that it could bake a loaf of bread out of a wheat field between the hours of sunrise and sunset. The outlay in stock and machinery on some of these bonanza ranches ran into enormous figures. But here, as in all new wheat countries, the productive power of the soil soon began to decrease.

Little by little the number of bushels per acre lessened, until the bonanza farmer found himself with not half the product to sell which he had owned the first few years of his operations. In one California town at one time a bonanza farmer came in and covered three city blocks with farm machinery which he had turned over to the bank owning the mortgages on his lands and plant. He turned in also all his mules and horses, and retired worse than broke from an industry in which he had once made his hundreds of thousands. Something of this same story was to follow in the Dakotas. Presently we heard no more of the bonanza wheat farms; and a little later they were not. The one-crop country is never one of sound investing values; and a land boom is something of which to beware—always and always to beware.

The prairie had passed; the range had passed; the illegal fences had passed; and presently the cattle themselves were to pass—that is to say, the great herds. As recently as five years ago (1912) it was my fortune to be in the town of Belle Fourche, near the Black Hills—a region long accustomed to vivid history, whether of Indians, mines, or cows—at the time when the last of the great herds of the old industry thereabouts were breaking up; and to see, coming down to the cattle chutes to be shipped to the Eastern stockyards, the last hundreds of the last great Belle Fourche herd, which was once numbered in thousands. They came down out of the blue-edged horizon, threading their way from upper benches down across the dusty valley. The dust of their travel rose as it had twenty years earlier on the same old trail.

But these were not the same cattle. There was not a longhorn among them; there has not been a longhorn on the range for many years. They were sleek, fat, well-fed animals, heavy and stocky, even of type, all either whitefaces or shorthorns. With them were some old-time cowmen, men grown grey in range work. Alongside the herds, after the ancient fashion of trailing cattle, rode cowboys who handled their charges with the same old skill. But even the cowboys had changed. These were without exception men from the East who had learned their trade here in the West. Here indeed was one of the last acts of the great drama of the Plains. To many an observer there it was a tragic thing. I saw many a cowman there the gravity on whose face had nothing to do with commercial loss. It was the Old West he mourned. I mourned with him.

Naturally the growth of the great stockyards of the Middle West had an effect upon all the cattle-producing country of the West, whether those cattle were bred in large or in small numbers. The dealers of the stockyards, let us say, gradually evolved a perfect understanding among themselves as to what cattle prices ought to be at the Eastern end of the rails. They have always pleaded poverty and explained the extremely small margin of profit under which they have operated. Of course, the repeated turn-over in their business has been an enormous thing; and their industry, since the invention of refrigerator cars and the shipment of dressed beef in tins, has been one which has extended to all the corners of the world. The great packers would rather talk of "by-products" than of these things. Always they have been so very poor!

For a time, the railroads east of the stockyard cities of Kansas City and Chicago divided up *pro rata* the dressed beef traffic. Investigation after investigation has been made of the methods of the stockyard firms, but thus far the law has not laid its hands successfully upon them. Naturally of late years the extremely high price of beef has made greater profit to the cattle raiser; but that man, receiving eight or ten cents a pound on the hoof, is not getting rich so fast as did his predecessor, who got half of it, because he is now obliged to feed hay and to enclose his range. Where once a half ton of hay might have been sufficient to tide a cow over the bad part of the winter, the Little Fellow who fences his own range of a few hundred acres is obliged to figure on two or three tons, for he must feed his herd on hay through the long months of the winter.

The ultimate consumer, of course, is the one who pays the freight and stands the cost of all this. Hence, we have the swift growth of American discontent with living conditions. There is no longer land for free homes in America. This is no longer a land of opportunity. It is no longer a poor man's country. We have arrived all too swiftly upon the ways of the Old World. And today, in spite of our love of peace, we are in an Old World's war!

The insatiable demand of Americans for cheap lands assumed a certain international phase at the period lying between 1900 and 1913 or later—the years of the last great boom in Canadian lands. The Dominion Government, represented by shrewd and enterprising men able to handle large undertakings, saw with a certain satisfaction of its own the swift passing from the market of all the cheap lands of the United States. It was proved to the satisfaction of all that very large tracts of the Canadian plains also would raise wheat, quite as well as had the prairies of Montana or Dakota. The Canadian railroads, with lands to sell, began to advertise the wheat industry in Alberta and Saskatchewan. The Canadian Government went into the publicity business on its own part. To a certain extent European immigration was encouraged, but the United States really was the country most combed out for settlers for these Canadian lands. As by magic, millions of acres in western Canada were settled.

The young American farmers of our near Northwest were especially coveted as settlers, because they knew how to farm these upper lands far better than any Europeans, and because each of them was able to bring a little capital of ready money into Canada. The publicity campaign waged by Canadians in our Western States in one season took away more than a hundred and fifty thousand good young farmers, resolved to live under another flag. In one year the State of Iowa lost over fifteen million dollars of money withdrawn from bank deposits by farmers moving across the line into Canada.

The story of these land rushes was much the same there as it had been with us. Not all succeeded. The climatic conditions were far more severe than any which we had endured, and if the soil for a time in some regions seemed better than some of our poorest, at least there waited for the one-crop man the same future which had been discovered for similar methods within our own confines. But the great Canadian land booms, carefully fostered and well developed, offered a curious illustration of the tremendous pressure of all the populations of the world for land and yet more land.

In the year 1911 the writer saw, all through the Peace River Valley and even in the neighbourhood of the Little Slave Lake, the advance-guard of wheat farmers crowding out even beyond the Canadian frontier in the covetous search for yet more cheap land. In 1912 I talked with a school teacher, who herself had homestead land in the Judith Basin of Montana—once sacred to cows—and who was calmly discussing the advisability of going up into the Peace River country to take up yet more homestead land under the regulations of the Dominion Government! In the year 1913 I saw an active business done in town lots at Fort McMurray, five hundred miles north of the last railroad of Alberta, on the ancient Athabasca waterway of the fur trade!

Who shall state the limit of all this expansion? The farmer has ever found more and more land on which he could make a living; he is always taking land which his predecessor has scornfully refused. If presently there shall come the news that the land boomer has reached the mouth of the Mackenzie River—as long ago he reached certain portions of the Yukon and Tanana country—if it shall be said that men are now selling town lots under the Midnight Sun—what then? We are building a government railroad of our own almost within shadow of Mount McKinley in Alaska. There are steamboats on all these great sub-Arctic rivers. Perhaps, someday, a power boat may take us easily where I have stood, somewhat wearied, at that spot on the Little Bell tributary of the Porcupine, where a slab on a post said, "Portage Road to Ft. McPherson"—a "road" which is not even a trail, but which crosses the most northerly of all the passes of the Rockies, within a hundred miles of the Arctic Ocean.

Land, land, more land! It is the cry of the ages, more imperative and clamorous now than ever in the history of the world and only arrested for the time by the cataclysm of the Great War. The earth is well-nigh occupied now. Australia, New Zealand, Canada, even Africa, are colonization grounds. What will be the story of the world at the end of the Great War none may predict. For the time there will be more land left in Europe; but, unbelievably soon, the Great War will have been forgotten; and then the march of the people will be resumed toward such frontiers of the world as yet may remain. Land, land, more land!

Always in America we have occupied the land as fast as it was feasible to do so. We have survived incredible hardships on the mining frontier, have lived through desperate social conditions in the cow country, have fought many of our bravest battles in the Indian country. Always it has been the frontier which has allured many of our boldest souls. And always, just back of the frontier, advancing, receding, crossing it this way and that, succeeding and failing, hoping and despairing—but steadily advancing in the net result—has come that portion of the population which builds homes and lives in them, and which is not content with a blanket for a bed and the sky for a roof above.

We had a frontier once. It was our most priceless possession. It has not been possible to eliminate from the blood of the American West, diluted though it has been by far less worthy strains, all the iron of the old home-bred frontiersmen. The frontier has been a lasting and ineradicable influence for the good of the United States. It was there we showed our fighting edge, our unconquerable resolution, our undying faith. There, for a time at least, we were Americans.

We had our frontier. We shall do ill indeed if we forget and abandon its strong lessons, its great hopes, its splendid human dreams.

## ALSO FROM LEONAUR
### AVAILABLE IN SOFTCOVER OR HARDCOVER WITH DUST JACKET

**THE 9TH—THE KING'S (LIVERPOOL REGIMENT) IN THE GREAT WAR 1914 - 1918** *by Enos H. G. Roberts*—Mersey to mud—war and Liverpool men.

**THE GAMBARDIER** *by Mark Severn*—The experiences of a battery of Heavy artillery on the Western Front during the First World War.

**FROM MESSINES TO THIRD YPRES** *by Thomas Floyd*—A personal account of the First World War on the Western front by a 2/5th Lancashire Fusilier.

**THE IRISH GUARDS IN THE GREAT WAR - VOLUME 1** *by Rudyard Kipling*—Edited and Compiled from Their Diaries and Papers—The First Battalion.

**THE IRISH GUARDS IN THE GREAT WAR - VOLUME 1** *by Rudyard Kipling*—Edited and Compiled from Their Diaries and Papers—The Second Battalion.

**ARMOURED CARS IN EDEN** *by K. Roosevelt*—An American President's son serving in Rolls Royce armoured cars with the British in Mesopotamia & with the American Artillery in France during the First World War.

**CHASSEUR OF 1914** *by Marcel Dupont*—Experiences of the twilight of the French Light Cavalry by a young officer during the early battles of the great war in Europe.

**TROOP HORSE & TRENCH** *by R.A. Lloyd*—The experiences of a British Lifeguardsman of the household cavalry fighting on the western front during the First World War 1914-18.

**THE EAST AFRICAN MOUNTED RIFLES** *by C.J. Wilson*—Experiences of the campaign in the East African bush during the First World War.

**THE LONG PATROL** *by George Berrie*—A Novel of Light Horsemen from Gallipoli to the Palestine campaign of the First World War.

**THE FIGHTING CAMELIERS** *by Frank Reid*—The exploits of the Imperial Camel Corps in the desert and Palestine campaigns of the First World War.

**STEEL CHARIOTS IN THE DESERT** *by S. C. Rolls*—The first world war experiences of a Rolls Royce armoured car driver with the Duke of Westminster in Libya and in Arabia with T.E. Lawrence.

**WITH THE IMPERIAL CAMEL CORPS IN THE GREAT WAR** *by Geoffrey Inchbald*—The story of a serving officer with the British 2nd battalion against the Senussi and during the Palestine campaign.

AVAILABLE ONLINE AT **www.leonaur.com**
AND FROM ALL GOOD BOOK STORES

www.ingramcontent.com/pod-product-compliance
Lightning Source LLC
Chambersburg PA
CBHW031615160426
43196CB00006B/142